HANDBOOK OF INNOVATIVE MARKETING TECHNIQUES

HANDBOOK OF INNOVATIVE MARKETING TECHNIQUES

by David D. Seltz
Seltz Franchising
Developments, Inc.

ADDISON-WESLEY PUBLISHING COMPANY
Reading, Massachusetts • Menlo Park, California
London • Amsterdam • Don Mills, Ontario • Sydney

Library of Congress Cataloging in Publication Data

Seltz, David D
    Handbook of innovative marketing techniques.

        1. Marketing. 2. Sales promotion. I. Title.
HF5415.S3686   658.8   79-27415
ISBN 0-201-07617-9

ISBN 0-201-07617-9

ABCDEFGHIJ-AL-89876543210

PREFACE

Never has there been a time of greater need for small businesses to utilize all possible tactics and strategies to maximize sales. Today's inflationary operational and promotional costs make the achievement of maximum market coverage with minimum capital outlay a business imperative. To accomplish this you must reach *all* potential marketplaces just as quickly, completely, and economically as possible.

That is the basic premise of the concepts outlined in this book. They combine sales and marketing techniques that can achieve maximum market penetration for minimum investment. Properly applied, they can make the crucial difference in profitability, growth, and even *survival* of a company.

Although many companies have benefited from the application of one or more of these techniques—some to the extent of *hundreds of millions of dollars* in sales—such special knowledge is virtually unknown to most businesses. These sales-generating concepts are simple to implement and most can be applied with a minimal capital investment. Consider one example: The *direct-sales* field is unknown or overlooked by many businesses. Yet it is a billion-dollar industry. One shoe wholesaler has 22,000 direct-sales representatives producing in excess of $50 million in sales per year on a "straight commission" basis.

Even the simple concept of "catalogue corners" has assumed immense proportions today. This is a system whereby noncompetitive firms serve as order-placement centers for companies that engage in large-volume catalogue sales. A small corner of a retail store is set aside and equipped with desk or table, catalogues, and order forms. The J.C. Penney Company has established "catalogue corners" in Thrifty Drug Stores. This concept produces multiple profit centers rapidly and with minimum investment.

The "Party-Plan" concept, which evolved from a promotional scheme used by Tupperware Corporation, has now found application in a myriad of businesses. Recently, a client of ours sold house plants on this basis. In one city of 250,000 population, some 200 house parties were conducted weekly, each producing average sales of $200.

These are *but* a few illustrations of the *many* concepts contained in this book. All of these concepts are practical and economical; all are proven sales producers. The business that uses them will enjoy a definite competitive advantage.

New York, N.Y.   David D. Seltz
September 1980

CONTENTS

CONTENTS

CONTENTS

SECTION THREE NEW ADVERTISING CONCEPTS

SECTION FOUR NEW IMAGE-BUILDING CONCEPTS

CONTENTS

CONTENTS

SECTION ONE

PROMOTIONS THAT GET "PLUS" SALES

CHAPTER ONE THE PARTY-PLAN CONCEPT

HOW IT WORKS

Briefly, this is how the Party-Plan concept works: Individuals are requested to invite friends and neighbors to their homes for a few hours of informal socializing and refreshments. Within this relaxed and congenial atmosphere the sponsor's merchandise or services are displayed and briefly demonstrated. The host or hostess receives a commission on sales—approximately 15 percent—plus a discount on personal purchases. Usually the majority of guests make purchases, often for significant sums of money. Equally important, they are exposed to the merchandise and learn of its advantages within the pleasant atmosphere of a private home. This invaluable consumer exposure and favorable identification of the sponsor's name and location virtually ensure subsequent additional purchases.

The Party-Plan sales concept is applicable to an extensive array of such products and services as kitchen utensils, apparel, art, boutique items, furniture, linen, books—practically everything and anything! For example, a company selling house plants via the Party-Plan concept recently achieved average sales of $200 per party, and conducted more than 150 parties a week within a city of 250,000 population.

A brain child of the Tupperware® Corporation, the sales party was conceived originally as a means of reaching homebound housewives who perhaps had spare time and needed supplementary income, especially during recessionary periods.

While at-home sales parties are still given chiefly by women, variations have been developed on Tupperware's successful theme. Inflation has created the need for second incomes, and today it's not unusual to find men hosting sales parties. Retired folks who feel strangled by too much leisure time and too little cash find the sales party a pleasant answer to both problems. Working people who have little chance to socialize on the job have shown interest in supplementing their income while enjoying the company of friends.

CAN IT WORK FOR YOU?

Probably! As we noted earlier, sales parties are adaptable to almost any kind of merchandise or service, and the number you can sponsor is limited only by the size of your community.

Sales parties are particularly suitable secondary retail outlets for drygoods and housewares or merchandise that can be accommodated easily in a home setting.

Consider these possibilities:

☐ **Bookstores** can sponsor meet-the-author parties where copies of a current book are sold and autographed. These can be conducted at lunchtime or after business hours, in the store itself or at people's homes.

☐ **Dance studios,** from disco to ballet, can sponsor gatherings or mixers to promote dance instruction.

☐ **Fabric or sewing-machine stores** can demonstrate dressmaking techniques.

☐ **Food establishments** (especially those featuring gourmet items) are especially adaptable to such parties. A caterer can offer samples of the menu to guests.

☐ **Housewares suppliers** can sponsor food preparation demonstrations, perhaps hiring the local equivalent to Julia Child. They might feature exotic utensils. The Chinese Wok, for example, is easy to use, fun to watch, and accommodates low-cost, healthy meals in one basic pan. The Cuisinart (or variations) "magic" hour would be another intriguing attraction.

☐ **Several noncompetitive suppliers** can cosponsor an event. For instance, the use of industrial or commercial equipment for home furnishings is a new, chic approach to interior design. Basically, it involves a new way of looking at functional objects—footlockers, for example, or plastic tubing, or steel restaurant sinks—as ornamental, rather than purely utilitarian pieces. Several such suppliers might team up with a decorator to sponsor an unusual and dynamic showing.

☐ **A gardening store** can sponsor an exhibit of its merchandise at the onset of spring, when yard enthusiasts are feeling their greatest sense of exhilaration.

☐ **A plant store** can sponsor a party, inviting new residents.

☐ **Hardware stores** have a wide variety of ordinary but useful merchandise. A store can sponsor several parties, each drawing attention to a specific group of related tools. One gathering might be devoted to minor home repairs, another to the variety and laying of tiles. Here the possibilities are endless.

☐ **Sporting goods stores** can display everything from skateboards to bicycles and "bring home" the message that exercise is healthy and fun. A separate fashion show would take advantage of the craze for fancy sneakers, jogging suits, and the new tendency toward style on the tennis courts.

☐ **A music store** can demonstrate a variety of instruments.

☐ **A bank** can run money-management parties: perhaps one for young couples and another for people on fixed incomes.

☐ **Investment firms** have a huge potential clientele, but most people must be convinced that savings accounts are not their only secure investment. These firms can sponsor parties that include brief discussions of art, antiques, and other collectors' investment areas, plus commodities and stock investments as appropriate inflation hedges.

☐ **A carpet store** can show new types of carpeting and demonstrate do-it-yourself installation. Tie-ins with current jobs in process might be arranged.

☐ **A beauty parlor** can offer a "free" set or haircut to customers in exchange for their appearance as models at a party.

☐ **A luggage shop** can sponsor a show featuring lightweight luggage for air travel, taking advantage of strategic timing before vacation season and graduation. Keep in mind the market of people whose jobs require travel, particularly young employees who want to be on the move. Another marketable item is sports-gear luggage. Members of teams, racquet clubs, and other physical fitness programs often take their equipment to the office for a game after work. They look for spaciousness, strength, and high quality to convey a "solid," executive, athletic image.

☐   **Home exercise equipment** is guaranteed to elicit lots of curiosity. These intriguing gadgets are amusing to try and can transform a sales party into a real event.

☐   **A drugstore** or other outlet for home beauty preparations can sponsor interesting demonstrations of new safe hair-coloring methods designed for home use. Henna, for instance, once came only in one color, red; now it is available in a variety of colors. Hair conditioners, plastic gloves, applicators, and other necessities can be featured as well.

☐   **Health-food** sales are increasing as people become more concerned about chemicals in their food. A party featuring health-food snacks is an ideal way of reaching that huge potential market. You might want to set aside a low-sodium foods corner, to show how painless a salt-free diet can be. If the event is held in a store, pass around sample cups of frozen yogurt. The popular natural grooming preparations—organic soaps, shampoos, cleansing creams—can be included in your demonstration. It helps if your salesperson is a glowing example of the benefits of a healthful diet: a vigorous person who knows about health foods and looks ten years younger than his or her age.

☐   **A magazine and newspaper dealer** has more merchandise to sell than ever before, as publications become more specialized. Give a browsing party, setting up racks stacked with new publications as well as the old standbys. Include new trade journals and magazines, plus the many publications devoted to the young, affluent lifestyle.

☐   **Antique dealers** can sponsor a party to "celebrate" the arrival of a particularly fine new shipment.

☐   **Florists** can make themselves known to the biggest party-givers in town by sponsoring a party for *them*. Invite representatives of new businesses or firms that might want the front-office prestige of a floral arrangement in the reception area. Plants, dried or green, have become an integral part of interior design for offices today.

☐   **Cosmetic dealers** can take advantage of marketing a line of goods that continues to increase in variety as well as in methods of application. Sell the cosmetics and give free lessons in their expert use.

☐   **Gift shops** are ideal for sales parties, perhaps keyed to theme (travel, exercise), or a color (pinks to reds, blues to greens), or a seasonal activity.

☐ **Toy stores** can show children and those who love them a good time to everyone's profit. As a gesture of goodwill, a few toys can be presented to the children's ward of a hospital.

☐ **A grocer** can demonstrate unusual food items and new time-saving cooking products. People are always interested in things that make their work easier.

☐ **An upholsterer** can display fabrics and demonstrate how to renovate old furniture.

☐ **A beauty-parlor operator** can give a one-lesson charm course, with all the latest beauty tips and tricks, while simultaneously taking orders for the demonstrated products.

☐ **A hardware store** can conduct a special showing of items that help save space around the home.

☐ **A decorating shop** can explain money-saving tricks that manage to accomplish striking decorative results.

☐ **A "do-it-yourself" fabrics store** can show new materials and also demonstrate how patterns make it easy for amateurs to create their own high-fashion clothes.

☐ **An appliance store** can demonstrate items that relieve the drudgery of housework.

SETTING UP YOUR OWN PARTY PLAN

Before conducting your first off-premises sales parties, investigate the possibility of insuring your merchandise, especially if the goods are valuable.

Then poll friends, customers, and suppliers to see what they think of a sales-party idea. At the same time, ascertain the names of potential sales-persons-hosts. Meet with them. Get a good idea of their ability to be congenial in a group while being businesslike in selling your product. Discuss refreshments and prices with them. Some party-givers might enjoy cooking, for which they would be paid above the usual commission, discount, and gifts. Work with the host or hostess on preparations, making sure mailings go out far enough in advance and contain an RSVP as well as the time, place, and date—details so obvious they can be easily overlooked.

If costs appear higher than you bargained for, keep in mind that 60 percent of your guests will buy a moderately priced, carry-home object. More important, you will be expanding your circle of word-of-mouth customers: *pure gold* to any business.

Remember these facts: Well-run parties usually result in sales to more than 60 percent of the people attending. Party selling allows you to reach customers in neighborhoods outside the normal selling range of your store. You can hold parties in the evening when your shop might ordinarily be closed, and you'll have a chance to demonstrate your products thoroughly to an audience whose very presence is an indication of their willingness to listen.

Four Steps
to Success
Like any other new merchandising endeavor, your sales-party effort will prove more rewarding if you precede it with some carefully planned groundwork.

First Be sure that you are offering the right products. Are they desirable? Salable? Get the advice of others—friends, relatives, prospective customers, and so on.

Second Appoint your party-plan "salespersons." Most likely these will be householders who undertake to invite approximately 10 friends, neighbors, or relatives to an informal get-together in their home, at which time your products will be displayed and described. As compensation, the householder receives a commission (percentage of sales). Refreshments are also served, creating a relaxed and congenial atmosphere.

Third Provide your salespersons with all the needed sales materials: order-taking forms, descriptive letters, brochures, etc. And, of course, make sure that you have your own sales talk down pat and that you have sufficient stock available to fill expected orders.

Fourth Bear in mind that those attending a party-plan event are good prospects to become salespersons who'll conduct sales parties in their own homes. Provide application forms for those expressing such interest. In this sense the party-plan concept contains built-in expansion capabilities. Sales can keep escalating with a ripple effect process.

CHAPTER ADDING NEW
TWO DEPARTMENTS

Greater profit without investment in additional plant, equipment, and personnel is *every* entrepreneur's dream. It's a dream that often can be achieved merely by *adding a new department* to the business. Practically *every* business has the potential for this type of expansion. The successful addition of a new department will increase store traffic and attract new customers. The decision as to what type of department best suits your individual operation should result from an intense survey of existing options, which may not be readily apparent to you. It is the purpose of this chapter to stimulate your thinking in this direction by offering various ideas and examples.

It might help to channel your expansion thinking into five categories:

1. Mail order

2. Product rental

3. Expanded product lines

4. Expanded services

5. Internal commission business

Mail Order Mail order should be the first marketing technique to demand your attention. If you are operating a retail establishment, a mail-order catalog sent to your own customer list has the potential to help you in two ways: Of course it will

9

produce mail orders; it may also increase your *store traffic* by attracting some customers you haven't seen for a long time. Controlling your mailings according to Postal Zip Codes, you can saturate contiguous territories within your trading or travel area and enjoy increased business volume.

You may be surprised by the mail-order results. In fact, after instituting a mail-order program, one retail bookstore found that mail sales outstripped in-store sales. Furthermore, in-store sales themselves expanded, resulting in a total retail business more than double that of pre-mail-order days.

Even relatively expensive items can be sold by mail order—for example, jewelry, coins, and a variety of other goods for which the cost of postage does not impose an onerous investment.

Product Rental

During inflationary times, discretionary spending may shrink and perhaps all but disappear. This means consumer spending for capital goods—that is, major budget items—may be deferred indefinitely. Yet the need for these goods continues to exist.

One mutually beneficial alternative is the rental of large investment items. Homeowners, for example, are prime prospects to rent chain saws, hedge clippers, earth-turning equipment, mobile lawn mowers, snow blowers, and a variety of less common items that have a one-time or occasional use. Special-event needs, such as party equipment (chairs, utensils, lawn tents, and cooking equipment) are popular rental items, as are camping and sports gear and certain photographic supplies. Less cheerful, but in constant demand, are all sorts of sickroom needs—hospital beds, wheelchairs, crutches, and walkers.

Nearly retail business can adapt itself to some sort of rental program. Examine the possible needs of customers in your trading area, decide what rental items will accommodate them, and then commence a direct-mail advertising campaign. You don't even have to make much of an investment in inventory—just line up a reliable supply source, because the rental market may prove better than you expect.

Expanded Product Lines

When you consider expanding your product line, remember this: You *have your hands on the prospects* already and can use the opportunity to demonstrate something new that will expand their "needs."

- **A plumber** can add a line of water conditioners.

- **A grocer** can add a line of toys to the store's display.

- **A tobacconist** can add a greeting-card department.

- **A dress shop** can add a rack of beauty aids.

☐ **A drugstore** can add a health-foods department.

☐ **A delicatessen** can go modern with the addition of a snack-foods bar, a cooking advice department, and a pantyhose rack.

Adding anything even remotely connected with your business will give you a chance to increase customer demand and so to make additional sales.

Expanded Services

Expanded services are more or less (but not exactly) "the other side of the coin" from expanded product lines, and in many cases they require less capital investment.

☐ **A photographer** establishes a film-developing service for those who take snapshots.

☐ **A gas station** offers automotive diagnostic services.

☐ **A furniture store** adds a department supplying interior-decorator services.

☐ **A dress shop** adds a convenient bridal-consultant service.

☐ **A house-painter** provides fire-retardant chemical spray service.

☐ **A home-alarm supplier** offers insurance at discount rates to customers installing its protective systems.

Internal Commission Business

Don't overlook the expansion possibilities involving collaboration with other firms or individuals. Such services as carpet cleaning, termite-proofing, and home-modernization can be offered under *your* trade name but actually performed by outside contractors who pass a commission on to you for developing the business prospect.

And here's a final idea for consideration: By allocating just a few square feet of floor space and investing virtually nothing in added overhead, you can establish a "catalog corner" at the rear of your store. After ensuring that prospective customers know you *have* such a department, you'll enjoy the additional profits that always result from increased store traffic.

CHAPTER THREE ESTABLISH YOUR OWN "BRANCHES"

AS MANY AS 100 OF THEM!
EACH EARNING MONEY FOR YOU
WITHOUT OVERHEAD COST!

Imagine the huge benefits you could achieve through the equivalent of 100 branch stores, covering your entire marketing area and serving as an effective sales force to attract orders for your store with minimal or even *no* increase in your present personnel and overhead.

It can be done!

Practically any merchant, in any community, can establish many such "branch" stores to help publicize and sell his or her products or services. All you need is a good imagination and the ability to inspire a spirit of cooperation among your fellow merchants. In the process you'll be helping them as well. Consider these examples:

☐ **A sporting-goods merchant** utilized window space in vacant stores to attractively exhibit sample products. (This merchant paid a nominal rental fee.)

☐ **A luggage store** devised compact see-through cabinets containing several selected luggage items. These were displayed in drugstores, supermarkets, and miscellaneous stores. The participating store received a commission whenever a sale was made from its exhibit.

☐   **A fast-service print shop** arranged for "booths" to be set up in all types of stores throughout the town. An accompanying sign stated: "Bring in your printing work before 5 p.m.—and have it returned by 10 a.m. the next day."

There are literally hundreds of branch-office possibilities in every community! Take some time to think about your unique situation and then explore the opportunities around you.

CHAPTER FOUR HOW TO REACH EVERY PROSPECT IN YOUR COMMUNITY

BOTH HOMES AND BUSINESSES— WITHOUT ADDING A SINGLE SALARIED EMPLOYEE

Would you believe that thousands of rugged individualists stand ready to work hard for you without demanding any salary! Well, it's true! These people are willing to engage in a distribution technique known as *direct sales.* If they make a sale, they earn a commission. No sale—no money. They will canvass a community, knock on doors, and demonstrate and sell your product directly to the consumer.

These men and women are not itinerant peddlers. That day has past. Before working an area, these salespeople inform the police of their intentions and obtain a local permit. Some firms telephone householders in an area and inform them that a representative will soon be calling personally. If anything, the direct-sales agent now has more prestige and responsibility than ever.

Before you dismiss such a sales technique as being undignified for your company, ask yourself this: "Which noteworthy companies engage in the practice of direct sales?"

How about the Fuller Brush Company?

Avon Products?

Electrolux Vacuum Cleaners?

Surely no products in their fields enjoy better reputations for quality and performance than these three.

Now, what other types of industries avail themselves of direct selling? More than a few come to mind:

- ☐ Greeting cards

- ☐ Pots and pans

- ☐ Plastic housewares

- ☐ Insurance

- ☐ Crafts

- ☐ Hobbies

- ☐ Costume jewelry

- ☐ Clothes

- ☐ Men's shoes

- ☐ Cookies

- ☐ Encyclopedias

- ☐ Home repairs

Even some of the world-famous department stores engage in direct selling. Both Macy's and Gimbel's now use this approach for selling such items and services as interior decoration, upholstery, draperies, furniture, and home modernization. Their direct-sales agents close the sales in-home on premises, in response to appointments often set up as the result of a direct approach to the home owner.

How effective is this sales method? *It is unusually effective!* In fact, it is so effective in closing sales that recent legislation has given buyers a "grace period" of several days in which to cancel signed sales contracts should they have second thoughts about the purchase. Implicit here is the fact that this method is sometimes effective enough to sell people things they don't really want. The impact of this legislation will probably be minimal, however, because after a product has been demonstrated in the home and becomes part of the normal domestic scene it is human nature to retain it.

Here's an example to prove the point:

A company "knocked on doors" to sell water softeners for the home. It charged $300 a unit. In this same community a department store sold similar equipment at one-half that price.

However, the direct sales of this item actually *tripled* those of the department store! Why?

The store must wait passively for people to recognize their need, then leave their home, travel to the department store, inquire for the product, and only then to purchase it. This is a lot to expect from potential customers when the product is not one that they have been conditioned to accept as a necessity.

The direct-sales company can demonstrate the product in the setting of its intended use, make customers aware of their needs, show them the benefits of the equipment, and close the sale at the peak of their desire.

What is the incentive for the direct-sales agent? Accelerated cash-flow, in most cases. Frequently, the down-payment made at the signing of the sales contract is kept by the agent as commission; only the contact itself is remitted to the supplying company. This encourages the agents to work at a pace that produces a high rate of sales.

And what is the supplying company's benefit? No fixed salary overhead, no drowning accounts, no expense accounts, no tension problems, no tax problems, no selling expenses—all profit!

Would it work for you?

CHAPTER FIVE MARKETING OFF-PREMISES TO ACCELERATE SALES

SOME IDEAS FOR EXHIBITS, HOME CONTACTS, "BEING WHERE YOU'RE NEEDED," AND INCENTIVES

Through a number of effective merchandising techniques you can take your product beyond the confines of your store or usual place of business and attract the attention of countless additional customers. Your increased visibility, accessibility, and—especially—your *convenience* for their patronage are guaranteed to bring you pluses in the sales column!

EXHIBITS

Exhibits or demonstrations of goods can be held in many places, directed toward specific groups of buyers within an exact area or toward a broader cross-section of the public. Well-tended booths or tables at community fairs or area events are certain to increase the range of your prospects. If your product is noncompetitive with their stores, local malls will often welcome your exhibit, especially in conjunction with seasonal promotions and holiday themes.

Such displays enable you to select and "show off" your best merchandise. They provide excellent publicity and help you attain the objective of *maximum local prospect impact.* Let's look at a few examples of what is and can be done:

☐   **An art gallery** gains publicity through art exhibits in its community; exhibits are held in churches, temples, hotels, office buildings, libraries, and so on.

☐   **Another art gallery** enlists the cooperation of some 20 local citizens who agree to exhibit paintings in their *homes*. There they are viewed by a variety of visitors, often leading to sales.

☐   **Still another art gallery** exhibits its paintings in local stores and restaurants.

☐   **A hardware store** demonstrates many types of cooking utensils.

☐   **A garden shop** exhibits its various garden and lawn products along with its unusual plants.

☐   **A music store** exhibits various musical instruments—e.g., electric organs that are easily mastered for home use.

☐   **A wedding salon** conducts bridal fashion shows.

☐   **A tile shop** exhibits ways to decorate the home or office through the imaginative use of tiles.

☐   **A lumber company** conducts exhibits for builders, carpenters, and others in the trade, featuring new products and construction methods.

☐   **A carpet shop** shows new modes and applications in carpeting.

☐   **A lingerie shop** exhibits new styles in robes, lingerie, and foundation garments.

☐   **A beauty parlor** shows new coiffures and methods of beautifying hair, including hair waving.

☐   **A ladies' apparel shop** has plenty of opportunity to display new styles in dresses, coats, slacks, suits, and other apparel items.

☐   **A luggage shop** shows latest types of luggage—valises, trunks, garment bags—featuring lightweight luggage for air travel.

☐   **A handbag shop** displays new handbag styles, focusing on new materials and colors in current fashion.

☐   **A cosmetic shop** uses party-plan events to exhibit new products and applications that aid beauty and enhance complexions.

☐   **A weight-reduction salon** can demonstrate techniques and shown how its courses help customers attain healthy and attractive body tone.

☐ **A health-food store** can provide opportunities for people to sample new or standard health foods and learn of their benefits.

☐ **A flower shop** can familiarize people with various kinds of fresh and dried flowers and arrangements, showing how they can be used creatively for home display and table decorations.

☐ **A gourmet shop** can offer samples of new delicacies.

HOME CONTACTS

Today's competitive market has led many businesses to pursue increased sales by taking their products or services directly to the homes of potential customers. Thus they need not rely solely on the traffic of passersby but can achieve greater coverage of the total market. Home contact can be initiated through a variety of channels.

Visual Surveys

☐ **A paint store** made a local visual survey of homes that needed exterior paint work. The homeowners were then contacted by telephone as a means of obtaining their patronage.

☐ **A roofing contractor** conducted a local survey of homes that appeared to have roofing needs. Friendly personal calls were made to the homeowners informing them of the company's services.

Free Tests or Instruction

☐ **A lawn-care service** offered to give a free soil test to homeowners, determining the acidity of their lawn areas. This opened the door to many new prospects who eventually became regular customers.

☐ **A bank** offered basic money-management courses directed at those who were inexperienced at handling household budgets.

Prospect Name Lists

☐ **A pet center** that featured a dog-grooming service obtained the names of area dog owners from the dog-license bureau as well as veterinarians. They contacted these prospects at their homes, informed them of the grooming service, and gained new clients.

BEING WHERE YOU'RE NEEDED

Other creative approaches for reaching and contracting prospective customers include the strategic concept of "meeting them where they usually are." Being in the right place at the right time is unusually effective in making sales.

Customers will respond to the convenience of patronizing you, often by making purchases that they would not otherwise consider.

☐   **A tea-and-coffee store** contacted business offices in its area, offering each the permanent loan of a coffee brewer with any ten-pound initial coffee order plus a minimum five-pound monthly order thereafter. This evolved into a flourishing operation that in time exceeded in-store patronage.

☐   **A grocer,** recognizing the continuing demand for such items as potato chips, pretzels, soda crackers, nuts, and confections, publicized and established a route delivering them to homes on a regular weekly schedule. Another, aware of the increasing use of soft drinks, such as colas, ginger ale, and diet beverages, established a route for weekly deliveries to local homes.

☐   **A baker** functioned similarly with baked goods; delivering bread, rolls, pies, and reviving for today's householders a once-traditional service.

☐   **A sandwich shop** utilized a rolling cart to deliver sandwiches and coffee to offices in commercial buildings in its area.

☐   **A florist shop,** recognizing that great numbers of people patronize shopping centers, arranged to have a "kiosk" established in the parking lot (occupying the space of two cars), gaily decorated with the florist's name and services and geared to take orders for flowers. This merchant anticipated impulse buying by customers of the other stores.

☐   **A Chinese restaurant** established a similar kiosk in a nearby shopping center, offering take-out orders of Chinese food.

☐   **A confectionery store** arranged with local shopping centers to permit its attractive show-case truck (with see-through windows) to roam through their parking lots exhibiting and selling novel confectionery items not normally obtainable in the shopping-centers' stores. These included such goodies as jellied and fudge-covered apples, popcorn balls, and cotton candy, which invited impulse purchasing—particularly for children—and sold extremely well.

☐   **A fabric store** arranged with local supermarkets and department stores (and in some instances, drug stores) to exhibit its racks containing fabric swatches. The attractive display directed interested customers to the fabric store. The supermarket or department store received 10-percent commission on resulting purchases.

☐ **A hardware store** developed substantial business by having a represen-tative visit community households selling pots and pans as well as mis-cellaneous utensils and hardware products known to have a high level of consumer need.

☐ **A tailoring establishment** specializing in custom-made suits for men made the rounds of local offices (equipped with swatches) to familiarize executives and other personnel of its services. In surprisingly many instances, the tailor's representative made the sale and was invited to take measurements then and there. Thus this tailoring firm has acquired a substantial number of customers who otherwise might never have thought about doing business with them.

INCENTIVES

To locate prospects in your area and acquaint them with your services, few devices beat the "free offer." This is particularly valuable where unusual or transient types of services are involved, but the appeal of a free gift is universal. Let's look at some suggestions:

☐ **A moving and storage establishment** offers a free booklet called "How to Properly Pack for Moving."

☐ **A hearing-aids store,** in an attempt to locate hard-of-hearing individ-uals in its area, offers an attractive gift to those who will submit names of friends or associates who are hard of hearing.

☐ **A dog-grooming service** obtained the names of dog owners in the area by offering free a special dish for dogs.

☐ **A tobacco store,** desirous of obtaining names of pipe smokers, offered a free booklet called "How to Properly Break-In and Smoke a Pipe."

☐ **An auto accessory store** regularly inserted circulars under the wind-shield wipers of cars parked in a nearby parking area offering a free car-polishing cloth or other low-priced gift.

☐ **A movie theatre** distributes free passes good for one admission if another admission is purchased at the regular price. Such passes are good only on off-nights, of course.

☐ **A travel agency,** to procure names of travel prospects, offers a free booklet describing cruises, interesting places to visit both here and abroad, bus tours, and general tips on traveling.

CHAPTER SIX ATTRACT CUSTOMERS IN GROUPS TO HEAR YOUR SALES STORY
—TRY SEMINARS!

You have probably seen ads publicizing *seminars* for all types of business executives. These seminars are usually conducted on a highly sophisticated level and in many cases it costs as much as $500 to attend.

You may ask, "How do seminars possibly apply to me, a small business owner?" Bear in mind that the *objective* of a seminar is to bring together, on an informal basis, people of mutual interests. Under these optimum conditions they can listen to authorities in their field discuss matters of common concern.

On your own level, you too can attract a relaxed, dedicated, "locked-in" audience. I am not alluding to one of the sophisticated, $500-admission extravagaznzas, but rather to small informal, intimate-concept seminars that can be conducted on a local community basis. Admission is free, or nominal.

SETTING UP THE SEMINAR

Seminars should be conducted on an informal yet authoritative level. Generally speaking, you should:

1. Determine where to hold it. In many instances it can be held in your own store if there is sufficient

space. In other instances, you may want to engage hotel or motel facilities.

2. Make the seminar authoritative by arranging for a "panel" of three or more qualified speakers. For example, the panel could be comprised of you (as the proprietor), a familiar local person who is a known authority on the subject and can speak from experience, and perhaps a representative of the manufacturer with whom you regularly deal.

3. Insert prior ads in newspapers and consider the use of direct mail to publicize the seminar.

4. Obtain *free* publicity in your local newspapers. Your seminar may be considered a newsworthy event, so write a press release. (Most weekly papers welcome prepared articles of local interest.)

SMALL-BUSINESS SEMINARS THAT HAVE WORKED

If the seminar concept still seems too sophisticated for your business climate, take a look at some of the small operations that have recently scored great success with it:

- ☐ **An interior decorator** conducted a seminar called "Newest methods for decorating your home." Sixty-five local residents attended, and many became continuing customers.

- ☐ **A plant and seed store** publicized and conducted a seminar on "Ways to achieve an attractive garden." Nearly one hundred customers within the community were enlisted as a result of this forum.

- ☐ **A jeweler** advertised a seminar on "When and how to wear jewelry—and how to select diamonds." This theme enabled the jeweler to share some professional expertise and demonstrate authoritativeness, thereby obtaining the respect and trust of the audience. Substantial sales were made as a consequence.

- ☐ **A hardware store** conducted a seminar on "How to fix things around the house." This seminar helped instruct people on the types and uses of hardware sold by the store. As a result, sales increased over 40 percent.

☐   **A bookstore** conducted seminars on "New books and authors," thus considerably expanding its patronage, particularly in the current best-seller market.

☐   **A travel agency** conducted seminars on various types of tours, e.g., "Scenic-spots tours," "Historical localities tours," "Golden-West tours," and so on. Tour patronage was achieved on a continuing basis as a result of these seminars.

☐   **A shoe store** offered a seminar on "Common foot problems: How to avoid them" and was thereby able to publicize a line of shoes designed to correct specific problems.

☐   **A gourmet shop** publicized a seminar on "How to prepare gourmet meals." Substantial patronage was gained from many who were interested in gourmet cooking but had been afraid to experiment with it.

☐   **An infants'-wear shop** sponsored a seminar on "Better care for babies," at which a pediatrician and child psychologist gave young parents sound infant-care advice. This created valuable goodwill for the store.

AUDIOVISUAL AIDS CAN HELP

Many small businesspeople find that audiovisuals (slides or films combined with voice) can help to expand interest in a seminar and at the same time minimize the need for "oratorical expertise" on their part (especially if they do not deem themselves good speakers). Here are some ideas:

☐   **A cosmetics store** sent mailings to area clubs, offering to show movies of newest cosmetics and their application. Many invitations were received.

☐   **A home-modernization firm** advertised movies of beautiful home modernization designs that were keyed to the current trends of that particular community.

☐   **A seed and plant store** contacted local Garden Clubs offering to show movies of the most beautiful gardens in their area. This attracted great interest and substantial patronage.

☐   **A travel agency** offered to show a series of movies called "Nationwide and Worldwide Travel Tours of Interest," which attracted an extensive interested attendance.

☐   **An art gallery** offered slides of selected paintings along with an instructional art-appreciation film. This, too, attracted substantial attendance and patronage.

One advantage of using films is that you may expect to receive invitations to show them before clubs and associations in your area. The program chairpersons of such groups as Kiwanis, Jaycees, Rotary, Lions, and Elks are always on the lookout for interesting presentations that will enliven their frequent meetings.

CHAPTER SEVEN FUNDRAISING IDEAS THAT CAN MAKE YOUR SALES ZOOM!

How would you like to have 50, 100, or even more enthusiastic salespeople working for you? Just think of the results that could have on your profits! But it sounds like an impossible dream, doesn't it?

Here's the surprising thing—it's quite possible to enlist a sales force of that size and never add a penny to your overhead expense budget! How? *By tying in your products with fundraising drives.*

If you are not familiar with this sort of operation, it probably sounds complicated and difficult. Well, it isn't. And remember this: it can be tremendously profitable!

ONE SUCCESS STORY

Here's the story of how one candy merchant did it:

Sam Sweet knew that a certain charitable organization was anxious to raise money for its ambitious annual program. Sam offered to supply boxed candy to the group at discount rates. They in turn could sell it to their members, friends, and to the public at its standard retail prices. The difference went to their treasury.

The members accepted the plan gratefully. Many were already buying the candy from time to time, and now they could have their candy and help their own cause, too! More than 100 determined salespeople descended upon their friends and neighbors. You can bet the orders poured in!

WHY NOT YOU?

There is no reason why this type of plan cannot be put to work effectively by almost any merchant. Keep one thing in mind, however: *It is usually best to offer a product or service that is generally known and has popular acceptance.*

☐ **A beauty shop** might offer a percentage of the price of each permanent wave received by a member of the group to its charity.

☐ **A bookstore** could offer certain books—especially those of particular interest to the organization—at discount rates.

☐ **A gift shop** is ideally suited to this type of tie-in. Its many desirable items appeal to a wide variety of people and include genuine necessities such as stationery, small gifts, and seasonal items.

☐ **A bakery** could offer cakes at reduced rates.

☐ **An appliance dealer** might find this the perfect way to reduce inventory on overstocked items.

The possibilities are endless, limited only by the imagination of the merchant. Here's another important point: You will not only boost your current business, but also make new friends and gain their valuable word-of-mouth advertising.

Remember, opportunities for joining forces with fundraisers were never better. America is a nation of "joiners." Every village, town, and city has its church, social, civic, political, and fraternal organizations. Virtually every one has an ongoing drive to fill its treasury.

Getting Started

The opportunity is there. How do you take advantage of it? Here are nine simple, tested rules that can help ensure success.

1. In selecting a group with which to work, try to find one with a leader or chairperson who is capable and energetic—the kind of person who "gets things done."

2. Help this chairperson set up a committee to see that the basic selling job is accomplished.

3. Assign members of the committee specific territories or tasks.

4. Make sure the committee meets at least once a week so that the progress of the campaign can be checked constantly.

30

5. Be certain that all committee members are thoroughly familiar with the product or service being sold.

6. Suggest telephone canvassing.

7. See that a portion of the time at each general meeting of the club is devoted to discussion of the fundraising drive. If a product is being sold, have order blanks available.

8. If the group has a publication, make sure it prints announcements about the campaign.

9. See that a letter announcing the sale is sent to all members. Here is a sample letter:

```
Dear Member:

    Here's exciting news for you and your club.

    By special arrangement with (your business), we are
now taking orders for (your product) at regular
retail prices.  Of course (your business) makes it
available to our organization at a cost lower than
retail.  The profit goes into our treasury.

    You need (the product), and your club needs the
money.  Ordering through our organization is quick,
convenient, and easy for you.  That's why this is
such an exciting project.

    An order form is enclosed.  Just mail or phone your
order to any of the people listed below.  Please do
it TODAY!

                                  Cordially yours,

                                    (Signature)

                          Fundraising Chairperson
```

By following these simple rules, you can make cooperation with fundraising drives a real boom to your business. The opportunities are enormous. It's up to you to take advantage of them.

FURTHER SUCCESSFUL VENTURES

Now let's examine some successful fundraising tie-in programs as applied by different merchants in different communities:

FUNDRAISING IDEAS THAT
CAN MAKE YOUR SALES ZOOM!

☐ **A lamp shop** enlisted the participation of the local Kiwanis Club to sell long-life lightbulbs to members and friends. The astronomical number of 10,000 bulbs were sold—indicative or the tremendous sales power of such programs.

☐ **An ornamental-candles store** enlisted the cooperation of a local women's club to sell specially boxed matched candle sets to their members and friends. The club's treasury received a commission of 25 percent on each sale. The club netted the sum of $325 and, of course, and candle store didn't fare too poorly in its own right.

☐ **A seed and plant store** contacted its local Boy Scout Council— numbering 104 strong—and arranged for Scouts to go door-to-door selling seed packets. Nearly 2000 of these packets were sold at 25¢ each. Both the Council and the merchant benefited substantially.

☐ **An enterprising hosiery store** cooperated with the local PTA in conducting a stocking sale that attracted the generous patronage of most members and their friends. A free "evening on the town," including dinner for two and theatre tickets, was awarded to the most successful salesperson. The same hosiery shop also enlisted the alumni of an area college to sell stockings as a part of their fundraising program.

☐ **A bakery** cooperated with a local church guild in its baked-goods sales. Even though many of the members baked their own specialties as a contribution, a substantial number of cakes, pies, and cookies were ordered from the baker, who provided them with a special discount price. Thus, in addition to aiding charity and achieving goodwill, the shop made a significant profit.

☐ **An enterprising antique shop** approached the guild of a nearby synagogue with the idea of organizing and presenting an antique fair to benefit their building fund. Other dealers were contacted and the affair turned out to be highly successful—40 dealers in attendance with refreshments provided. Money was raised from admissions, commissions on sales, dealers' fees, and refreshment receipts. *And,* each antique dealer came away with a substantial number of sales!

☐ **A hair stylist** offered special percentages to the fundraising drive of a local civic group for all customer referrals. Special certificates were provided to members, enabling identification of the referral source.

CHAPTER EIGHT USING PREMIUMS

HOW "GIVEAWAYS" CAN HELP YOUR BUSINESS

How should merchants use advertising specialties in their business? What types of specialities should be used? How can they build traffic and sales? In this chapter, we will look at 23 ideas and proven ways in which small businesses may profit from the use of advertising specialties and "giveaways."

1. Build prospect lists Give a gift to each customer who recommends ten friends who may patronize you. The premium thus helps expand your prospect lists.

2. Get your product and firm talked about If your giveaway item bears your name, then every time it's used or seen your name is noticed . . . and usually "talked-about." This recurring attention leads to subsequent buying action.

3. Open doors Few things can get you or your salespeople ushered into a prospect's home or office more quickly than presenting a premium as your "business card." Thus, you actually get to see the prospect *by invitation,* an opportunity coveted by all who sell for a living, since it indicates that a sale is half-made.

4. Build goodwill Giving away specialties builds goodwill with everyone, everywhere and also helps "control" your distribution area. If, for example, you're now doing business on block A and want to attract customers from block B, what better way is there than to pinpoint your promotions to the *exact groups* you desire to reach? Distribute goodwill builders and advertising specialties in the controlled area of your choice.

5. Symbolize your product The specialty that bears your product identification, trademark, slogan, or picture of your store is an *effective* and *constant* reminder to your prospect. Specialties can also be created in the *image* of the product.

6. Try a birthday plan Few things please an individual more than being remembered on his or her birthday—especially if it's done with a gift. Why not send a gift to your customers (even to prospects) on their birthdays? That's one way for "beating out" competition and enhancing your trade.

7. Increase store traffic Offer premiums for minimum purchases—for example, $5.00. Thus you're encouraging a constant flow of store traffic. Offering free gifts has the magnetic effect of drawing people into the store.

8. Stimulate dealers and clerks Offer premiums to your dealers and clerks as rewards and incentives towards their best performance. It's surprising how a gift brings out *extra* effort in an employee. Often a gift is more attractive than a cash payment. Help your dealers and clerks by giving *them* gifts to offer to prospects and customers, thus galvanizing their sales efforts.

9. Reward visitors Give specialties as "souvenirs" to visitors in your store, factory, or warehouse. This gesture of hospitality builds a tremendous amount of goodwill and creates in people friendly, personal feeling towards your firm.

10. Leave things behind If customers are out, or merely want to "think it over," you can make sure they remember you and your product by leaving behind a specialty containing your advertisement. It's an ideal "memory-prodder."

11. Acknowledge orders with a prize Instead of the negative message evoked by your invoice, why not initially respond to your customer with the positive message of a thank-you that includes some free advertising specialty. It shows appreciation and breaks through the usual cold business barrier that separates seller from buyer. Just a few cents outlay may lead to thousands of dollars in additional orders.

12. Acknowledge new customers The first contact your new customer has with your firm should be a friendly one. Why not reward the order and thank your customer for giving it to you by sending along a specialty with your friendly personal mesage?

13. Acknowledge your errors It's so much easier for the customer to "forgive" errors if an attractive premium accompanies the explanation. Harsh attitudes dissolve when your approach is one of personal concern.

14. Acknowledge interviews Your selling visit can be a much more fruitful one if you begin it with a "thank you" for the appointment and offer an accompanying specialty. Sending a specialty is effective *after* you've received the interview, also.

15. Announcements Whatever you want to announce will be seen more effectively and will receive greater response when a giveaway is involved.

16. Questionnaire plan Many firms have successfully "opened doors" through the use of questionnaires. The prospect is asked for some facts concerning use of the products, and specialties are given as rewards for his or her cooperation. Many respondents become customers, and helpful suggestions for product improvement may be uncovered.

17. Conventions and trade shows Are you planning to exhibit at a convention or a trade show? Handing out specialties is an ideal method for gaining attention and ensuring that people remember your product.

18. Direct-mail attention-getter In your direct-mail promotions offer a premium for making purchases, for answering questions, or for recommending friends.

19. Letter gimmicks Specialties have proved to be effective in dramatizing messages in sales letters. For example, a comb in an envelope ties in with the message "*Comb* the market . . . you'll not find a product as good as ours." A key might go along with "Here's the *key* to big savings on your part."

20. Commemorate anniversaries Is it your tenth anniversary? Twenty-fifth? What better way to commemorate it than by giving out specialties and calling attention to the reliability and stability of your firm?

21. Tie-in sales As a means of "pushing" slow-moving products, a specialty can be offered if the customer buys a specified item. (No need to mention that it's a slow mover.)

22. Collect past-due accounts There's a saying, "Sugar attracts more flies than vinegar." Thus will friendliness collect more bills than hostility. Try enclosing a specialty with your "past-due" notice.

23. Control patronage A big advantage of the specialty is that you can distribute it exactly and only where you desire; hence you can select the exact patronage you want through pin-pointed distribution of premiums.

CHAPTER NINE NEWCOMERS IN YOUR AREA

HOW TO TAP THIS WELL OF POTENTIAL CUSTOMERS

A MARKET WITH MANY NEEDS

Despite energy shortages and costs, we continue to be a "society on the move." Statistics point out that more people are relocating more often, as industrial trends change and individuals seek better job opportunities and improved life-styles. The old family homestead has become a rarity.

In most instances these "mobile" citizens will buy or even build a home in their new locality. Thus newcomers have a wide range of immediate needs as they begin to set up their homes.

Necessary services

- ☐ Electrical
- ☐ Plumbing
- ☐ Carpentry
- ☐ Heating
- ☐ Glazing
- ☐ Automotive
- ☐ Legal
- ☐ Medical
- ☐ Babysitting
- ☐ Insurance
- ☐ Landscaping

Necessary merchandise

☐ Furniture
☐ Appliances
☐ Carpeting
☐ Curtains
☐ Hardware and tools
☐ Paint and wallpaper
☐ Lawn care materials
☐ Pets and accessories

This is only a partial inventory. New arrivals are also in need of the standard essentials in grocery, clothing, drugstore, and cosmetic items. According to one recent estimate, the sum of $350 million is spend annually by newcomers alone. Since families on the move tend to be of greater than average affluence, their needs and purchases tend to be more substantial in scope. The merchant who attracts the initial patronage of these newcomers is the merchant they generally stay with; a kind of built-in loyalty and buying momentum generally prevail. Thus it is a great advantage to any merchant to be *first* in attracting the patronage of newcomers.

How to Find Them

Name lists of newcomers can be obtained through various sources, including the Telephone Company (new phones), utility companies (gas and electric), realtors (involved in selling or renting homes), County Clerks (who hold records on property transfers), and moving companies (whose vans have done the moving job).

How to Win Them

It is obvious that newcomers will appreciate being "greeted" by local people who welcome them to the community and give them a free introductory gift of merchandise or services. Gratitude established at this stage tends to endure.

The best procedure is to greet the newcomers immediately upon their arrival (either in person or by mail) and offer them a free gift or a substantial discount for their initial patronage. A number of organizations specialize in locating these newcomers and contacting them on the merchants' behalf, offering them the special gift or discount in addition to those of other noncompetitive merchants in the community. One of these is Welcome Wagon. Another is Getting to Know You.

Virtually all types of merchants can link themselves profitably to this approach. For example:

☐ **A cleaning establishment** offers "two for the price of one" on the first cleaning order.

☐ **A florist** delivers a free welcome-to-your-new-home bouquet or plant.

☐ **An electrician** offers a ten-dollar discount on his initial services.

☐ **A hair stylist** gives a free set or cut.

☐ **A drugstore** supplies a free "hospitality kit" containing various items and provides emergency-telephone-number stickers for the medicine cabinet.

☐ **An apparel store** offers a discount on initial apparel purchases or perhaps a "two-for-one" bargain within a certain price range.

☐ **An automotive shop** gies a free motor lubrication.

How to Keep Them

Despite the great effectiveness of this hospitable approach in attracting the newcomer to your store for the initial purchase, it behooves you as a merchant to take advantage of this contact with a proper follow-through. When the customers come to your store initially, make them *feel really welcome and important!* Be sure to take their name and address and recontact them thereafter in a similar friendly spirit to invite their further patronage. Perhaps you will be able to extend to them the privilege of a charge account or acquaint them with new merchandise or services that may be of special interest to them. You may want to inform them of special customer accommodations (e.g., free delivery, late-hour services, or a special quick-service program). If you always greet them by name and make them feel important, the advantage of becoming one of their first "friends" in a strange community will ensure their patronage for years to come!

CHAPTER TEN THE RENTAL CONCEPT

HOW IT CAN MULTIPLY YOUR REVENUES AND PROFITS

WANT MORE INCOME? TRY RENTING!

Here's a simple idea that has helped many small businesses substantially increase their cash intake almost instantly.

Instead of merely selling their products, they also *rent* them!

The success of this idea is based upon a simple point of psychology: Many people dislike the commitment of large purchases. It's a big decision. They're not sure whether their need justifies the expense . . . whether they'll be satisfied . . . whether they can actually afford the cash outlay. Usually these people say, "I'll think it over and let you know." They rarely return.

Here are examples of how this plan has been profitably used:

- [ ] **An appliance store** offered to rent TV sets for a nominal fee (e.g., $10 a month). Eighty percent of the renters ultimately made a purchase.

- [ ] **A furniture store** offered to pay a "warehousing" fee of five dollars a week for six weeks to people who would agree to "store" furniture in their living rooms. Forty-five percent of those "storing" furniture purchased the sets after growing fond of their attractiveness and comfort.

☐   **A used-car dealer** offered to rent its used cars at a weekly rate. After driving the cars for a while, many renters decided they liked them and subsequently purchased those cars.

☐   **A typewriter store** had difficulty selling two-hundred-dollar typewriters. A rental offer ($20 a month) brought 65 *purchasers* within two weeks. The store successfully expanded its plan to include adding machines and dictaphones.

☐   **A music store** sold pianos and organs but found most prospects hesitant to make such "big-ticket" purchases that could not be justified as necessities. Their rental plan removed hesitation and tripled sales.

☐   **A sporting goods store** rented fishing tackle, motor boats, baseball equipment for teams, and so on. Eighty-six percent of the renters ended up purchasing.

Analyze your own business. How can *you* arrange a rental plan to increase *your* sales potential?

CHAPTER ELEVEN
AUCTIONS CAN WORK FOR YOU
THEY SEIZE ATTENTION AND INCREASE PATRONAGE

The excitement and challenge of an auction stir the imagination and invite participation. Recognizing the emotional electricity that auctions seem to generate, many merchants have adapted them with great success to attract increased patronage.

Merchants in a shopping center, neighborhood, or community can organize a group auction event, sharing publicity and building local enthusiasm. Actual Auction Dollars can be devised and printed, especially if it becomes an anticipated annual celebration. These are awarded with designated purchase amounts (much like savings stamps) and, once or twice a year, credited toward bids on merchandise, supplementing customers' real-dollar bids.

Individual merchants can hold auctions, of course, but the advantage of a spirited group effort is worth considering.

Let's look at just a few of the many commodities that can be auctioned successfully:

☐ **Art** (to achieve sale of selected paintings) can be auctioned in the dealer's own gallery or in conjunction with the charitable activities of local organizations.

☐ **Antiques** are enjoying unprecedented popularity. Such an auction will generally attract a large and spirited group, many of whom will bid substantial amounts for items they like.

☐ **"White elephants"** can be any overstocked, outdated, or slow-moving merchandise. Proprietors usually hold such auctions on or about their own premises.

☐ **Automobiles** are often auctioned by overstocked used-car dealers. Bidding is usually established on an item-for-item minimum.

☐ **Phonograph records** that haven't moved can be grouped with currently popular discs and auctioned off as bargain packages.

☐ **Luggage** never loses its value, yet some items simply don't move well. To effect turnover of such sleepers, an auction can prove most helpful.

☐ **Books** require ample display space, and most dealers' shelves are limited. To reduce stocks of books whose sales have dropped or that never quite made the best-seller lists, an auction does wonders. Who can pass up a book bargain?

☐ **Carpets and rugs** are items that householders can usually talk themselves into needing—*if* they think they're picking up a bargain. Auctions thus provide wonderful means for clearning excess stock.

☐ **Greeting cards** take up space and storing seasonal cards from one year to the next is a nuisance. Plenty of bargain-hunters are willing to bid on boxes of greeting cards at an auction.

☐ **Fabric** is another item easily auctioned to individuals who can't resist a bargain on something for which they *might* have a future need.

☐ **Furniture** may well be the most auctionable merchandise of all. Dealers who find themselves overstocked can advertise and conduct a gala auction sale that is bound to liquidate their surplus in short order. Few householders can resist "needing" a desired article—or even an entire suite—if they feel confident of getting it at the lowest possible price.

Keep in mind the familiar boastful words, "I *won* this at auction!" *Won!* Although the speaker indeed offered the highest sum of money, he or she is considered a *winner*—and you can be the one who awards the prize!

Let's face it, auctions are fun!

CHAPTER TWELVE
LET YOUR AUTO OR TRUCK DO SOME SELLING

By its very nature, your automobile or truck has constant mobility. It travels throughout all sections of your business and maintains its visibility wherever you park it. Instead of considering your vehicle as merely a means of transportation, examine its possibilities as a roving "billboard" that can provide valuable free advertising wherever it travels.

Many ingenious approaches have been devised by all types of merchants who utilize their vehicles to publicize and dramatize their products or services. Some go so far as to decorate the entire side of their truck with lifelike illustrations of products, while others display actual merchandise, develop an eye-catching gimmick, or prominently letter their name and location. Whatever the approach, its result is *increased exposure to the public*.

☐ **A hardware dealer** has an actual ladder mounted on the roof of his automobile, thus prominently exhibiting one of the store's best-selling items. On each rung of the ladder is lettered a one-line advertising message. His telephone number appears on the bottom rung.

☐ **An electrician** painted his panel truck white. Lettered colorfully on the truck is a list of services he offers. His address and phone number are prominently displayed.

☐ **Grossman's Lumber** trucks are known for their simple but imaginative lettering: "Here comes Grossman," states the front of the truck; the rear of the truck says, "There goes Grossman." Listed along the sides are some of their products.

☐ **A druggist's** truck is outfitted with a removable panel sign that can be changed weekly to announce new offerings.

☐ **A restaurateur** custom-designed a truck in the shape of a giant frank-furter, one of the restaurant's specialties.

☐ **A stationer** attached a small showcase to the rear of the truck to display interesting products. The displays are changed regularly.

☐ **An appliance dealer** has a basic message on the side of his panel delivery truck: "Barney is delivering another *Gas Dryer* today."

☐ **A toy store** has a huge balloon mounted atop its delivery truck. The balloon can be inflated and deflated with a simple air-pressure mechanism installed in the vehicle. When the balloon is fully inflated, it reveals a message: "The Best Toys for Good Girls and Boys." The driver hands out small balloons with the same message to children who gather around the truck at its various stops.

☐ **A bakery** truck has the characteristic bakery odor emanating from within (*mmmmm . . .*). Every time the truck stops to make a delivery, the entire neighborhood gets a good appetizing sniff. For those who can't resist such temptation, the baker carries a selection of stock items.

☐ **A pizza parlor** that delivers pizza and other Italian food specialties to area residents has attached to the side of its delivery vehicle a large pouch containing oversized menus and a "Take-One" sign. When the truck is parked, passersby are thus encouraged to take home a menu, which nearly always leads to future patronage.

☐ **A TV sales and repair business** has an actual television set mounted in the curbside of its delivery van. When the technician is making a house call, the set operates for the benefit of passersby. Likewise, when the van is parked in front of the shop, the set is always turned to a seasonal sporting event or some program of general interest.

☐ **An oil company's** delivery truck bears an oversized thermometer indicating the outside temperature. During off-season months it displays a sign detailing a 10-point preseason oil-burner and furnace checkup offer.

You may have some ideas of your own! Whether your vehicle is large or small, your message bold or sedate, it will be carrying word of your business throughout the community.

CHAPTER THIRTEEN HOW MAIL-ORDER CAN INCREASE YOUR SALES

Mail-order is a thriving, productive sales medium that has virtually built some of the biggest merchandisers in the world and provided a substantial profit to thousands of small operators. However, most merchants never use it. Why? Mainly because they haven't considered its potential for their own operation.

Here's how a few small businesses have made mail-order work for them:

☐ **A grocery store,** often complimented on its homemade preserves, decided to make them available through mail-order.

☐ **A camera shop** does film developing by mail—and includes a mail-order blank for more film with each processed roll.

☐ **A furniture shop** does a brisk mail-order business in its "assemble-it-yourself" line of furniture.

☐ **A meat market,** widely known for its delicious steaks, quick-freezes and mails the frozen steaks, three to a box.

☐ **A hardware store** sells hobby and home-crafts tools by mail through advertisements in specialty magazines devoted to those interests.

☐ **A gift shop** periodically sends special gift lists to potential mail-order customers. A steady business results, especially during the holiday season.

□　**A beautician** packages favorite items used in the shop and sells it by mail as a good-grooming kit.

□　**A printer** gets a steady flow of orders for business cards and stationery by running ads in business magazines.

MAIL-ORDER SUCCESS FACTORS

There are many reasons for the success of mail-order sales. Some people, because of age or illness, cannot leave their homes. Others, in remote locations, find it difficult to get to stores. The natural way for them to shop is by mail. Many people *like* to shop by mail, actually *prefer* it to other types of shopping. They enjoy reading about the products offered and welcome the expectation of waiting for the postman to deliver the order.

Mail-order allows a merchant to operate outside the physical selling range of the store, and opens new profit potential. Properly handled, mail-order business tends to be repetitive business, an advantage to any operation.

GETTING STARTED

As a small merchandiser, you can operate a mail-order sideline either through direct-mail promotion or through advertising.

Direct mailing of sales material and order blanks to prospective customers is favored by most merchants because it gets the undivided attention of the reader and allows more space to tell the "story."

An advertisement that includes your mail-order blank is useful when you are offering an outstanding bargain that will be recognized without a strong sales pitch. If your product holds special appeal for a particular group of people and you can reach them through a magazine or paper devoted to their interest, then an order blank within the ad is recommended.

Mailing List Sources

If you decide on the direct-mail method, your first need will be a mailing list. Your established customers are your best prospects, of course, but you'll want to explore other sources. For a small price your town or city clerk's office purveys the local directory (sometimes called a "sheet list"), which will further help you to select potential customers according to age or occupation. The telephone company or moving firms may supply names of new residents.

Mailing lists may be purchased from brokers devoted to this business. Their charge is anywhere from five to ten cents a name. But there are these advantages: brokers' lists contain the names of many confirmed mail-order buyers. These lists are broken down and grouped in such a way that you may be able to get a list tailored quite precisely to your needs.

48

What Kind of Return Can You Expect?   Response varies with the product offered and the impact of the sales message. Two percent is considered a good return, or twenty responses per thousand letters. Using these figures you can decide whether the product or service you are offering would lend itself to successful mail-order.

VALUABLE MAIL-ORDER TIPS

1. The best days for customers to receive mail are Tuesday and Wednesday.

2. Color printing will *double* the selling power of your letter or brochure.

3. Make sure you get a good printing job. If your letter is sloppy or cheap looking, the customer will inevitably get the impression that you run a slipshod business.

4. In writing your letter, make a strong sales pitch by fully describing your product and its advantages. Avoid *exaggerated* claims that the product cannot possibly live up to. Such claims will only leave customers feeling they have been "taken."

5. Illustrations are especially helpful in selling products that are not well-known.

6. When you receive an order, forward the merchandise promptly. Keeping customers waiting or forcing them to inquire about why they have not received their goods usually discourages further business.

Properly operated, mail-order means profits. You owe it to yourself to discover whether or not it can help your business.

CHAPTER FOUR-TEEN

"STICK-ONS"
A POWERFUL SALES TOOL THAT DRAWS REPEAT BUSINESS

A great asset to any merchant is dependable repeat business. Steady, established patronage is most profitable because it involves minimal promotional cost; the advertising investment is made but once, at the time of the customer's initial order.

An effective tool in accomplishing this is the "stick-on," an adhesive label imprinted with your company name, phone number, and perhaps a brief advertising message. Stick-ons can be attached appropriately in your customers' homes to keep your name in their minds and for quick reference when they need your services.

This inexpensive promotional item can often make the difference between your or your competitor receiving the customer's next call. You have effectively installed a permanent advertisement that accomplishes several things:

1. Simplifies the process of calling you.

2. Reminds the customer of your previous satisfactory performance.

3. Indicates your reliability and eagerness to be of further service.

    4. Reinforces the association of your name and your particular product or service in the customer's mind. To this extent you and your company eventually become synonymous with the type of product or service you provide.

Let's look at some time-tested examples of businesses that use stick-ons:

☐ **A TV repair service** attaches to the repaired TV set a sticker giving the service's name, address, and phone number for future repair calls.

☐ **A druggist** supplies an emergency-phone-number sticker to be attached to the customer's medicine cabinet. Included, of course, is the phone number of the drugstore.

☐ **A typewriter repair service** attaches to the repaired machine a sticker giving its phone number along with the projected date when typewriter is due for its next overhaul.

☐ **An automotive transmission specialist** attaches a sticker in the car projecting the date (or mileage) when the automatic transmission may next need attention.

☐ **A piano tuner** fastens a neat little sticker on the back of an upright piano or inside a grand piano, specifying when the piano should next be tuned, and including, of course, the tuner's address and phone number.

☐ **A liquor store** furnishes customers with a sticker to post in the liquor closet or on the bar. It gives the store's name and phone number along with a statement of its delivery policy.

☐ **A picture framer** places a sticker on the back of framed pictures, giving the shop's address and indicating that all types of frames are available.

☐ **An exterminator** pastes a sticker inside the kitchen cabinet or broom closet indicating the date of service when a return visit should be scheduled.

☐ **A stationer** affixes stickers to boxed merchandise, indicating the store's name, location, and phone number.

CHAPTER FIFTEEN TELEPHONE SALES IDEAS

WHY TELEPHONING PAYS OFF

Your telephone can become a powerful selling medium. Its judicious use can increase your list of prospects, establish continuing customer communication on a highly personal level, and greatly augment your sales. New and inactive accounts will show response, and active accounts will react more favorably through frequent telephone contacts.

Low Cost

A telephone call will achieve at relatively low cost a personal contact that can be surpassed only by an actual visit. The telephone puts you in touch with your prospect on an intimate conversational basis.

PLAN YOUR CALLS

For maximum effectiveness, it is essential that you develop a properly organized approach to telephoning. The amount of time invested in preparation will quickly pay for itself when your calls carry exactly the customer impact that you have in mind. A list of the prospects you wish to contact is of primary importance.

Prepare a Brief "Pitch"

It is wise to prepare a written specimen of your proposed telephone conversation and time yourself so that this "pitch" does not exceed one minute. Just as a personal visit, your personality becomes the all-important factor.

Your presentation will succeed or fail according to the image evoked in your prospect's mind. Not only your choice of words, but also the very tone of your voice will attract or repel and ultimately determine your results. Years ago, the telephone company based a public-relations campaign on the theme, "It's the voice with the smile that wins." This is an important fact to keep in mind when contacting your prospects by telephone.

Let Your Customers Talk

In your telephone sales talk, try to summarize the advantages of your proposition in one or two sentences. Whatever you do, *don't* deliver an "oration" to the faceless individual. Speak in conversational tones. Envision the person with whom you are speaking as a typical prospect, and act as though you were sitting across from him or her and taking face-to-face. As in talking face-to-face, allow "resting spots" in your telephone talk so that your prospect has an opportunity to say something or ask a question here and there.

Reinforce Your Ads

Telephone calls are highly effective when geared to a current direct-mail program. A call can be made as a follow-up to your letter or as an announcement that a letter will be forthcoming. In either case the telephone calls attention to the importance of your mailing and adds a personal note that can't help but improve its results.

Keep Records

Worth repeating is the importance of properly organizing your telephone program and adhering to a plan. You should arrange to make a specified number of calls each day, setting a daily minimum of ten calls, for example. Your list of prospects should consist of a card or chart for each, listing pertinent statistics and allowing adequate space for notations about the results of your calls. There should also be space to indicate call-backs, along with their dates and circumstances. (The illustration may serve as a guide.) As you make your calls, enter them faithfully on the chart. Few things are so embarrassing as calling the same prospect twice.

WHOM TO CALL

You can focus your telephone campaign on acquiring new customers, getting in touch with old ones, or on keeping current accounts lively—or you can effectively use this method to make contact with all three areas of your market.

Finding New Prospects

New account prospects should be compiled from name lists available from varied sources. It is considered sound strategy to probe and test different name groups until you have established which groups or lists yield your best

```
┌─────────────────────────────────────────────────────┐
│              TELEPHONE RECORD                         │
│                                                       │
│  Name: _____       │
│  Address: _____        │
│                                                       │
│  _____        │
│  Telephone no.: _____        │
│  Date of initial call: _____        │
│  Talked to: _____        │
│  Results: _____        │
│                                                       │
│  _____        │
│  Comments: _____        │
│                                                       │
│  _____        │
│                                                       │
│  _____        │
│  Call-back date: _____        │
│  Results: _____        │
│                                                       │
│  _____        │
│  Comments: _____        │
│                                                       │
│  _____        │
│                                                       │
│  _____        │
└─────────────────────────────────────────────────────┘
```

customer potential. After this discovery, concentrate your fire on those areas that have proven to be most worthwhile.

 Inactive accounts can often be revived and returned to active sales status through a telephone call with a strong personal touch. Such calls make customers feel that you really value their patronage and have a genuine personal interest in them. You may be surprised at the results. Recent test telephone campaigns of this type have succeeded in producing revived sales in up to 35 percent of the contacts made.

Active Accounts

Active accounts solicited by telephone can prove particularly productive. A phone call now and then indicates that you appreciate their business and it reminds them about another order they've been thinking of placing with you. Also, it gives you an opportunity to bring to their attention new products and services, as well as information about new uses for your product, improvements, price changes, and so on.

WHEN TO CALL

Bear in mind that certain hours of the day are better than others for making specific telephone calls. This depends largely upon whom you are directing your sales pitch toward:

Homes   Homes, it was once felt, should be phoned in the afternoon if you wished to speak with the wife and the evening if you wished to speak with the husband. Changing employment trends now indicate early evening is the most likely time to reach both householders.

Stores   Stores should be phoned in the morning or mid-afternoon, *never* during their busy noon hours.

Businesses   Businesses should be called at hours that seem convenient to their individual operations. *Builders,* for example, should be contacted before 9:00 a.m. *Other service agencies* should be contacted early in the morning, before they embark on their day's itinerary. Times are more flexible for those who work on their own premises.

THREE MAGIC WORDS

There is considerable magic in the announcement, "Long distance calling!" Many firms make effective use of the special service and rates offered to business by their telephone company. Such service may enable you to reserve time for making an unlimited number of long-distance calls into a given area, each with the operator's own lyrical announcement of "Long distance calling!" However, instead of paying so much per call, you are billed a flat overall monthly fee—to put it more bluntly, you pay a "bulk" rate. The telephone company helps further by supplying you with directories for those areas you arrange to call.

SOME SUCCESS STORIES

Yes indeed, the spoken word can be highly persuasive and most effective. If you don't take advantage of your telephone, you're missing an awfully good bet! Consider the following uses, and see which one might apply to you:

☐ **Firm 1** (*in the infra-red industrial heating field*) used the phone to arrange appointments prior to the sales visit. This saved considerable time and frayed nerves on both sides and led to a more receptive attitude on the part of the prospect.

☐ **Firm 2** (*in the typewriter sales and service field*) contacted all past customers on their list asking whether the typewriters they had purchased needed servicing. This goodwill type of phone contact was appreciated; it impressed customers with the reliability of the organization and led to a good percentage of orders for new typewriters.

☐ **Firm 3** (*in the closed-circuit-television field*) used the telephone to conduct conference "sales chats" among their dealers. Each dealer was urged to make ten phone calls the next day to inactive customers and report back (also by phone) with the results achieved.

☐ **Firm 4** (*in the kitchen-cabinets field*) used the phone to notify area residents of a scheduled Open House in their showroom, at which prizes would be featured.

☐ **Firm 5** (*owner of a drive-in hamburger stand*) successfully used the phone to announce (1) their grand opening; (2) special discounts for family patronage; (3) appearance of celebrities on a specific date; and (4) special take-home gifts for the children.

☐ **Firm 6** (*in the formal-wear rental field*) successfully used the phone to contact college fraternities, informing them of the advantages of their policies and rates. Similarly, they have phoned caterers, political organizations, wedding coordinators, and so on, to ensure that these related firms are aware of their convenience. The telephone has proved a big factor in their business.

☐ **Firm 7** (*in the sauna-bath field*) regularly uses the phone after each sauna installation to inquire how customers enjoyed their initial use of the sauna and whether the installation was satisfactorily and courteously performed.

☐ **Firm 8** (*in the record-keeping and tax-preparation field*) phoned small businesses in the area to inform them of a special booklet, "How to Save on Your Taxes," that was available at no charge. This provided a *door opener* for their followup visit.

☐ **Firm 9** (*selling prepackaged novelties from from racks installed in stores*) telephoned area residents to inform them that these racks were now in their neighborhood stores and contained a variety of unusual tricks and games.

☐ **Firm 10** (*in the industrial soaps field*) "leased" long-distance telephone lines on a monthly charge basis. Their ten salespeople contacted all industrial firms and institutions within the radius of this phone connection, selling to them on a "money-back-if-not-satisfied" basis. This proved so effective that the firm tripled its business in one year. New localities are "saturated" by phone on an average of one a week.

☐ **Firm 11** (*a rug-cleaning business*) established a policy of phoning customers every three months to see whether another cleaning job was desired. This proved effective in stimulating a continued flow of business.

☐ **Firm 12** (*in the credit and collection field*) used the phone very effectively to contact all past and present customers and request referrals to their business friends. This effort yielded an average of three referrals per call.

☐ **Firm 13** (*a lawn-care specialist*) established a telephone canvass that contacts all residents of a neighborhood in which a job has been completed. "We have just done some landscaping for Lee Jones, your neighbor," they explain, "and while we're in the neighborhood, we can also take care of YOUR lawn at special prices!"

POINTS TO REMEMBER

To get new customers Compile your prospect list, using the phone directory, street directory, or other convenient register. Phone these individuals with an attractive *specific offer* that enables an easy decision and doesn't commit them to a big expenditure. (Your aim is to establish initial patronage, no matter how small.) One firm phones to offer free consultation; another offers to show the prospect what their firm has done for a competitor or neighbor. A laundry offers free cleaning of a tie with each order.

Introduce yourself by emphasizing "no obligation" and that your call will take only a few minutes of their time.

To maintain goodwill of current customers An occasional phone call builds valuable goodwill and serves to reinforce your relationship with a regular customer. One firm stresses a "special offer" that they feel the customer will appreciate being informed of at once, by phone. Another firm phones to extend best wishes on customers' birthdays (carefully recorded and filed at the time of their initial patronage). Another makes an informal, friendly call expressing concern when a customer hasn't been seen for a while. Such calls win the customer's gratitude and help ensure maintained patronage.

Off-hour telephone sales Many small retailers engage telephone-answering services (usually available for about $8 a month) and then advertise that customers can place orders at "any time of day or night." In some instances this encouragement of impulse ordering has increased business as much as fifty percent.

Your telephone personality Speak naturally, in a conversational tone, just as if you were speaking to a friend sitting nearby. Use a "you" (rather than "I") approach — stress what you can do *for the prospect.* Give those whom you call plenty of chance of participate by asking them questions.

CHAPTER SIXTEEN PROMOTING FUTURE BUSINESS THROUGH PRESENT JOBS

If your operation is one of service, installation, home maintenance or improvement, every job provides a unique opportunity to attract additional customers in the same area.

PERSONAL CONTACT

While working in a neighborhood, take some of your own time to visit other homes nearby. You should know each prospect's name, and make your approach friendly, casual, and brief:

"Good afternoon, Mr. Smith, I'm Lee Jones of Jones Associates. You may have noticed that we're doing some work for the Greens down the street. While we're in the neighborhood, we'd like to offer you folks the same fine service at a similar low price . . ."

This type of low-key, personal approach has tremendous sales potential. If you happen to be working in coveralls, don't let that deter you—it may even help. (After all, a housepainter or landscaper wouldn't be expected to do much work in a three-piece suit!)

The fact that your work is in progress offers splendid documentation— it *proves* that you are active and successful in your field.

If the current job is being done outdoors, or if your customer encourages neighbors to drop by and view interior work, your prospects will have the opportunity to actually *watch* you perform. In this context they usually manage to identify your services with their own needs. Confidence is engendered while sales resistance is reduced. The fact that their neighbors seem pleased with your work further ensures the likelihood of their future patronage.

VISUAL ADVERTISING

Whenever and wherever you perform your services, consider the possibility of visual advertising. An attractive, easy-to-read sign need be your only investment. Just place it where it can be seen by neighbors and passersby.

☐ **A kitchen modernization firm** might set up a sign outside the house announcing, "Another Custom Kitchen by Caswell."

☐ **Housepainters** have been using this device for quite some time: "Another Outstanding Paint Job by Mazarro Brothers" says it all!

☐ **A lawn-care specialist** can do likewise: "This Lawn Is Receiving the Tender Loving Care of Lou's Landscaping, Inc."

☐ **A real-estate agent** will find it effective to post an on-site sign stating, for example, "This store has been rented through Harvey Green Realty Associates."

Analyze your own services. What type of sign would be applicable to what you are doing? We know some companies who have built a substantial part of their businesses around these on-the-job promotions that reach new prospects while work is proceeding for their neighbors and associates.

A popular variation of the on-site sign is the "door-hanger," a simple, eye-catching card designed to attach easily to the doorknobs of houses. The illustration shows a sample of one format that can be inexpensively printed and quickly personalized to suit an individual neighborhood.

You're Invited to Watch

AJAX PAINTERS

Paint the Home of Your Neighbor

Name: _____

Address: _____

Date: _____

Time: _____

We will be pleased to have you observe the quality of our work. We know you will be particularly pleased at our low rates. We'll be glad to estimate your home. No obligation! Come look—you'll be glad you did.

CHAPTER SEVEN-TEEN PROMOTIONAL "EVENTS" AND CONTESTS— THE DYNAMIC DUO!

THEY'LL PEP UP BUSINESS IN COUNTLESS WAYS

Even the most thriving business occasionally becomes somewhat sluggish. Does yours need a stimulant? Why not try a little showmanship! With minimal expense you can tap your imagination and originality to stage a promotional event or sponsor a contest that will create community interest, attract new patrons, and rekindle the enthusiasm of established customers.

Let's examine just *some* of the things a well-timed event or contest can do:

☐ **Stimulate** and increase store traffic.

☐ **Supply** the customer an incentive to purchase.

☐ **Avoid** seasonal "drop-offs."

☐ **Encourage** attendance at product demonstrations.

☐ **Add** action appeal and a new twist to your advertising.

☐ **Combat** competition. If prospects feel they have a chance to win or save by buying from you, they'll ignore your competitor.

☐ **Introduce** a new product or line.

☐   **Expand** the customer's uses of an established product.

☐   **Convince** people to buy greater quantities of your product or continue to use it over an extended period. (The incentive may involve purchase of several units rather than one, or the repeated use of the product.)

☐   **Interest** the public in naming a new product.

☐   **Secure** customer testimonials.

If you distribute your merchandise through a number of outlets, a promotion or contest can help in these ways:

☐   **Enlist** dealer cooperation in obtaining more display space. Retailers know that a contest has customer appeal; if they feel that store traffic and sales will receive a boost, they'll gladly tie-in with you.

☐   **Inspire** dealers to stock larger quantities of your product or expand their current stock into a full or wider line.

☐   **Pep-up** your sales force. A contest gives them something concrete and new to talk about, something through which they can persuade dealers to increase orders and expand their focus on your product.

☐   **Familiarize** the public with a change in product name or package design.

☐   **Call attention** to a newly instituted premium plan.

PROMOTE WITH A FLAIR FOR FUN

Your primary objective in a campaign of this type is to attract attention, so don't be afraid to try the unusual. Time-tested promotions and contests often bring great success, but chances are good that the more off-beat and humorous your ideas are, the better they'll accomplish your goal.

You might want to sponsor a team or weekly athletic event. But it doesn't have to be men's softball! Discuss the idea of a "whacky" competition among your neighboring merchants. People could be encouraged to represent your store in a local tiddly-winks, croquet, marbles, or hula-hoop tournament. Frisbees, yo-yos, jacks, and paddleballs have faithful (and often skilled) fans of all ages. Ongoing scores and pictures of the teams in action could be posted in your windows, along with messages of encouragement from your patrons. At the end of the "season" one team can be awarded the championship of the local FOOLympics.

Entries in the more staid events, such as soap-box derbies, turtle races, walkathons, and bikeathons still generate much public interest, of course.

Another twist is to capitalize on current local events. You might look for tie-ins with coming movies, for example. If a horror film is due, invite folks of all ages to draw or construct (to scale) any large portion of a would-be monster. The ugliest of these parts are used to assemble an actual monster. Everyone whose parts were used to create the final monster receives movie tickets, while the monster is displayed prominently in your window.

Utilize all window space or open area for such feature events and faithfully post the progress of each contest.

Such unusual goings-on provide welcome feature stories and pictures for the local newspaper. Make sure the editor gets the word! Keep publicity in mind when planning your attraction and try to make it as colorful as possible. Besides luring more patrons it is also an excellent opportunity for FREE publicity. And the more talk that it stirs, the better!

SOME SUGGESTIONS FOR SALES-BOOSTING PROMOTIONS

☐ **Wheel of Fortune:** At varying hours of the day, a large wheel is revolved. Individuals holding the "lucky number" from your advertisement or brochure win a prize.

☐ **Crazy Auction:** For example, start bid high . . . and work down to ridiculously low price bids.

☐ **Postcard Payoff:** A postcard (with your ad) contains a chance number on it . . . good for a designated item or discount when brought to the store.

☐ **Balloon Bonanza:** The store is dresed up with balloons. Free balloons are given to the kiddies, and your newspaper ad centers its theme around balloons.

☐ **Food Festival:** Many effective, appealing promotional opportunities exist for food items—World Food Fair, Meat 'n Taters, Let Them Eat Steak, and so on.

☐ **Art Show:** Sponsor an art show, exhibiting the best entries in your establishment. Price them for sale. Try to obtain entries from prominent people, and expect to "discover" some local talent.

☐ **Western Week:** Decorate store and dress personnel in Western motif, play Western music, hang reward posters, and feature Western money (discount coupons).

☐ **Group Project:** Ask everyone to donate squares for the "biggest quilt in the world," or string and cord for an enormous string ball. Naturally the article will be displayed prominently in your store and its progress should generate much interest.

- ☐ **Traffic Builders:** Trading coupons . . . special "ridiculous bargain" days . . . Wishing Well for customer drawings (winner has "wish come true") . . . mystery gift-pack . . . fashion show . . . these and other gimmicks will bring people inside.

- ☐ **Accent on Youth:** Offer free tickets to local baseball games . . . sponsor clubs for teenagers . . . feature record and tape specials . . . display interesting local hobby collections or student crafts.

- ☐ **Giant Spotlight:** Try a "follow-the-lights" promotion by positioning a giant spotlight in front of your shop. As its beams reflect in the sky, curious people will seek out their source.

- ☐ **Store Anniversary Celebration:** Offer prizes to oldest customer, youngest customer, largest family group, most recent bride and groom, and other "superlatives" who visit your store.

- ☐ **Dutch Auction:** Trade-ins, used or shopworn items, discontinued items, and overstocked "bargain buys" can be moved, and everyone can join in the fun.

- ☐ **Cash Refund:** During one specific day of the month, the full purchase price is refunded to customer—slips are handed out for each day of the month. A drawing is held on the last day of the month. Those holding the lucky slips are to get full refund.

LUCKY WINNERS

Lucky Fifth Sale Give out numbered coupons to people entering your establishment for one hour in the morning and one hour in the afternoon. Every *fifth* coupon entitles that person to a small prize of some kind. This idea should keep them coming in!

Lucky Thirteenth Sale One merchant of our acquaintance runs an annual clearance sale at which time he credits $10 for every *thirteenth* sale, actually ringing a gong outside the store whenever a thirteenth sale is made.

Lucky Number Surprise From an alert retailer in a small town comes this idea: Compile a mailing list of community residents and assign a number to each. Display six numbers on your bulletin board each day; those having "lucky numbers" will be surprised (and delighted) with the news that they are entitled to $10 worth of merchandise *free*. With proper publicity, this idea can really increase store traffic!

Lucky Baby   Originating with an infants' wear store but good for public relations for any establishment, is the idea of awarding a gift to the first baby born in the community each month.

Lucky Birthday Cake   A unique and attention-getting store anniversary celebration is one in which a 100-pound birthday cake is featured. Baked into it are a dime, a thimble, a wedding ring, or any assortment of items you choose. Customers are invited to have a piece of the cake and those who find a concealed item in their slice receive prizes.

Lucky Telephone Number   One retail establishment has used this idea repeatedly with success. It may work well for you. Periodically it conducts a "Surprise Day" at which time randomly selected phone numbers and their subscribers' initials are scattered throughout the store's full-page newspaper ad, along with the name and price of an article. Those finding their initials and phone number in the ad need merely show them to the store manager and the particular item is theirs — *free*. Certainly this is a way to ensure that your ad is carefully read!

Lucky "Dollars from Heaven"   In conducting this promotion, one organization hired a helicopter to hover several hundred feet above its premises, slowly circling about in the beam of a giant spotlight. Numbered circulars advertising the store's sales event were dropped from the helicopter. One hundred "lucky numbers" were listed inside the store, redeemable for five dollars each.

Lucky Cleanup   If you were to run a related promotion (as perhaps a "Clean Sweep" Sale), you could award a vacuum cleaner to the holder of a lucky card drawn from those deposited in a box during the week of your sale.

Lucky Family   Here's a promotion to surpass all the rest, especially in today's inflationary climate where everyone worries about their living expenses. Who could resist dropping by to register for *an expense-free month for the entire family?* The outlay is substantial, but the interest and goodwill that will surely result should more than offset your expenses. Several small stores in a shopping community might well put their heads together on this one, sharing costs and enjoying group publicity.

At no obligation, with nothing to buy or write, invite customers to enter their names in a Grand Drawing. They need not even be present if their name is drawn to receive the following:

Rent or mortgage—up to $400

Food—up to $800

Heating fuel—up to $100.

Electricity—up to $50.

Telephone—up to $30.

Movies—up to $25.

Hair stylist—up to $50.

Babysitter—up to $75.

Laundry and dry-cleaning—up to $30.

SEASONAL PROMOTIONS

Your special events and extravaganzas will attract the desired attention, but to keep business lively throughout the year consistent month-by-month features and themes are in order. These can be considerably less flashy, but they'll provide the variety in atmosphere and advertising that tells people your business is thriving. And so it will be, if you cater to the seasonal interests of your customers!

January
- ☐ After-Christmas sales and clearances.
- ☐ Safety campaign slogans for New Year's ads.
- ☐ Gift certificates to new members of a community.
- ☐ Large calendar display in store showing community events during coming weeks and months.

February
- ☐ Displays honoring National Boy Scout Week.
- ☐ Valentine's day promotion (very colorful).
- ☐ Lincoln's Birthday.
- ☐ Washington's Birthday.

March
- ☐ St. Patrick's Day sweepstakes.
- ☐ Easter focus (eggs, bunnies, and apparel).
- ☐ "Mad Hat" Contest (employees design hats from merchandise, publicity is generated, and judging is staged in store).

April
- ☐ April-Fool sale (with *you* as the fool for offering bargains).
- ☐ *Revolutionary* sales spectacular.
- ☐ "Spring is here!"

May
- ☐ Mother's Day.
- ☐ Baseball season has begun—a good theme here.
- ☐ Flowers, gardens, things that grow.

June
- ☐ Father's Day promotion.
- ☐ Vacation features.
- ☐ Outdoor fun.

July
- ☐ Fourth of July promotion might include nonexploding firecrackers in barrel bearing name of your establishment and "Our (product) is not a dud."
- ☐ "Sizzling" summer values.
- ☐ How to *beat* the heat—create displays that look (or even feel) cool.

August
- ☐ Big-Top theme. (Stock a big tent with fine buys and refreshments.)
- ☐ Back-to-school promotion.

September
- ☐ Labor-Day clearance.
- ☐ Back-*at*-school promotion (perhaps a contest for children).
- ☐ Fall "harvest" of values.

October
- ☐ Columbus-Day sale. ("*Discover* our values!")
- ☐ Halloween promotions and contests almost create themselves.
- ☐ World-Series spectacular. (You might rent a TV set and place it in your window so that passersby could keep up with the games.)

November
- ☐ Thanksgiving. Invite a live turkey to spend some time in your store window (or substitute some good illustrations of turkeys). Sponsor a "free drawing"—winner gets bird!
- ☐ Christmas (have sneak previews of holiday goods and a special "male-only" night for Christmas shoppers).

December
- ☐ Christmas and New Year promotions abound. This is a good time check store housekeeping, cleanliness, and lighting. Don't skimp on special services. Decorate attractively—tie-in your window display with the store's interior.

CONDUCTING CONSUMER CONTESTS

Nearly everyone enjoys the spirit of competition, which is why a consumer contest is one of the surest ways to make new friends and win new customers. The possibilities are all but unlimited, and you can be sure there is a contest that will suit your business perfectly. Prizes don't have to be particularly expensive. You may prefer to award credit vouchers, merchandise, or cash, of course—but don't overlook the *unusual* variety of prize. A short vacation in a neighboring town, a servant for a week, or an old car or bus may be things your contestants have never experienced or owned before. They may enjoy receiving a tree, an engraved trophy, or merely an ornate certificate of distinction. The spirit of the contest is the main thing; if your approach is right, people will enthusiastically enter the competition regardless of its reward. Advance news of the event should be well posted on your premises.

TYPES OF CONTESTS

Contests can be as far out as your imagination want to take them, but a few basic formats usually come to mind:

- ☐ **Best entry:** Letter about your product, statement in 25 (or 50) words or less, slogan, last line (for a limerick or jingle), list of product uses, illustration for your ad, idea for new way to use product, and so on.

- ☐ **Photos:** Cutest baby (customers vote); match-the-twins. Who (or where) is this? (Identification of old pictures from around the community.)

- ☐ **Name something:** A new product or combination of food items; a game or way of using a product; a pet that you keep in your store or window (*it* could be the prize).

- ☐ **Marathon:** Chair rocking, rope skipping, dancing, piano playing, knitting, gum chewing, chess playing, see-sawing, swinging . . . anything that involves continuous motion and will attract spectators.

- ☐ **Treasure hunt:** Conceal something in your store or elsewhere in town, give clues (the familiar Easter-egg hunt can be adapted in many ways). Search for some unusual or long-lost item (e.g., 1935 telephone directory or oldest citizen in town.)

- ☐ **Guessing game:** How many beans in a bathtub? Bottle-caps in a jar? Buttons in a box?

- ☐ **Superlatives:** *Most* freckles; *biggest* ears, feet, dog, cat, rabbit; *fastest* gun draw, ice-cream eater, puzzle-solver; *longest* beard or hair, *funniest* face, *tallest* man, *shortest* woman, *most elaborate* sundae or *most unusual* recipe, *prettiest* smile, *smallest* handwriting, and so on.

You may also be interested in considering the traditional talent contest or competition involving skilled athletic accomplishment, *especially if these areas relate in any way to your products.*

INTRODUCING
YOUR CONTEST

In conducting your consumer contest, you'll be looking for all the publicity you can get, so don't be bashful about seeking it. Let your product show—let everyone know *what* and *who* is sponsoring the contest. Don't be afraid of repetition in your advertising; it adds emphasis and achieves clarity.

Be convincing! Make *every* contestant feel that he or she has an equal chance to win. Use every means at your command to encourage dealers or suppliers to tie-in with your efforts.

Play up your first prize, but don't subordinate lesser prizes too greatly. Let people know there are plenty of opportunities to win something.

If merchandise prizes are being offered, don't allow them to overshadow your product. Remember—it's *your* product that you're trying to sell!

**Rules for
Rules**

1. Make sure your rules are perfectly legal and do not violate any lottery laws.

2. State the rules thoroughly and clearly, aiming for simplicity in wording and layout of copy.

3. Give contestants a sample of what they are to do. (For example, if it's a puzzle contest, show a sample puzzle and a clear explanation of how to solve it.) If the contest has intricate points, issue a booklet explaining them.

4. Make the entry blank large enough so that it can be filled out easily and plainly.

5. Advertise the contest in the same media in which you advertise your product.

6. Display the rules prominently in your store. In your ad, keep them clearly separate from your promotional copy.

**And don't
forget to . . .**

. . . Specify the closing date (emphasize postmark requirement, if there is one).

. . . Explain how ties will be decided.

. . . Specify where to send entries.

. . . List prizes clearly, showing first, second, third, and so on, in complete sequence.

. . . Indicate that judges' decision will be final and entries are nonreturnable (if this is so).

. . . State when and how winners will be announced.

SOME EYE-CATCHING CONTESTS THAT ATTRACT PARTICIPATION

Matching Card Halves
Here's an idea to maintain loyalty as well as to attract new business: With each sales slip, give the customer a sealed envelope containing one-half of a card illustration. You'll be working with a number of card illustrations, so it's purely a matter of chance (depending largely upon how often the customer comes in) as to whether he or she gets two matching halves. Publicity—such as immediate posting of winners' names—will build interest and get people to feel that they, too, have a good chance to win. This gives them a good reason to return often.

Guessing Contest
While this idea may have originated with a drugstore, it can be used by practically any store with a display window. The idea is to place in the window a large pharmaceutical jar filled with simulated pills (M&M's, for example). Contestants must guess how many pills are in the jar, jotting down their guesses, as well as their names and addresses, on a piece of paper that they deposit in a convenient ballot box. You can award prizes weekly, changing the number of pills. Your window will attract the attention of many passersby to your merchandise display as well.

Slogan Contest
Apparently never losing its popularity is a contest that awards prizes for slogans that expand a statement such as, "I like to shop at _____ because. . . ." Ask a few prominent local figures to serve on your panel of judges.

"Grow-the-Biggest-Squash" Contest
A "corny" type of contest is often very appealing. Located in a rural area? Publicity and goodwill will result from a contest for the biggest squash grown by local student farmers. You provide the necessary seeds, and later award prizes to the most successful boys and girls. This could be expanded to include

categories for several types of vegetables. In a nonrural area, try a sunflower competition. Incredibly tall sunflowers can be cultivated in a sunny corner of a yard or alongside a house!

Poster
Contest

Offer prizes to local students who submit the best posters advertising your establishment. In announcing prizes, display the winning posters—and runners-up—in your window or inside the store. This contest could extend over a period of time by assigning a separate month to each of several age categories.

Melting-Time
Guess

Much interest is attracted by this contest, in which a cake of manufactured ice is placed in a window. A straw hat or some durable product from your inventory is frozen into the middle of it. Passersby are invited to come into the store and record their guesses as to how long it will take for the ice to melt and the object to become unfrozen. Prizes, of course, are awarded to those coming closest to the actual "unfreezing" time.

"Guess Its
Age" Contest

As we saw it done, a runt pig was displayed in the window—but the type of animal you use is up to you. The contest is open to children under sixteen who are asked to guess its age. To narrow this down, require that the age be guessed in years, months, and weeks. Then ten (or more) children guessing closest to the actual age are awarded prizes.

Swimming
Meet

You really get "in the swim" with this competition, which can be held in a community pool, or that of a local school or college. Offer prizes of season tickets to a nearby swimming pool or amusement park, plus listed prizes from your own stock of merchandise. Your local paper's sports section should give this one a lot of publicity!

Spelling
Bee

Invite local high-school students to compete in an annual spelling bee. If you're persuasive, a local TV station may see fit to broadcast the semifinals and finals. The resulting community interest can build valuable goodwill for you and your business.

Dressmaking
Contest

Adaptable to any establishment that caters primarily to women, this contest for nonprofessional dressmakers offers prizes for the home-sewn dresses judged best in design and workmanship. It will encourage women to visit your store and further ensure that you'll be mentioned in conversations with others who share their interests.

**PROMOTIONAL "EVENTS" AND CONTESTS—
THE DYNAMIC DUO!**

Baby Contest

Arrange a "party" for babies of the community and offer prizes for the prettiest smile, the reddest hair, the bluest eyes, the baldest head, the rosiest cheeks, the loudest howl, etc. Advertise well, and invite as "special guests" any high-schoolers or retired people who are in the business of babysitting. This gesture of goodwill should combine with the merriment to make it an occasion every-one will remember—and you know what that means for business!

Silver-Coin Exchange

Here's a guessing contest that automatically provides word-of-mouth adver-tising! A dealer advertises that five persons in the community (not employees of the firm, of course) have been given silver coins (or ten-dollar bills) to carry with them. Anyone who asks a "secret carrier" the proper question (e.g., "Don't you think Smith & Co. is great?") wins that coin (or bill). (One merchant reported that by the second day all coins had changed ownership; needless to say, the store's name had been mentioned hundreds of times.

Most Words from the Letters in Your Store's Name

Another way to keep your name in the public eye is to offer prizes for the longest lists of words using only the letters in your firm's name. If your trade name is very short (Al's TV) or its letters limited (Zeke's Pizza), add a *brief* slogan.

Smallest Handwriting Contest

Here's an idea that will be talked about and *written* about. Offer a prize to the person or persons who write the name of your establishment (or whatever appropriate line you choose) the greatest number of times—*on an ordinary postcard.* You might want the line to mention some feature of your store; for example "The Smith Co. sells Brown-Jones Shoes." Display all entries on a bulletin board in your store.

Most-Intelligent Pet Contest

Many people own pets, and their affection is such that they'll happily vie for prizes to prove *their* pet is the most intelligent. Find a suitable auditorium, gymnasium, or park in which to conduct your contest. Announce "preliminar-ies" and later conduct "finals." These contests attract widespread participation and invite much publicity. Expect to review a great variety of pets. Dogs and cats will be entered, of course, but monkeys, roosters, and even pigs may join the fun. In one case a dolphin's entry had to be rejected when no tank facilities could be made available.

Costume Contest

In this contest, prizes are offered for the most original designs for costumes that can be made at home from relatively inexpensive materials. You might specify fancy dress balls, masquerades, Halloween, or St. Valentine's Day costumes, or have a category for each. The winning designs are made into costumes, which are then displayed in your store windows. A panel of judges could be drawn from the faculties of local schools—art teacher, sewing teacher, drama coach, etc.

Rooster-Catchers
Get the Bird—
and a Bonus

Here's a "bird" of a field event that was used effectively by one retail establishment. A number of fast-running roosters were released, each carrying a tag good for $5.00 on a purchase. Those nimble contestants who caught the roosters kept the birds and redeemed their tags toward merchandise, as well.

SECTION TWO

NEW SALES CONCEPTS

CHAPTER EIGHTEEN PROSPECTING FOR CUSTOMERS

"Prospecting" for customers is a lot like prospecting for gold: It requires plenty of *digging*. Moreover, it requires digging with the right *tools*—in the right place and at the right time.

Whether you are selling a product or a service, the extent to which you *prosper* is governed by the extent to which you *prospect*. And that isn't just a matter of quantity, but quality and continuity as well. In other words, reach out with a well-prepared sales program and plenty of follow-up.

ESTABLISH A PLAN

To be successful, your prospecting program must be planned thoroughly and executed carefully. Three essential steps demand advance consideration:

1. **Determine whom** you want to reach.

2. **Decide how** best to reach them.

3. **Organize your program** for maximum results from time and effort. (In this connection it is important to maintain an alphabetical file, as well as a date file that tells you when various contacts should be followed up.)

WHOM TO CONTACT

Determining whom you want to reach may at first seem rather elementary. You may say to yourself, "Since I know my product, I should certainly know my prospects." For example, someone in the jewelry handicrafts line says, "My prospects, of course, are *women*." Someone selling Finnish sauna baths answers, "My prospects are *homeowners*." Someone in the toy business responds immediately, "*Children!*"

In the broad sense, of course, each would be right. However, such general categories are tantamount to "ot-shooting" rather than precision rifle shooting at specific targets. It is important to aim individually at the various component facets of your market rather than to scatter your fire indiscriminately. The difference between concentration and hit-or-miss can be the difference between success and failure. Concentrating your fire on one segment at a time can, in the overall picture, multiply your results as many as ten times.

**Be
Specific** It is highly essential to take a microscopic view of your market. Ask yourself, "What specific uses do our products have that will make them desirable to select groups and encourage their wider use?" With this provocative question in mind, let us analyze the market for the three businesses mentioned above and consider some precise groups that would be logical prospects.

**Jewelry
Handicrafts**
- ☐ Junior achievement groups
- ☐ Geriatric groups
- ☐ Women's clubs
- ☐ Church groups
- ☐ Earning fund programs
- ☐ Industrial firms (employees' handicraft classes)
- ☐ Schools (student handicraft classes)
- ☐ Party-plan promotions (see Chapter One)
- ☐ Hospital rehabilitation groups

**Finnish
Saunas**
- ☐ Hotels and motels
- ☐ Health spas
- ☐ Hospitals
- ☐ Gymnasiums
- ☐ Massage parlors
- ☐ Individual homes

Toys
- ☐ Manufacturers who feature premiums to attract business for their own products
- ☐ Earning fund programs
- ☐ Mail-order firms (game-of-the-month or toy-of-the-month plans, gift catalogs, etc.)
- ☐ Private kindergartens and schools

HOW TO
REACH THEM
Once you have thoroughly explored your possible markets and determined exactly whom you want to reach, it's time to decide with which method or combination of methods you will best accomplish this:

- □ By mail
- □ By telephone
- □ Through media ads

Mail
The first step is to get prospect lists. These are obtainable through mailing-list brokers, city directories, trade directories, reverse telephone directories, referral names. You can use such varied types of mailings as postcards, self-mailers, letters, brochures, and samples.

Telephone
This is a highly personalized and particularly effective approach. The telephone can be used (a) to activate inactive customers; (b) to initiate sales contacts (informing customers of a sale, a new development, etc.); (c) as a dynamic direct-mail follow-up. The direct mail introduces you and in effect "opens the door." The follow-up telephone call now personalizes the mailing. The call can be brief, since details concerning the offer have been provided in the mailed literature; hence maximum attention and sales potential can be expected.

Media Ads
Media advertising provides improved market penetration and image exposure. It's also a means of achieving the impact of repetition on your prospective customers. Local media includes community newspapers and magazines (specifically pinpointed to your area), trade or professional magazines (targeted to the specific business of your prospective customers), and the electronic media of radio and TV.

In budgeting for advertising, strive to use media proven for their results. Proceed cautiously! Start small, test your results, and expand according to sales and cash flow received from particular media. Also ascertain that a chosen publication has minimum "waste" circulation—and instead targets the greatest possible concentration of prospective customers as contrasted with *non-*prospects.

CHAPTER NINETEEN BRINGING INACTIVE CUSTOMERS BACK TO THE ACTIVE FOLD

Exactly what causes once-active customers to become inactive?

In some instances, of course, loyal patrons move away or are forced by practicality to deal with a similar business that has opened closer to their homes.

In most cases, however, little grievances—usually figments of their own imagination—have led to their inactivity. A fancied slight or discourtesy, an inadvertant overcharge, an imagined inferiority in service or product—such things assume monumental proportions. Forever after, false pride will discourage them from patronizing your business unless *you* do something about it!

Often, just a little initiative on your part—a letter or a personal call—provides the "push" needed to win back these customers, converting them into active accounts again. Try it with *your* "dead" account list—watch how you've suddenly added dozens (perhaps hundreds) of profitable accounts to your books.

HOW TO REVIVE INACTIVE CUSTOMERS

By Mail Write a short, friendly note, telling your inactive accounts how much you miss their business. Let them know that you value their business, that you are wondering just what could have happened since their last patronage. Were they displeased about anything to do with the handling of their account? Is there anything that you can do to make up for their displeasure? Ask for a definite reply.

One plumber who dealt mostly with men enclosed a cigar in the letter as a "reward" for the time customer took to read and answer the letter. A TV-repair shop offered a gift to the customer on his next visit to the shop.

By Telephone The fact that you take the time and trouble to telephone an inactive account is bound to have a positive effect. If there is some sort of gripe, if someone else is giving them better service, or if your price is not in line with that of your competition, a phone call will give you the opportunity to present your side of the case. Usually it gets the account back onto your books as well.

By Personal Visit If this method of following up on your inactive accounts is at all possible, it is likely to produce the most effective results for your. Face-to-face with an individual, you'll find out more about the situation than through any other means. Besides, if you can resell them during the visit, you have a much better chance of walking away with an actual order instead of a promise.

By Incentive Many times, an inactive account can be revived through the offer of a "special deal," a "premium gift," or perhaps some sort of a special "reacquaintance" discount. Most people love a bargain or "something for nothing." Some of your lost customers might have been weaned away from you by just such methods, and an inducement on your part could just as easily lure them back. Turnabout is fair play.

CHAPTER TWENTY ANSWERING 42 COMMON SALES OBJECTIONS

Whoever seeks to sell a product or service is bound to encounter "objections" from a number of prospective customers. To the extent that these objections can be anticipated and answered promptly, properly, and believably, sales will increase and the seller's business will continue to prosper.

In responding to objections, there is one cardinal rule to remember: *Don't be afraid to talk back to your prospect!* Answering objections firmly and adequately only increases your customer's respect for you. Your answers indicate confidence in yourself and your product, as well as knowledge about what you're selling. A constructive answer, therefore, puts you one step closer to making your sale.

Study the range of objections on the following pages. Many of them are probably the same ones you encounter every day in your own business. Compare your usual answers with the suggestions we've made. You may recognize some of your own words, but you may also come up with new ideas that will help your answers to be more effective.

Finally, as a constructive exercise in salesmanship, without looking at the answers, write down *every* objection you can think of; then, next to each write down your response. Refer to this list continually until it becomes a part of you. Soon you'll be handling objections with ease.

It costs too much. "I agree that is sounds like a lot of money in dollars and cents, but over a one-year period my product can help you save at least twice its cost in reducing your operating expense. So you see it does not cost—it pays!"

Your price is too high. "Our price *is* higher than many inferior competitive products. But actually you save money by buying from us. You pay only 10 percent more for a product that will give you 100 percent more service and satisfaction."

We tried it . . . It didn't do the job. "My customers constantly praise the job it does. I feel there must have been some misunderstanding. Was it used correctly? I will be glad to demonstrate its proper use—right in your own shop (home, office)."

Our present equipment is satisfactory. "I am sure you have obtained excellent service from your present equipment. But until you try ours, you'll never know what you have missed in better performance and increased savings. Our equipment makes the difference between being 'satisfied' or being 'enthusiastic.' We are *so* sure you will want it that we are willing to put it on approval!"

I'm over my budget now. "All the more reason why you should buy now! By the end of the year my product can achieve savings that will help bring your budget into line."

I can't afford to gamble on a new product. "I do not *want* you to gamble! All I ask is that you use our product for a week. Try it yourself. In fact, I'll even come to your plant (home, office) and show you *how* to use it. At the end of the week, if the product is not satisfactory, return it to us."

I haven't got time to listen to your story. "Could you spare the time if I paid you $5 a minute? My story takes just that—five minutes—and $25 will be the weekly savings I'll demonstrate to you through the use of my equipment."

I'm using a competitive product that's satisfactory. "Satisfaction is a matter of degree. A Ford satisfies a lot of people. On the other hand, we both know many folks who won't buy any car but a Volkswagen. All I ask is an opportunity to demonstrate how you can get *increased* satisfaction from using my product."

I have a closer source of supply. "You will find our service just as quick . . . perhaps quicker. We always ship "rush" orders by air. Our deliveries are often faster than local deliveries. As proof, here is a list of customers in this area who find our service to be outstandingly helpful to them."

We've been dealing with our present supplier for thirty years. "Fine . . . but it is often wise to have an alternative supplier. It gives you a solid basis of comparison and far better purchasing control."

I'll refer your story to the "powers that be." They'll make the decision. "I know you'll give my story an adequate presentation. However, questions are bound to arise on details, and these can only be answered by someone who is thoroughly familiar with the entire proposition, someone from our company, who knows our policies. Our product holds such great benefits for your firm. I would feel terribly disappointed if you missed out on them because of some misunderstanding that I could answer easily if I were present. I would appreciate an opportunity to attend the meeting with your executives . . . to help you just in case any question arises."

I can't get the boss's "okay."   "I'm glad to know you tried. That means *you* are sold on my proposition and what you need is a little help to present all the facts clearly. I can do that for you, if you'll introduce me."

We can get a better deal from your competitor.   "Would you mind outlining exactly what sort of a deal they have offered you? Perhaps I can help you weigh the advantages of each proposition. Or maybe we can offer you the same terms."

We buy only from established firms.   "I understand your point, and I used to have a tendency to feel that way myself. However, I should point out that while we are a relatively new organization, our management is composed of people with long experience . . . some of the most successful and highly respected individuals in the industry." (A brief but folksy history of who founded your company—and why—will be very helpful.)

Your competitor offers a better guarantee.   "Our firm has been in business for 25 years. I'm sure you'll agree that this couldn't have happened if we weren't able to back up our product 100 percent. I have never encountered a customer who felt that we failed to fully back-up every one of our products."

Come and see us again . . . after you have been in business for a year.   "Unfortunately, present indications are that within a year the cost of our product (or service) will be considerably higher. Our service can be useful to you now as well as in future years. So why not take advantage of our low introductory price."

I can buy cheaper, elsewhere.   "I have no doubt of that, but can you be *sure* you're getting the same value for your money? Our firm has a longstanding reputation for fine quality. Further, as you know, we stand four-square behind your purchase. On a substantial expenditure of this type, I think you'll agree that quality and guarantee should be two of your most important considerations."

Your competitor's bid was lower.   "I'm really surprised at that! I would like to be absolutely certain that we were figuring on identical specifications. In our business there are so many details—when we compare estimates, we often find two widely different figures on the same job because of a misunderstanding of the specific requirements. Just to assure you that you can expect the same quality of workmanship that our proposal offered, may I take a look at our competitor's estimate and specifications?"

I am overstocked on similar products now.	"The fact that you are overstocked may explain why you need our product . . . perhaps the other products are not really 'similar.' Our product enjoys consistent turnover and the likelihood of overstock is remote."
I still have most of your last order.	"Fine . . . then let me help you build a sales-stimulating display. While we're at it, we can tell what items may need "fill-ins."
I am overstocked with your product.	"That's unusual. Our merchandise generally moves fast. Tell you what . . . if you'll buy more now, so you can handle a possible rush of orders, I'll supply you with promotional materials (ads and displays) that have really boosted sales for other merchants." (Supply examples: Jones & Co. sold this much; Smith & Co. sold that much using these materials.)
I don't like your firm . . . had an unpleasant experience.	"I am sorry to hear that. Would you mind explaining what happened? If you were offended in any way, my firm would like to know . . . so that they can make restitution. I am sure they would already have done so if they had been aware of the situation. You can be assured of my complete cooperation in setting things right."
Your competitor gives better service after purchase.	"I haven't run into any complaints about our service, but let me assure you that I will be completely responsible for the handling of your account. You can contact me at any time between my visits to you and rely upon my complete cooperation. We'll give you any service you may possible need in connection with your purchases."
We don't use enough of your product to warrant buying the new model.	"If that is true, then I must be at fault . . . for not making clear to you the many ways in which our product is designed to help your firm cut costs (increase profits). I should like to make this clear to you in even more emphatic terms by demonstrating our new product, which has even more spectacular cost-saving (profit-building) features."
I understand Jones & Co. had a bad experience with your product.	"I am sure that misunderstandings occur in your business occasionally, too. There are generally two sides to every issue. Frankly, I know nothing of Jones's difficulty, but if you want, I will get the details from our plant and tell you about them on my next visit. Meanwhile, let me show you how our product can give your firm a truly wonderful experience."
See me again, when I return from my vacation.	"I realize how busy you are, getting ready for your trip. But wouldn't you enjoy it even more if you went away feeling 'Boy, did I just negotiate a good deal for the company?' And you will . . . when you hear what I have to offer you."
I am too busy to consider all the facts right now.	"How much would you say your time is worth? Ten dollars an hour? Just *five minutes* of your time can earn you as much as $300! Let me show you how my product earns you at least this in day-by-day savings."

Your equipment would mean expensive alteration of our methods . . . the benefits aren't worth the cost.	"If you will permit me, I would like to make an analysis of your operation to show you how long it will take the increased production (which our product assures) to completely amortize not only the expense of your procedural alterations, but also the cost of the equipment itself."
Your product does not fit in with this year's program.	"My product is specifically designed to help you make more money, and that is the very reason you are in business. If making money fits in with your program this year . . . or any year . . . our product fits in with your program."
The quality difference does not justify the additional cost.	"That may appear true on the surface. But considering the added years of service our product quality assures . . . the higher trade-in value that is yours at any time . . . not to mention the prestige of using our equipment, the cost difference is actually more than justified. It's like comparing a meal at the Waldorf-Astoria to one at Burger King."
Your credit policy is too rough.	"Our terms are pretty standard with the rest of the industry. Fundamentally, they represent the most that can be given in order to assure you top quality. And which would you prefer—a few days extra credit or 50 percent added product value?"
Your competitor's product must be better; it is more widely used.	"I agree with your *second* statement. My competitor's product does have far broader distribution. That is because it is 'mass-produced,' designed as an all-purpose product. Our philosophy is just a little different. We feel that the best results are obtained with a product specifically designed to do a certain job . . . particularly when the job is an important one. Therefore our product is designed according to rigid standards, specifically set to give you the best possible results."
I will have to get additional bids.	"I am glad you are going to do that. They will help you to appreciate better the many factors that go into producing our product. However, be sure your other bids meet identical specifications. Our price is as low as you will find for the same quality, so beware of lower bids. In the long run, what appears to be 'cheapest' may often prove to be most costly—and our work is *guaranteed.*"
I will buy it on one condition . . . that I have exclusive rights.	"I want to help you sell our product in any way I can, but have you considered that demand for an item actually rises in proportion to its number of outlets? The more outlets products have, the more advertising and publicity they get. And demand generally increases proportionally for all the selling agencies."
I have not had any calls for your product.	"You cannot expect many calls if the public does not know you carry the product. Display it and promote it, and you will get plenty of demand. Let me explain what other dealers have done to increase sales of our product."

ANSWERING 42
COMMON SALES OBJECTIONS

Business is bad. I do not want to buy. "It seems to be bad for everyone but us—we're receiving bigger orders every day! Maybe what you need is a really 'live' line of goods that will attract customers . . . a line that has the right kind of promotion behind it, like ours does."

Your company is too small to give us the service we require. "Our size means *better* service for you! In a large company, a customer too often becomes just another number on a ledger sheet. With us, you are 'one of the family' . . . a valued member in whom we have a personal interest. You'll get the best results from the best possible attention."

Can I return the merchandise I don't sell? That's the only way I will buy it. "You know as well as I do that selling on consignment is the straightest road to bankruptcy. You wouldn't *want* to do business with a firm whose position was that insecure. Who knows when you might find there was no longer a business to return merchandise *to?* Our product is planned to *move* from you to consumers . . . not from you back to us."

I am not interested. "What was that? *Not interested* in making $100? That is what you will save in a year by using our product!" or "*Not interested* in adding one-half hour of spare time to each day? That is how much our product saves you!"

I do not want to deal with so many separate suppliers. "I know how you feel, but remember that your customers like to shop in the place where they find the largest selection from which to choose."

Your product's quality is too good for my trade. "Better quality merchandise can help build your customers' confidence in your store and help stimulate business. It can actually elevate your trade in addition to enhancing your establishment's esteem."

I will buy when your price is lower. "I don't predict the future, but I can say that with the great demand we are getting there is a good chance prices will rise." Or, "That is going to be quite a long way off—you must make sales in the meantime. You will need stock to tide you over."

CHAPTER TWENTY-ONE
HANDLING THE PRICE OBJECTION

Salespersons in all lines are increasingly aware that they have entered a period of the tough sell. Rising costs and slower sales have put a profit squeeze on manufacturers. Specialty salespersons, along with others, are finding that prospects are today more concerned with price than they have been for some time past.

In this situation a review of ways to handle the price objection can be both timely and valuable. You must be prepared when a new prospect or a reorder customer says, "Your price is too high." How prepared? By *taking a fresh look at your product and learning all there is to know about it,* especially any exclusive features that give *you* an advantage.

When your prospect says, "Your price is too high," how can you build a strong and convincing answer to overcome this obstacle? Let's look at a few approaches.

Justify Your Price

One way is to *justify* the price you ask. Follow the lead of a specialty salesman who sells plastic-boxed hardware specialties to store owners: "When the customer says my price is too high, I answer with what I call 'building my blocks of value.' Like a kid building something on the floor, I talk quality of materials, special process of manufacture, durability, superior workmanship, special design, customer satisfaction, and finally dealer profit. I show them how, by getting slightly higher prices from their own customers, they make more than if they were selling an inferior product at a lower price."

Agree . . . But Explain Why

Another way to handle price objection is to concede the fact that your price *is* higher, thus robbing customers of part of their defenses. "Yes," you can say, "my price *is* too high if you are thinking of greeting cards at a dollar a box. But our cards are made for the discriminating customers like you, who want to be remembered for the cards they send." Then point out the superior design, colors, printing, paper stock, and messages that distinguish a quality product from an inferior one. Building your customer's prestige will do much to overcome price.

Demonstrate Superiority

Use showmanship to meet the price objection. Whatever it is you sell, be prepared to demonstrate superiority. For this purpose, secure samples of competitive products; study their literature and compare their merits with those of your own product. You should find certain advantages in your product that the others lack. When face-to-face with the prospect, draw up a chart showing these comparisons, emphasizing the added benefits your product gives. As you talk, price will become less and less important in the buyer's thinking.

"I can't afford it," is often heard as a general objection to any spending. In this case showmanship can help, too. A salesman who sells products for cleaning household furniture and draperies, and performs the work himself, welcomes this objection. Tactfully selecting a small chair or hassock, he demonstrates the glowing results as he talks to the prospect. Usually this effect is so pleasing that he secures an order to do further work at the customer's convenience.

Many other products lend themselves to effective demonstration with similar results. It is important to place the item in its most effective setting so that the contrast between "before" and "after" produces the strongest impact. The desire for permanent possession and enjoyment will often suggest ways through which the prospect can arrange to "afford" it.

Cite Possible Losses

Often, a description of *losses* the customer may experience by not buying is more effective than stressing the benefits exclusively. Insurance policies, alarm systems, and various kinds of safety equipment are among the commodities that lend themselves to this method of meeting the price objection.

In one case an insurance salesman had presented a health package that his prospect agreed was satisfactory in *every* way. The individual did not feel ready to pay the first premium, however. He told the salesman that he'd think it over, and suggested the salesman return in a month.

94

"That, of course, is up to you, Mr. Jones," the salesman replied. "But what if, during that month, a costly accident or illness occurs in your family? You agree, don't you, that you need the policy and can pay for it?" The prospect admitted these facts. "Then why go for a month without our protection? You'll feel happier if you sign up now and have no risk hanging over you." The customer signed.

Always Stress Value

Price objections may take many forms and you may be destined to meet them more often from now on, but with a little psychology you *can* overcome them. Just remember that successful answers start from one basic point—*value*. When you can show prospects that your product will provide *more* of what they want, price begins to lose its importance. But you must be prepared to show this convincingly. Resourcefulness in developing new answers to the price objection will be well worth your time and effort.

CHAPTER TWENTY-TWO

"TIP CLUBS" CAN BOOST SALES

One highly prolific and ongoing source of cost-free prospect leads is the "Tip Club." This mutual-assistance approach has become increasingly popular among businesses throughout the United States. There may be one in your community. If not, you can pioneer the concept and win thanks as well as business. A properly conducted "Tip Club" can help sales as many as 10 to 20 times, depending, of course, upon the size and activity of its membership.

WHAT ARE "TIP CLUBS"?

Tip Clubs are not lavish country clubs. Nor, as the name may imply, are they clubs organized to dispense tips on horses or stocks. The businessperson's Tip Club is organized by noncompetitive merchants in a common selling area, as a means of increasing their sales.

Simply stated, ten or more businesses within a given area form a club and arrange to meet at regular intervals for a common objective. They can be diverse businesses, representing practically any product or service that seeks to reach the same prospect group. The only strict provision is that they be noncompetitive with one another. The resulting Tip Club functions for the mutual exchange of prospect leads.

"TIP CLUBS"
CAN BOOST SALES

The success of such a club is based on the premise that each business member is usually familiar with his or her clients' needs above and beyond the products or services he or she supplies. Hence one club member "tips" another member, who may be able to provide the additional needs or services.

It's amazing how many such tips are obtained—*almost on a daily basis*—and how many sales result!

Tip Club members often make the initial contact for their referral, and it's not unusual for them to set up an actual interview and demonstration.

A Glance at How They Work

Assume, for instance, that you sell grocery products, and Rick Schaub, a member of your Tip Club, sells store fixtures. Rick has contracted to supply fixtures for a new grocery store. While talking to his customer, Rick asks what brands of grocery products the store expects to handle and mentions that he has a friend in the wholesale grocery business whom he can recommend as to product quality and service. If the grocer seems interested, Rick will offer to have you contact him, perhaps even suggesting that the three of you have lunch together on some convenient day.

At another time, you may have a customer who is planning a store alteration. Now you have the opportunity to mention Rick Schaub as a reliable person who can provide an excellent selection of up-to-date fixtures. A similar introduction is arranged.

Isn't is logical that this cooperation between members of a Tip Club can substantially multiply the sales of each member?

STARTING YOUR OWN TIP CLUB

If no Tip Club exists currently in your business community, you're probably wondering at this point if one would work for you. It certainly would! But like all innovative business techniques, its degree of success will depend greatly on the care with which you launch it.

First, it's important that your membership consist of eligible business people. They should be noncompetitive, but they should call upon or service the same general types of business prospects. For instance, if you sell to retail stores, a list of your membership might include sellers of bread, insurance, coffee, cigarette vending machines, real estate, commercial laundry services, and moving and storage facilities, along with one general contractor—all of whom deal with retail merchants.

This list can be greatly enlarged, of course, by including sellers of other lines of goods. However, care should be taken to limit membership to those who are sales representatives in the true sense of the profession. Do not enroll "desk" types, or telephone and "inside-the-store" salespeople.

98

A THREE-POINT FORMULA

To get your own Tip Club started, use this three-point formula:

Sell yourself. Become convinced in your own mind that a Tip Club can be a highly effective sales generator for you and other members.

Sell one other . . . or maybe two. They will each sell one or two other noncompetitive salespeople, who in turn will sell still others. The first thing you know, your club will expand just like a chain letter.

Plan your first meeting. Set a specific date, not more than a week ahead, for your first meeting. Prepare an agenda and run it like any other club, maintaining meeting schedules and keeping things on a businesslike level.

SUGGESTED PROCEDURES

Regularly scheduled meetings should be held, preferably on Mondays, because Monday signals the beginning of the business week; therefore anyone who receives a tip can arrange to act upon it sometime that week . . . if not immediately. Luncheon meetings are better than evening meetings because those attending will have their minds on business, not on hurrying to get home.

Each meeting should last about an hour and a half. During the meal, the Secretary calls the membership roll, a brief discussion of old and new business takes place, and then the President asks for current tips.

Each member, in rotation around the table, rises and gives his or her tips. It is vitally important that quiet be maintained while tips are being given. Questions regarding individual tips should be held until the end of the meeting.

The Tip Club should have a certain amount of procedural formality in its organization. Officers should be elected, committees appointed, and rules established. Each member should fully realize that he or she is a part of a select group that has been formed for everyone's mutual benefit. It is essential that each member fully realize his or her responsibility to the other members, for it is upon this vital interaction that the success of the Tip Club depends.

Maintaining Order

Since Tip Clubs are organized for business and not social purposes, a certain amount of discipline must be maintained. The luncheon meetings have a serious purpose, and maximum attention is essential as each member offers his or her tips. For this reason it is a good idea to establish a "penalty system" wherein fines of $1 or more are levied upon members for inattention or interference while tips are being given. Lateness or absence from meetings for reasons other than illness can also be considered punishable offenses.

Excessive absences may indicate that a member considers other personal matters more important than the Tip Club, and should result in that individual's being dropped from the club when they reach a specified number. In most cases it has been found that, shortly after a Tip Club is formed, there develops a substantial waiting list of interested people who wish to join. Often this waiting list is larger than the membership of the organization itself, and a disinterested member can be replaced immediately by one who is enthusiastic.

Establishing Ethics

Due to the nature of the Tip Club, it is imperative that a Code of Ethics be established and impressed upon the membership. The Code acts as protection against competition from outsiders or against possible resentment by a member's customer that the member may have given out his or her name as a tip. A useful set of club ethics includes the following:

- Tips are strictly confidential. No member will mention a tip he may have heard in the club on the outside.

- No competitor of any of the members can ever attend a meeting.

- The meeting must always be held out of earshot of nonmembers.

- No comments will be made by anyone during the tip presentation.

- Each member must guarantee his product and service to the satisfaction of the club membership, to ensure against resentment by a customer at whomever may have given out his or her name as a tip.

Optional Features

Numerous innovations are possible within a Tip Club to make it a more effective instrument than just a tip-giving exchange. Some Tip Clubs print their own business cards and lists that include the names and busineses of all who are members. When a member calls at a new place of business, he or she leaves the list and personally guarantees the services of the fellow Tip Club members, explaining that the club, as a whole, endorses each of its members and the products or services offered.

A practice that can greatly increase the effectiveness of the club is for its members to maintain contact with one another during nonmeeting intervals. Thus a midweek phone call from one member to another can assure immediate action on a tip which otherwise would have to await the next scheduled meeting.

It's a good idea to charge more for a Tip-Club meal than the club's actual cost—enough to cover expenses. A club in California, for example, pays

$5 for the meal but charges its members $10. The difference constitutes the club dues, and at the end of the year it is "lumped" with the money collected from fines to form a fund from which the Tip Club's annual social function is paid.

CHAPTER TWENTY-THREE GETTING THE MOST FROM EACH DAY'S SALES EFFORTS

SELECT AND KNOW YOUR MARKET

Learn right from the beginning to whom you are selling and exactly where you are going to sell each day. The entire world is not an open market for every product. Successful salespeople realize this, and that is why they find and fix their market before they "leap." On the basis of careful preliminary investigation, these successful reps select a specific territory, narrowed down to those prospects who are likely to buy. They make sure that every one of these prospects will be contacted, for the solitary prospect that they carelessly miss might very well turn out to be their *big sale.*

KEEP A STRICT SCHEDULE OF REGULAR WORK HOURS

Once you know your territory and the prospects you are going to contact, fixing and keeping a schedule of work hours is easy. This is most important if you want to "sell" all eight hours of every day. Determine intermediate sales goals for yourself, directing your full attention to the selling job; start at the same time every day and faithfully stay with the prepared program, finishing at the same prescribed period every day. After a while, you will find selling a joyful habit and a big profit. With a little determination, neither interruptions nor disappointments can divert you from your main selling goals: personal accomplishment, prestige, and profit.

BE POSITIVE AND ENTHUSIASTIC

There is no room for negative thinking in the personal makeup of a salesperson. "Turn-downs" are a normal part of any business. Therefore, brace yourself against discouragement. Remember—successful selling is based on *averages*. Prepared with select prospects and a feasible schedule to work by, you must meet the people who will buy each day, and you *must* make a set average number of sales.

PREPARE A FOLLOW-UP PLAN

Salespeople should plan their itineraries so that they can call back a prospect every thirty days. This can be vastly simplified by implementing a plan designed with call-backs in mind.

The "Spiral Plan"

The "spiral plan" is just such a plan. You simply follow the squares, intensively and scientifically working your territory into big sales and earnings. House-to-house and store-to-store salespeople have found it especially successful. Here's how it works:

Step A Select the general area of town that offers the greatest sales potential.

Step B Obtain a street map or take a plain sheet of paper and draw a simple checkerboard street plan of the selected area. Nothing fancy is needed—you don't have to be an artist. With the use of a ruler or even the edge of a card or envelope, just draw lines in a square as shown in Fig. 1, and write in the street names.

Step C Pick out an intersection near the center of the selected area and mark it with a dot or cross. Using this spot as a corner, draw a heavy dotted square around an area consisting of several blocks that you consider to be the cream of the general area you selected (we recommend using a colored pencil or pen). This is going to be your area of concentration for the next few months.

Step D Cover one side of the square each week for one month. Wherever a sale is not made, tell the prospect you will return in thirty days. Leave whatever promotional literature you have, so that during this time the prospect can become better acquainted with your product.

Step E Start walking. Figure 2 shows how your square will look for the next four weeks.

On the fifth week, STOP! Before you start a new square, *return to the area covered during the first week*. Revisit *every* unsold prospect. By now, they have had a chance to examine your literature and think it over, and you have

FIGURE 1

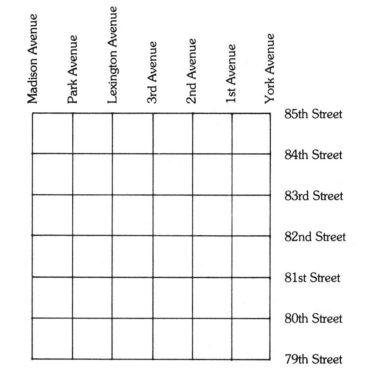

FIGURE 2

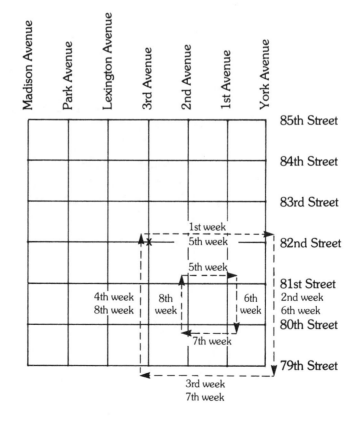

proven your reliability by returning in thirty days, true to your word. Now these prospects may be quite ready to do business with you, and the sales you make on these call-backs will take but half the time and effort of an initial contact.

Step F On the sixth week you are ready to start a new square in the spiral. Since making call-backs during the fifth week did not constitute a full week's work, you have more time and a smaller area to cover for new business in the sixth week. The sixth week simply repeats the pattern of the fifth week—only now, you revisit the area originally covered during the *second* week and make call-backs. Then you proceed with the new calls in the smaller square.

   The seventh and eighth weeks repeat the patterns of the fifth and sixth weeks. During week seven, the area of week *three* is revisited, and in the eighth week you will revisit the unsold prospects of week four before new calls are made.

   By the end of eight weeks you have made call-backs on all of the first month's unsold prospects and have visited new prospects, some of whom you will revisit within the next four weeks. Needless to say, it is important to keep a simple, accurate record for yourself, showing the dates of the original calls, call-backs, and results.

   After you have completed your square, then what? You are ready for the final step in the Spiral Plan!

Step G Start a new big square. Repeat all the steps you took in the first big square, depending on the size of your original square—whatever is practical. If after six weeks you find that you have just about reached the center, simply start a new big square at that point. There is no fixed rule about the size of the town, the nature of the neighborhood, or the degree of customer flexibility. Every addition of "master" squares increases your territory; eventually it will look like that shown in Fig. 3.

   Your individual plan must be tailored to your personal needs as influenced by the nature of your product, the town in which you are selling it, and a careful self-analysis of your own capabilities and limitations. Your ultimate plan may bear little resemblance to the plan we have suggested. But the important thing is that YOU HAVE A PLAN! *Now work it!*

FIGURE 3

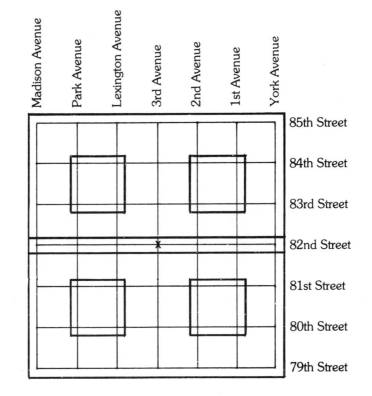

CHAPTER TWENTY-FOUR SELLING COMPLETE SYSTEMS

Two basic goals govern the day-to-day operation of all successful salespersons.

☐ To receive preference over their competitors.

☐ To make multiple sales per customer.

It is widely recognized that most items of a kind are somewhat similar. They share common characteristics and perform prescribed functions. All lighting fixtures produce illumination, for example, and all typewriters type. All brands of tape decks record and play sound, and one aquarium is much like another as far as the needs of fish are concerned.

THE "SYSTEM" AS A CONCEPT

One dynamic sales approach, which can clearly distinguish your product from that of your competitor, derives from the all-encompassing word *system*. What we mean by system in this context is the benefit. By selling a *system* you now offer your customer a *concept* rather than a mere product. You are, in effect, offering a series of benefits composed of your products or services. Together, these things distinguish your products and subsequently make you "noncompetitive"—even though your component items essentially resemble others on the market.

Additionally, by dint of selling *systems* you can now sell many units of your product line to a single customer under a single sales contact. Your particular system can embrace as many as a dozen or more individual products. Always bear in mind that the customer is buying the system, not the product alone.

**Some Examples
of How
It Works**

John Fergusson, a lighting fixtures salesman, advanced a lighting *system* rather than a specific lighting product. His lighting system included a multiplicity of specific benefits: relief from eye strain, energy economy, enhancement of room decor, expanded reading capacity, and so on. To obtain the total benefits available in John's system, a customer should purchase as many as twenty different components; hence John is selling one concept but *many* products!

Equally important, the systems concept makes John *noncompetitive.* Other lighting salesmen sell products, but individually they lack the many advantages of a lighting system.

Anne Neal, whose product was typewriters, promoted a "creative corner system" rather than a typewriter alone. The creative corner included a typewriter, a compact portable desk, accessible filing trays, a two-drawer filing cabinet, a thesaurus, a dictionary, a book of quotations, a reading lamp, a typewriter stand, and other products to facilitate the thinking process. The complete system sold for $850—quite a contrast to the usual $200 sale of the typewriter alone. Anne's approach—selling a *concept* at an expanded cost—also stimulated more purchases of her typewriters. In reality, Anne's typewriter differed little from other $200 typewriters, but her systems approach distinguished *her* from others and made her *noncompetitive.*

Dan Frisbee made a system sale through similar resourcefulness. Dan sells lighting, including all types of bulbs, tubes, grilles, and special installations. Part of Dan's territory is the New York waterfront, and one day he called on an important Naval Station. The minute he entered the office he was conscious of a yellowish glare which he recognized was almost certain to produce eyestrain. A few minutes' observation of the clerical workers confirmed his suspicion.

When he went in to talk with the purchasing officer, he mentioned the condition he had observed and offered to correct the lighting on the spot. The officer agreed, and Dan went out to his car and brought back a box of bulbs which were presently installed by maintenance workers. The result was an entirely different white light that gave immediate relief to the staff.

Gaining permission to look around the building, Dan found an entertainment hall with colored walls. The effect of the existing lighting was to dim objects at a little distance and make them hazy. He knew the need here, too—

110

bulbs of a different color that would work *with* the walls instead of *against* them. Two days later he made that change and shortly afterwards secured the contract for lighting the entire building. He was able to show his prospect that buying the complete system not only saved money through a volume purchase, but also assured uniformity of performance—every item in the system complemented the others, as it was designed to do.

SELLING YOUR OWN SYSTEM

Any salesperson whose product lends itself to the system type of selling can increase volume sales by organizing for the job. Those who are most successful usually follow these steps, which, in some cases, will be taken over a period of time:

- ☐ **Gain complete knowledge of your product;** know what it can do, and what benefits it will produce under various conditions.

- ☐ **Learn about your prospect** and be well-informed about his or her business before calling.

- ☐ **Visit the prospect's entire premises,** if possible, to ascertain problems.

- ☐ **Talk with everybody** who can affect the purchase decision, especially the potential users of your system.

- ☐ **List the problems** you find and work out corrective measures, stressing the benefits that will result.

- ☐ **Draw up a formal proposal** (if the type of industry requires it) setting forth all your findings and recommendations.

- ☐ **Present your proposal** to the *individual who has the final buying decision* if you possibly can. Emphasize any support your plan has received from others with whom you have talked in the company. In addition, stress the reliability and reputation of your company and its products and support these claims with testimonials or other evidence from satisfied customers.

- ☐ **Constantly reiterate the chief benefit** to the customer—reduced expense, greater production, bigger profits, better operation.

- ☐ **Ask for the order** or contract, and suggest a date for installation.

Selling total-requirement systems is not *easy.* What makes it worth the effort is the exceptional combination of advantages to the customer and to you, as well.

Once you have made the sale, you achieve a higher prestige in the selling profession. Now you must make sure to provide close supervision and service until your promised results begin to show. Your customer will appreciate this, and often may bring problems to you for discussion and decision, thus making you a consultant. Depending upon your judgment and help, he will continue to buy from you with confidence and reward you with valuable word-of-mouth advertising.

One word of caution: The length of time you hold the account will depend entirely upon you. Don't begin to take things for granted, avoid responsibilities, or "alibi" occasional failures. Remember, there are other companies—just as good as yours—hungrily awaiting their opportunity.

CHAPTER TWENTY-FIVE THE ART OF "CREATIVE" SELLING

IMAGINATIVE WAYS TO BOOST SALES

Nearly every type of business requires some form of selling—whether your product is a hamburger, technical expertise, or a work of art worth thousands of dollars. *Creative* Selling enables you to sell more products or greater quantities of a product to more people. In many businesses it can make the difference between roaring success and bare subsistence.

WHAT IS "CREATIVE" SELLING?

Creative selling is *imaginative* selling. It's the difference between timidly *asking* prospects if they can use your product . . . and *showing* them not only *how* they can use the product but also *why* they *must buy it!*

There is an important point of psychology involved here: If asked whether or not they *want* a thing, few prospects will want the product—the instinct is to say "No." If shown why they *need* something, most prospects will recognize such a need—now the instinct is to say "Yes."

This little formula has the dynamic potential to double your annual income!

Creative selling requires more than a mere demonstration of a product or service and its uses, however. It requires wrapping the product with excitement and drama—with living, breathing BENEFITS—that make your prospects look beyond the product itself and into their own lives. You must allow them to envision how this product can do something to improve the very quality of their existence—starting right now!

Creative
Salespeople
in Action

Jed Burton was one of our favorite creative salesmen. His product was very, very ordinary . . . a wrench. Practically everyone has a wrench; few feel that they need a new one. Hundreds—perhaps thousands—of salespeople compete to sell wrenches.

What made Jed different? Before he started to sell, he sat down to think: How could he command the immediate attention of his prospects? What could he say or do that would get across the wrench benefits as quickly and dramatically as possible? *Eureka!* He had it:

"I'm here to sell you one thousand tools for the price of one . . . !"

The fantastic bargain-value of this offer "stopped" the prospect. Jed received an audience—in fact, when he used this approach, *every* prospect gave him a receptive hearing. He could now get into his selling talk, explaining how the wrench he sold was indeed capable of doing a thousand tasks.

Jed's one simple approach accomplished three vital things. First, it "stopped" the prospects and caused them to listen; second, it seized their interest; third, it dramatized the benefits of Jed's product, enabling prospects to envision all the things it could do for them. Needless to say, Jed's sales soared. With the help of one sentence, his income jumped considerably above its former figure.

A further example of creative selling is seen in the case of Bob Henderson, who sold typewriters—another very ordinary product, you'll agree. Like Jed, Bob recognized that he'd make few sales by just asking people if they wanted a typewriter. He had to dramatize some benefit that his typewriter would give them . . . do for them . . . that the prospect never realized before. Suddenly it came to him:

"I have something sensational to show you—an actual IDEA-MANUFACTURING MACHINE!"

Every prospect stopped to listen and look. Bob now had a responsive audience to hear him explain the smoothness of the typing that enabled easy "idea-manufacturing," how prospects could type faster and express themselves better with this typewriter than others. It worked!

Still another example comes from a friend of ours, George Cole. George sold subscriptions to a travel magazine. On the surface, you'd say this is a tough item to sell—who actually *reads* travel magazines? Yet George earned upwards of $35,000 a year. His approach:

"How would you like to buy a trip through Europe for only a dollar?"

This "stopped" people, and they listened. He then explained how the current issue took them on a "fascinating, romantic trip through Europe . . . almost as if you were there in person." The next issue would take them through South America . . . and so on. All for the subscription price of only $12.00 per year.

It's easy to see why George's income was so high.

Another of our favorite creative selling approaches was that of Dolph Stonehill. His product was a photocopying machine that reproduced letters, office forms, and documents. There were several brands on the market. He analyzed the benefits and concluded that his machine saved business firms a great deal of money each year over usual duplicating methods. He now created an apporach that would best get this across:

*"I have something to show you that will interest you very much—*a MONEY-MAKING MACHINE!"

People listened. A *money-making machine* . . . this they had to see! Dolph now found it easy to get into his selling pitch, demonstrating how the machine actually "made money"—lots of it—for business firms, through the savings they realized each year. It could do so for the prospect's firm, too!

Creative selling takes on many forms. However, the goal should be symbolized by the first words of an approach, promptly proclaiming and dramatizing how the product will benefit the prospect.

A *survey* approach was used by Howard Holmes, a printing salesman. Few prospects had responded when he asked whether or not they needed printing. Virtually *all* responded when he offered to give them a "free, scientific analysis of their office forms and letterheads."

Another firm, selling shrubbery, built up a $30-million-a-year business offering prospects a free sketch of how their landscape could look. They "sold" *beauty,* but earned their profits from the sale of shrubbery!

Showmanship is an important component of creative selling. Fred Torket, an awning salesman, carried a Polaroid camera with him and took snapshots of retail businesses with awnings that looked shabby. His approach was to show prospects an actual photo of their store along with a photo of another store (that of a customer) recently equipped with fine, new awnings!

DEVELOP YOUR OWN CREATIVE STYLE

How can you become a creative salesperson? With a little thought and ingenuity you can easily be as imaginative as Jed, Bob, Doph, and the others who have so successfully increased their sales. Just keep the following points and questions in mind:

Know your product
What are its outstanding uses and benefits?

Know your prospects
What do they want and *need* that your product can supply?

Be curious
Get ideas from all available sources: other salespeople, customers' house-organs, trade magazines, newspapers. Maintain an "idea bank." Jot down your ideas, file, and use them. Review them often—they'll nudge dozens of creative ideas into practical applications.

Be a perfectionist
Before seeing the prospect, take the time to sit down and consider exactly what you're going to say . . . and how you're going to say it.

Expect the sale!
Creative selling breeds self-confidence. When you're sure that prospects need what you have, and believe in your mind that they *will (must)* purchase it—they usually will!

Study your markets
Where can you find new markets for your products? How can you introduce new uses for them?

Bring out the full strength of your creative talents! In future years when you review your sales career, the chances are you'll find *your own imagination* was what helped you stand out among the pack!

CHAPTER TWENTY-SIX
UNUSUAL APPROACHES LURE BIGGER SALES

One of the most successful merchants we've known, whose sales eclipsed those of others in his field, attributed his success to being a "daze-crasher." Our curiosity impelled us to ask, "What in the world is a *daze-crasher!* And how does being one help sales?"

He answered, " 'Daze-crashing' is more or less the knack of being able to dramatize the benefits of your products in your very first words.

"Normally, people have a dazed—or unthinking—reaction to sales approaches. They're usually on the defensive if you ask them to buy anything, even though they may need it. Their unthinking, automatic response is usually negative."

"This," he continued, "is what I mean by daze-crashing: Before seeing a prospect, I ask myself what there is about my product or service that offers this prospect exceptional benefits? How can I get this across in a few words—as graphically and dramatically as possible?"

Inevitably this approach evoked quick interest. It dispelled the prospect's natural defensiveness and gained our merchant a responsive audience. Thus jolted from his or her ''daze,'' the prospect listened attentively to the finer details of the sales presentation.

USING PHOTOS AS ATTENTION-GETTERS

The instant-developing Polaroid camera can become a versatile sales-promoting instrument. Why? Because it offers a *personalized* touch that is bound to attract prospects' attention and capture their interest.

☐ **An office-furniture salesperson,** upon entering her prospect's office, snapped a quick Polaroid shot of the existing desk arrangement. Subsequently she showed the prospect the photo, and pointed out how her own line of furniture could improve the office's appearance and increase efficiency. Intrigued and surprised to see the photo, the prospect readily absorbed the suggestions, and usually made a purchase. This individual averaged sales to seven out of ten prospects—a fantastic record for the office-furniture field.

☐ **A store-awning salesman** in Pittsburgh snapped a quick picture of his prospect's store (showing the existing awning) *prior* to making his sales approach. He then displayed before-and-after photos to the prospect: first, the photo he just took, showing the window as it now looked; second, a photo from his presentation book, showing the window as it would appear when equipped with a new awning. The visual comparison usually convinced the prospect.

☐ **Landscaping services** have used the photo-approach with great success. Enterprising salespeople take photos of existing grounds and yards in their area. When they meet with a prospect, they show the current shot as a "before" photo and offer in comparison a photo of the beautiful landscaping that could be accomplished through their services.

☐ **A home-remodeling contractor** increased his business substantially through the use of pictures. He took photos of a number of area homes that appeared to be likely candidates for exterior remodeling. Carefully matching each "as-is" photo with a photo of a similar structure that had been attractively remodeled by his firm, he mailed them out to the respective prospects. Attached was a friendly letter calling attention to the comparison: "You'll notice that we've enclosed a photo of your home as it appears today. We think you'll be interested in comparing it with the Anderson property on West Street, which we had the privilege of working on a year ago. The homes are similar in architecture and size . . ."

OTHER UNUSUAL APPROACHES

We can't emphasize enough the importance of putting your imagination to work for you. Those personal touches that others overlook, especially when they make your prospect feel "important," can spell success. Here are a few:

Birthday Greetings

In this grim, impersonal world, a friendly, considerate approach is appreciated. Dan Robins, who runs a Colorado auto repair service, capitalized on sentiment and increased his business. He cleverly obtains the birthdates of his customers and faithfully sends them greeting cards. Effective? Dan points proudly to the fact that most of his customers have remained loyal to him through the years, staunchly refusing to deal with anyone else.

Special Surveys

Try to sell someone something and they automatically say "No!" That's an instinctive reaction. However, offer a *free survey* and the tendency is to say "Yes!" You have converted your image from that of a canvasser to an *expert consultant* whose opinion is respected. For example, Ted Stone (representing a home-heating-oil firm) offered to conduct a free study of prospective customers' oil-heating systems to detect sources of leakage and waste. His approach—offering a desired service—won the respect and gratitude of the householders and, in most cases, also won their oil trade.

We want to emphasize, in connection with this approach, that it should be based on a sincere and knowledgeable desire to evaluate the prospect's needs objectively. It should not be used as a subterfuge for the sole purpose of "pushing" an immediate sale.

Turning the Tables

Often the reversal of a usual trend helps jolt a prospect into attention. For example, Beth Miller (who sold advertising specialties) reasoned that prospects were customarily contacted at their place of business—where they were generally under business tension. She reversed the trend by contacting them at home. The very unusualness of this approach appealed to most prospects. They were appreciably more relaxed and responsive in their home surroundings. Beth's sales increased substantially.

Getting Leads and Introductions

Sue Blake makes it easy for her customers to give introductions to their friends and acquaintances who may be able to use her product. Sue has a printed card which reads as follows:

```
┌─────────────────────────────────────────────────────────┐
│                                                           │
│   To ─────────────────────────────────                    │
│                                                           │
│             Introducing Ms. Susan Blake,                  │
│                 who represents                            │
│            THE COLOR-GLO CORPORATION                      │
│                 Manufacturers of                          │
│          Fine Paints and Designer Wallpapers              │
│                                                           │
│                   ──────────────────────────             │
│                                                           │
└─────────────────────────────────────────────────────────┘
```

Thus it is a simple matter for customers to fill in the new prospect's name at the top and add their own signature at the bottom. There is no search for a sheet of paper. Time is saved and the customer can concentrate on thinking of prospects for Sue.

Whe she contacts the new prospect, Sue carries with her the tangible endorsement of a friend. Another plus!

Offers to "Pay" for Prospect's Time

Jim Prescott sells roofing to homeowners. Often his prospects believe that their roofing is in satisfactory condition and that no repairs are necessary; hence they tend to react negatively when he attempts to make his presentation.

In anticipation of this, Jim has developed an approach that proves highly effective in gaining his prospects' interest. He takes a half-dollar from his pocket and hands it to the prospect. "Will that pay for three minutes of your time?" asks Jim. "That's how long it will take to tell my story."

Usually the prospect responds to the humor and novelty of this approach and allows Jim to proceed. Ninety-eight percent of them return the half-dollar when he's finished. Jim's story is that roofing often wears in various spots, leaving the homeowner unaware until a heavy rain damages walls, paint jobs, and possibly even expensive equipment and furnishings. Jim explains that a simple low-cost roof inspection at regular intervals can guard against such damage. The half-dollar approach wins the prospect's attention and allows Jim to tell his story.

Offer a Ball-Point Pen

Lynn Carter has found that ball-point pens inscribed with her company's name are excellent daze-crashers. They are also great *gate*-crashers! Receptionists who accept pens usually soften their attitudes and help Lynn get in to see the boss, who also tends to be more receptive when handed a gift pen. Ball-point pens imprinted with your firm's name are quite inexpensive when ordered in reasonable quantities.

Astrology— A Star Attraction

One retail establishment placed a card in its window offering a free monthly horoscope. Astrology enjoys wide popularity, and many interested passersby enter the store to receive their horoscopes. Once inside, they naturally notice the attractive displays of merchandise and respond to the friendly greetings of the salespeople. (Monthly horoscopes for each sign of the zodiac can be purchased or compiled easily from those printed in astrology magazines.)

BUSINESS CARDS THAT GAIN AN AUDIENCE

Ever have trouble getting *in* to see a business prospect? Is the receptionist or the prospect's secretary your barrier? Here are several examples of business cards that have served as the key to many a prospect's closed doors, gaining attention and often ultimate purchase. They cost little or nothing, so give them a try!

The Ordinary Business Card

A business-machine salesman we know encountered a good deal of difficulty getting past receptionists. One day, on inspiration, he took out one of his business cards and on the face side wrote the word "OVER." On the reverse side he wrote, "I can show you how to reduce your office overhead by $5000 a year." Handing the business card to the receptionist, he asked that it be sent in to his prospect—a man he'd previously been unable to see on several visits.

Everyone wants to reduce costs, so naturally the prospect's curiosity was aroused. Furthermore, the personal handwritten message on the card seemed to stress the urgency of this salesman's call and to demand immediate action. Thus the prospect was swayed to invite the salesman into his office and let him "tell his story."

Once there, the salesman explained that his business machine, operated by only one employee, could accomplish the work of several clerical employees, and do it in less time. Thus the business would save $5000 a year in salary hours for an investment of only several *hundred* dollars for the machine. The once elusive prospect soon became a regular customer.

This method of approach can be used effectively in sales of insurance, office machinery, factory equipment, business service—in fact, almost any field in which a money or cost savings can be demonstrated clearly.

The "12½%" Business Card

One salesperson of our acquaintance, who sells infrared industrial heating to factories, used this approach to make his point quickly: He ordered a business card with a large "12½%" occupying about four-fifths of the card area. At the bottom of the card, in very small (6-pt.) type, was listed his name, address, and the telephone number of his firm.

The card was sent in to the prospect, whose curiosity about the meaning of the "12½%" usually led to an interview. Once inside his prospect's office, the salesman explained, "That's the savings percentage you can realize with infrared heating as compared with your present system. Let me show you why . . ."

Cartoon Business Card

A closed-circuit-television salesman prepared a cartoon-type business card aimed at a prospect's sense of humor. An artist's sketch of a group of navy men on duty at a small desert island shows a signalman reading "wig-wag" signals through a pair of field glasses and translating them to this officer. The signals are being sent by a lone individual in a rowboat, far out on the water. The message: "He says he's Baxter of Jones and Company, Sir, and he requests permission to come aboard!"

Baxter gets in to see three out of every five prospects. Whatever *your* line may be, if your prospects can enjoy a little chuckle, they'll be more willing to see you.

Business in Rio

Although this is not a business *card* as such, it is another novel way of getting past the gate of an overprotective receptionist:

Ruth Jenkins sells advertising space in a trade publication that is read widely in Latin America. She was usually turned down when she approached a receptionist with a request such as "Please tell Mrs. Flynn that Ms. Jenkins of *Magniscope Magazine* is here to see her."

What a difference her new approach has made! Now Ruth says to the receptionist, "Please tell Mrs. Flynn that Ms. Jenkins wants to see her about some *new customers* in Rio de Janeiro!"

"New customers" is a magic phrases to any businessman and Ruth is always admitted quickly. Once in her prospect's office, Ruth explains that in Rio her publication has thousands of readers who would be ideal customers. She assures the prospect that her publication is the best means of getting a sales message across to this market. Ruth's record of sales runs six out of every ten prospects she interviews.

THE ABSENTEE APPROACH: LEAVE SOMETHING BEHIND

Enterprising salespeople are not daunted by the discovery that a prospect isn't in. Instead of shrugging their shoulders and walking away, they are prepared to take advantage of such a situation by leaving some eye-catching clue of their visit.

122

Shipping Tag
Attached to Door

An entrepreneur specializing in home landscaping and lawn service uses his prospect's absence as a selling tool. On an ordinary shipping tag he writes: "Stopped by today to discuss some interesting facts about the present condition of your lawn. Sorry I missed you. I'll return next Thursday at 8 p.m."

He attaches the shipping tag to the front door of the house. Arriving home, the prospect is intrigued with this personalized message and usually makes an effort to be present when the salesman returns at the promised time.

A Larger Card
with Your
Personal Touch

Your prospects see hundreds of business cards, most of which look unremarkably alike. For leave-behind purposes, a larger card with a clever message will be far more impressive.

One business-service salesperson leaves a well-designed 6×9-inch card that includes her picture and a brief message reproduced from her own handwriting:

"Sorry I missed you . . . came to show you how to get 50% more production from your present office staff. Will be back on _____ and hope you'll have just five minutes to listen to my story."

If this sounds a bit like a political handout, remember that successful politicians are in reality successful salespeople. This method will pique your prospects' curiosity and make them eager to find out just how you can help them.

CHAPTER TWENTY-SEVEN BUILDING REPEAT BUSINESS

You may have heard the "old saw" that says, "Friendship has no place in business." Please don't believe it for one moment! Friendship can be one of your greatest assets, for friendship means loyalty, and customer loyalty brings *repeat business.*

A truer adage is this: "With your first sale you make a friend . . . with your repeat sales, you make a profit." And that's the important thing to remember, for it takes more effort to sell a prospect who is unfamiliar with the product, the company, and you, the representative, than one who has experienced the benefits which your combined performances provide. Once your customer has been convinced that your product solves a problem or supplies a need, that you company offers quality and integrity, and that you are personally interested in seeing that he or she gets maximum benefit from what you've sold, *then* that customer becomes a "pushover" for the repeat sales that bring profits.

The misguided individual who coined the "old saw" could not have been a salesperson, for the statement shows no understanding of the true art of selling. Show me the salespeople who have friends and I'll show you the ones who are making a success of their efforts!

The fallacy of reasoning lies in the fact that selling is a necessary element in almost every phase of our human relationships, and successful selling as a profession is rooted in the ability to make friends. It's easy to meet people, if you really want to; but it's an *art* to make people your friends and to keep their friendship glowing and growing. And the basic technique of this art is selling yourself.

When you sell, you supply—or serve—the needs of others. Who can help but be friendly with one who serves them well? Continue to serve your friends well, whether they be on the social or business level, and your relationships will grow, blossom, and result in mutual warmth and satisfaction. Do ill to either business or social friends and your relationships will deteriorate.

Like friendships on the social level, business friendships must be earned. You gain the respect and affection of your customers in direct proportion to the effectiveness of your service to them. Good friends are good customers whenever possible. When they need what you're selling, they call you with an order; if you call upon them, they'll extend themselves to think of something they can buy from you. So, in your selling career, do your best to make friends —from them will come your profits. Above all, *keep* your friends by serving them well in whatever ways you can, for your repeat sales and extra profits grow in direct proportion to your friendships with your customers.

It's a friendly act to drop in on customers after their purchases have been delivered, just to be sure that everything associated with a transaction has proven satisfactory. Be sure your customer understands the use and operation of every purchase. If it is an item that must be assembled after delivery, see that all parts have been shipped and are in good working order.

If you determine that something may be missing or defective, don't wait for your customers to discover it. Call it to their attention; then get on the phone and call your employer. Request your shipping room to send a replacement part just as quickly as possible—by special messenger or taxicab—so that the assembly can be completed while you are still on hand to support customer enthusiasm. This is the kind of service customers will appreciate. Obviously, you are doing your level best to take complete responsibility for which they rightfully believe they have paid. Even though something may have been defective or missing, their interest and enthusiasm are not given a chance to die, because *you* are there—waiting it out with them—ensuring that things are as they should be before you leave.

In the future when you call on these customers, they'll be glad to see you. You are a friend who has served them well. You are honest and responsible. Therefore, when a new need arises, they will naturally want to do business with you.

Fortunately, it isn't always necessary to turn your plant upside down in order to give your customers service. Efficient inspection techniques generally assure that most products are in good condition when delivered. (If quality control begins to slip, don't hesitate to discuss the matter with your employer.) There are hundreds of little ways, however, through which to assure customers of your continued interest in them, thereby maintaining the friendships that pay profits in repeat business. In the remainder of this chapter, we'll examine a few of the methods used successfully by outstanding salespeople in a wide variety of fields. Study them and keep them in mind. You'll find many occasions in your selling career when one of these ideas may be just what you need to provide your customers that extra little business-building service.

Help Your Customers Profit from Their Purchases

Basically, your customers are interested in their own profit. They seek ways to increase their worth . . . worth that will bring recognition from family, friends, and the entire community. But most of all, whether they know it or not, they seek their own recognition of added worth—the attainment of increased self-esteem.

When we speak of *profit* and mean *money,* we are singling out the most obvious benefit a customer may gain from dealing with you. Since it is so obvious and easy to understand, it is the means through which we most often strive to demonstrate continued interest in customers. However, we must remember that profit in terms of money alone is simply representative of all the other benefits that people like to realize for themselves. So in considering *profit* here, let's use the term in its all-inclusive sense, meaning *benefit that satisfies a customer's ultimate goal of increased self-worth.*

Birthday Cards

Many salespeople offer a continued note of interest and friendship to their customers through remembering birthdays. They go to some effort to find out the date, consulting a secretary, the personnel department, or a mutual friend. When the date comes 'round, they drop the customer a card. Who doesn't feel friendly toward the person who remembers their birthday? Our egos are fed when we know that someone has given us this extra bit of thought. When we need something that this person can supply for us, we are naturally inclined to call upon him or her. Yes, here is a very simple and inexpensive way to extend goodwill to our customers, stimulating their friendship and beckoning business in our direction when their needs arise.

Supplying a Related Product or Service

A men's shoe salesman, Jack Stanley by name, keeps careful records of customers on whom he calls in person. On each customer's card he lists the style and color of each shoe purchase. Keeping his cards in a tickler file by date, Jack is able to tell exactly when each customer purchased shoes from him, and three months later he sends the customer a waxed shoe-polish cloth "to help impart a brilliant shine to the shoes we sold to you . . . and to show our appreciation for your patronage." As a reminder of other possible products the customer might want to buy, Jack includes an illustrated shoe catalog.

Telephone Selling

Under the proper conditions, the telephone can accomplish miracles of selling, particularly when you're trying to get repeat business. An occasional friendly telephone call to customers lets them know you're thinking about them and often reminds them of something that you can supply. We can't always personally visit all the people we'd like to see, but a phone call is "the next best thing to being there." It's a good plan to set aside fifteen minutes, or one-half hour a day to telephone old customers. Each evening select four or five customers to contact by telephone the following day. You'll maintain many pleasant relationships and often find your efforts more than rewarded by the repeat business that may be yours without even asking.

Supplying Information

Market trends, competitive activities, new developments in the field . . . these areas of information are important to any businessperson who is trying to run an organization at a profit.

As a salesperson, you are out on your territory, constantly coming into contact with others who talk ideas, developments, and collectively provide a wealth of generally useful intelligence. You can actually become your customers' source of intelligence, to the mutual advantage of all. Being out in the field and seeing all kinds of people in every kind of business, you often hear and learn considerably more than your customers, who are tied to office-running routine and desk work. So it often pays to keep your eyes and ears open for information that your customers can use.

Sarah Snodgrass is a sales representative for a haberdashery manufacturer, and her territory covers several states. Sarah has earned the undying appreciation of her five biggest customers. Why? Because whenever she runs across a new type of promotion, a new item (not manufactured also by her own firm) which has profit possibilities for them, or anything else that she believes can help her customers improve their business, Sarah sits down and writes them a letter.

Sarah's letters have earned her the respect and loyalty of the "big five" mentioned above. She earns a fine income every year from the repeat business of these customers alone. It would take a lot of doing for a competing sales rep to break through and get an order from any one of them. And here's the big plus: If Sarah were to leave her present firm, there is an excellent chance that all five accounts would follow her and change their lines.

Sid Schoenbrun uses a different technique to supply information to his printing customers. Sid digests worthwhile material from a large number of trade magazines in different fields each month. With this material he gets out a varityped market newsletter and sends a complimentary copy to all his customers. The customers appreciate his interesting digests of trade news, new developments, market trends, and promotional methods. They read his newsletter with enthusiasm . . . including the subtle plugs for his own printing business, with which the letter is liberally sprinkled.

Sid finds that during the ten days following each issue his repeat business orders swell to a peak. More old customers call for estimates and place orders than at any other time of the month. This certainly indicates the effectiveness of Sid's method of encouraging repeat business!

Offering
Gifts

Tom McDougall is a house-to-house silverware salesman. Now silverware isn't the kind of item that a person buys often. Consequently, once Tom makes a sale he's pretty much out of his customer's mind for a while. But Tom doesn't let this condition prevail indefinitely. A year after the silverware purchase he drops the customer a line explaining that he has a free "anniversary" gift, if the customer will just let him know (by mailing an enclosed business-reply card) when a visit would be convenient.

The free gift is a box of initialed matchfolders, which are both useful and decorative. Tom's customers are always glad to receive them and appreciate Tom's thoughtfulness. Tom, of course, uses the visit as an opportunity to get new leads from his old customer . . . friends who may be interested in the purchase of silverware. Additionally, he points out what wonderful gifts his silverware items make for Christmas, weddings, birthdays, and other occasions. The next anniversary of the purchase brings another letter from Tom.

Through this simple means of communication, Tom has developed a number of steady customers for a line of items that one rarely thinks of in repeat-business terms.

CHAPTER TWENTY-EIGHT TESTED TECHNIQUES THAT CLOSE SALES

Questions that Elicit Commitment

This is a method wherein the salesperson seeks to get the prospect's agreement on each point made during the sales presentation. By answering "Yes" to progressively important questions along the way, a prospect is more likely to reply "Yes" to the *big* question that closes the sale. One automobile salesman engineers it like this:

> "Isn't that body a wonderful shade of blue?"
> "Yes," the prospect agrees easily.
> "Rides smoothly, doesn't it?"
> "Yes," the prospect agrees again.
> "Handles like a baby carriage, doesn't it?"
> Further agreement.
> "As cars go these days, don't you agree that the price . . . the low maintenance . . . and the extra mileage make this a wonderful value?"
> The prospect can do little but continue to agree.
> "Then you'll want to accept delivery today . . . won't you?"

Having agreed to all the good points, and actually being in the market for a car, the prospect now finds it very difficult to say anything but "Yes" to this final question, which is actually the sales clincher.

Another advantage of this method is that a negative answer will alert you to the prospect's possible objections or concerns, enabling you to alleviate them before asking the final question.

The "Consultant" Method

Most people like to believe that their knowledge of what they buy is equal to (or better than) that of any salesperson, and their egos are reinforced when you seek their advice. Soon after starting his presentation, a salesman of vacuum cleaners says to a customer, "I can tell from the way you're looking at this that you're an expert in household equipment. You know what good performance is, so when you see this machine in action, I won't have to say any more about it. It meets all underwriter requirements, so just let me put it to work and you can judge it according to your highest standards."

After receiving a compliment on their technical expertise or judgment of quality, most prospects will find it hard to disagree with your evaluation of your product.

This technique can be especially effective if you sell to prospects in their own homes. Learn to judge at a glance where they place their values, and relate this in some way to what you're selling. Mention their tasteful eye for color, their fine antique coffee table, their superb stereo system, their well-behaved child—anything that can be linked to a conclusion of "So of course you'll appreciate what I have to show you. . . ."

Trial Closes

These are questions through which you give prospects a choice between two alternatives. You seek a favorable answer to some major point that will reveal their thinking and give you the green light. You don't ask *what*—you ask *which.*

A cash-register salesperson might say, "Here are the two models I have been talking about. Now *which* of the two do you prefer?"

The home-study salesperson: "Shall I send the books to your office or to your home?"

A greeting card salesperson: "These beautiful cabinets come in three sizes and designs, Mr. Hamilton. Which will fit best into your store and give you the optimum display?"

Practically every product offers opportunities for the use of trial closes—at the right time. Don't try to force a decision too early in the sale. If the prospects feel they are being pressured, they will resent it and defeat your purpose.

Emphasizing a Single Feature

If you remain constantly aware of your prospect's every reaction, you can soon spot the feature or benefit that most appeals to him or her. In furniture, it may be distinctive design; in life insurance, some unique feature of the policy; size, versatility, or warranty terms loom large in other product areas. With most prospects, economy ranks high—but convenience, beauty, or novelty often supply what they desire most. In any case, once you have identified what feature intrigues them, concentrate on showing how superbly your product provides it, and at the right time ask for the order.

Summary of Principal Advantages

In most presentations there comes a time for *review*. A prolonged discussion may drift into side issues, and sometimes the prospect actually forgets points or confuses them, particularly if the item is new or unfamiliar. At this point, a short summary of the main advantages will refocus the prospect's thinking and illustrate again the benefits of buying. Some salespeople accomplish this by ticking the points off on their fingers. Others use a series of colored cards, each stating one point, which they lay down in order on a table or desk. Here again it is possible to stress the one or two advantages that have had most appeal.

Closing on an Objection

Frequently, the sales discussion will reveal one objection that seems to be blocking a final favorable decision. The prospect may have mentioned the objection, but may possibly be holding it back. To get action, you must concentrate on removing this. You can say, "Is there anything about my product that I haven't made clear?" Or, "Is there something else worrying you that we haven't discussed? Please tell me what it is and let me clear it up."

If the prospect has shown serious interest and the interview has been friendly and businesslike, nine times out of ten he or she will come out with the objection. This narrows the closing of the sale to a single point. Respond to it completely and try again for the order.

Special Inducements

Nearly everyone welcomes that "extra something" that expresses gratitude for their order. Depending on your business, sales incentives can run the gamut from ten-cent items at the door to such things as radios, watches, desk sets, or savings bonds. Sales to stores climb when you can offer special deals, extended credit terms, or a chance to buy before prices go up. Used in accordance with company policy, inducements can be powerful closers.

Advantages and Penalties

Stressing the advantages of owning your product activates the basic urge that leads to closing the sale. Introduced and repeated throughout the presentation, they build the prospect's desire to the highest point and concomitantly reduce the importance of price or other negative factors. Dramatizing the advantages is more effective than mere statements:

In talking with a storekeeper, a systems salesperson might explain, "With just simple organization and control of your business operations, you could hear an extra five-hundred dollars a month 'ring up' on your cash register."

A swimming-pool dealer may observe, "With this pool in your yard, every weekend will be just like a vacation—without even taking the car out of the garage!"

An equally *effective* method for hastening the close is to remind them of the *penalties* they may suffer from not putting your product to work:

A seller of business machines can tell an office manager, "Every month you continue with your present system will cost your company hundreds of dollars. Why not start saving that now?"

A seller of pest-control devices might look out at the customer's garden and remark, "What a pity all that beauty could be damaged by insects when you can prevent it at such little cost."

A life-insurance salesperson can ask, "Wouldn't it be comforting to know that your family would be protected no matter what happens?"

A home-repair service representative might warn a homeowner, "Mr. Johnson, you can't afford to let your house go any longer. A few gutters, leaders, and lawn spouts installed now will prevent much worse damage that could run into a lot of money next year!"

The Power of Silence

Let's assume that your description of the penalty of delay plus your reassurance of complete satisfaction still fail to close the order. You have covered everything, have made sure the prospect knows all that he or she needs to know.

What else can you do? In the face of refusal, ask just one more question: "Are you *sure?*" The next step is up to them. They will start to explain, hoping to satisfy both of you. One of two things may happen:

They may raise some entirely new objection, one not mentioned before. This may be the real "roadblock." Handle it well and you may get an order.

They may come up with valid reasons why they can't buy now. Accept them and set up a mutually agreeable time for a call-back. They may indicate their generally favorable attitude toward your proposition and hint that a positive decision will be made at that time. But don't take anything for granted. Prepare for that next call as carefully as you did for this one.

If you want to increase your number of successful closes, the methods described here can help you. If you have any fear of the closing process, they should eliminate it; closing should be the perfectly natural result of all that has gone before. If the prospect is qualified to buy your product and has shown genuine interest in it, closing is always possible. It can happen at any time during the sales presentation.

The increase in your closings will depend on your skill in handling your closing tools. With your opening words you must elicit the prospect's desire to buy and then increase it, without apparent pressure, at each stage of the sale. The methods outlined above will enable you to accomplish this—if you use them correctly. Study them, practice them, and adopt them to your specific selling situation. Collectively they map the surest road to the top ten-percent.

CHAPTER TWENTY-NINE MAKING THE MOST OF YOUR TERRITORY

Are you the *explorer* or the *scientific* type of salesperson? Do you judge your territory's value on its geographic size alone? Or, like a laboratory scientist, do you constantly study and analyze your assigned area . . . trying to learn more about its basic nature and to bring out is hidden profitable potential?

If you are constantly beleaguering your sales manager to expand your territory, or if you find yourself casting envious eyes at the larger areas covered by your colleagues, consider these two facts:

☐ The smaller your territory in terms of square miles, the more time you can spend in actual, profitable sales effort and the less time you need waste in nonproductive travel.

☐ Your best sales aids are the recommendations of satisfied customers. These are achieved far more effectively within a concentrated area where customers are known to one another.

Explorers seldom become rich; the fact is that they seldom know very much *about* their discoveries. Actually, the explorer is a sort of "bird-dog" for the profit maker, showing the way to new potentials but seldom around to reap the benefits of their development. Columbus knew but an infinitesimally small part of the great and wonderful land that he discovered. Henry Hudson knew nothing about the lush New-York-State valley that bears his name—only about the river up which he sailed. Ferdinand Magellan could hardly be considered a great world authority, albeit he was its first circumnavigator.

On the other hand, consider the scientists. They study and analyze an apparently dead and inert piece of ore, for example. Without moving from their laboratory, they break it down into useful compounds and elements. Still dissatisfied, their curiosity leads them into further study and experiment. They break it down even further and discover the energy of its atoms . . . with their enormous power, so great that just a few pounds of the ore can drive a ship around the world . . . heat and light a great city for a year . . . or (may we have the good sense to avoid the eventuality) blow the entire earth to "smithereens."

Similarly, successful salespeople continually study and analyze their territory in order to develop its last "ounce" of potential. They know it has possibilities far greater than are realized through one or two calls upon each prospect. They don't worry about saturation, competition, or territorial wealth. Instead, they learn as much as they can about how their product or service can satisfy the wants and needs of every prospect. They learn current product applications and create new uses, some of which even their employer may have been unaware. They sell and resell within their territory until they are absolutely sure that every prospect and customer has been sold "to the hilt."

Aside from their product and such promotion as their company may supply, *all the salesperson has to work with are his or her territory and his or her time.* Proper knowledge of your territory tells you when and where sales are most likely to be made. Proper use of your time enables you to spend more of it in actual selling to customers, thereby deriving more personal profit from more sales made.

Too many salespeople treat their territories on a hit-or-miss basis. They operate like Sunday fishermen, casting their lines once or twice into one part of a lake and, not getting a bite, moving on to another area. (Fishing, too, can be carried on scientifically, taking time to study the habits of fish in various waters; but most weekend anglers are out for pleasure and rely largely upon hunch.) As a salesperson, you are out to earn a living . . . to get the results that put money into your pocket. You must operate scientifically to make the most of your opportunities.

Let's start from scratch. You've got a new job, selling, and you plan to make it your life's work. You've been assigned a territory or given a prospect list. How are you going to *make the most* of it?

Isn't it logical that you organize yourself to operate efficiently before you even start to sell? Let us assume your prospect cards are alphabetically arranged when they are handed to you. The first three names are Ames, Benjamin, and Clark. Ames and Clark are in one part of your territory and Benjamin in another part. Wouldn't it be more sensible to call on Ames and Clark at one time and Benjamin at another time, rather than to make your calls alphabetically? Obviously, you'll save time and avoid call-backs if you are so organized as to cover all the prospects in one area at one time.

To organize your territory properly, the first thing you need is a map. It makes no difference whether your territory is part of a small town or an area covering several states, a map that clearly shows the location of your customers and prospects is the most useful aid in organizing your selling efforts.

Second, divide your territorial map geographically—according to region, town, neighborhood, and block—so that you can cluster and schedule your contacts on a methodical section-by-section basis, conserving precious time. Call-backs, too, should be clustered according to geographical proximity. Plan to make call-backs within ten days from the original contact.

Third, and *most important,* be *prompt* in filling customer orders. KEEP YOUR PROMISES! Customer goodwill and repeat patronage ensue from reliable sales follow-through.

CHAPTER THIRTY: INCREASING THE SIZE OF EACH SALE

One of the best ways for a small business to reduce its selling expense is by increasing the size of each sale. Customers are always glad to get more for their money, even though they may initially have to pay a little more than they intended. Here are some ways to cash in on their natural bargain-hunting instinct:

Many items normally sold one at a time can be packaged in lots of three or more and sold readily with a small price concession. An example is tennis balls, which come packed in a vacuum can. Nobody expects to buy *one* tennis ball—the unit of three is accepted. Beverages, drugs, and food products offer many opportunities to enlarge the unit of sale through attractive multiple packaging.

Increasing the number of units in a standard assortment will mean additional purchases. Glassware, china, and tools can be made packaged in sixes instead of fours, for example.

Appeal to a hobby and offer special packages of products pertinent to the hobby. Thus a large-volume, big-ticket sale is possible in each instance. Special package deals for gardeners, lawn experts, and marine enthusiasts get quick attention.

Gifts are a year-round business, and customers will respond to new appeals as holidays and anniversaries roll around. Combining two or three related items for one special event will prove successful.

INCREASING THE
SIZE OF EACH SALE

Economy has the greatest appeal to customers, and offering larger packages of standard items at a small concession will always draw trade. Food, drugs, cosmetics, paints, and beverages are examples.

You can build a customer's feelings of importance by recommending additional items that will complement a purchase: new tables to go with the couch, some curtains to match the spread, shutters to enhance the vinyl siding, patio blocks to surround the pool, a telephoto lens for the camera—or merely some fries to munch with the burger!

Here are some ways that merchants increase sales:

- ☐ **A meat market** offered a holiday "package" including a turkey, a ham, and prime steaks to carry the householder from Christmas through New Year's Day without further shopping. A savings of $5.00 was offered, and the butcher exceeded his greatest previous sales.

- ☐ **A silverware shop** increased the traditional six-place-setting wedding gift to *eight* during the month of June and offered appreciable savings to its customers. The jeweler then expanded the basic idea to serving dishes and Sheffield plates.

- ☐ **A sporting goods dealer** developed a "family plan" as Spring approached. Tennis, golf, and fishing equipment was offered at substantial savings if purchased by members of one family. The merchant tied the plan to occasions when gifts would be appropriate—graduation, Mother's Day, and Father's Day. This spread the payments over a period, although the base price remained the same.

- ☐ **A clothing store proprietor** used fashion appeal to increase sales of men's apparel and accessories. He set up special displays in the men's suit department showing stylish apparel combinations for business and evening wear, attractively coordinated with varied accessories. The customer was thus influenced to purchase other apparel items inclusive of accessories.

CHAPTER THIRTY-ONE
RETAIL PROMOTIONAL IDEAS

Do-it-Yourself Display

Capitalizing on the do-it-yourself trend, an Akron, Ohio, dealer finds it extremely effective to create a "do-it-yourself" window display twice a year— just after Christmas and just after Easter, times when most people are looking for ways to reduce expenses. His window features five or six household items that could be built or repaired by a customer. These displays may include unpainted furniture, a dog kennel, a television cabinet, an old bicycle, even a "knocked down" automobile engine. Alongside each item he displays the parts and the tools needed to build or repair it. He lists prices of the materials, comparing the total cost of the do-it-yourself projects with the cost of buying new or paying for professional repairs. This store has become a regular information bureau for people who like to work with their hands (and for many who don't), thereby creating much goodwill, gaining enormous popularity, and cornering the do-it-yourself market throughout the community.

Excursion Ticket to Various Departments of Store

A Louisville, Kentucky, department store mailed a long ticket, similar to an excursion ticket, to prospects in the community. Its heading: "EXCURSION TO BETTER LIVING." Each stub directed the prospect to a different department in the store, listing items therein that could be used for home improvement.

Profit-Sharing Plans

A retailer in Newark, New Jersey, has inaugurated a profit-sharing plan whereby customers can earn a five-percent discount on their purchases.

143

Customers are asked to save their sales slips, and at the end of each quarter-year they are entitled to turn the slips back to the store for either cash or merchandise. This practice not only builds goodwill for the dealer, but also discourages customers from shopping elsewhere (even if another store should be more conveniently located) once they have accumulated a few slips.

Calendar
Mailings

Last year, a building-materials dealer in Des Moines, Iowa, added to the store's goodwill by sending out a calendar. It's main illustration was a scene in a carpentry shop, and of course the dealer's name was tastefully but prominently lettered. On the back of each month's calendar sheet were instructions and diagrams for making two or three home-workshop projects.

Postcard
Specials

A retailer in Evansville, Indiana, mails out postcards to his customers and prospects four times a year. On the card he lists a group of items and their prices. He offers SAVINGS OF 20% on those items to customers who *bring the card to the store with them.*

Build Free
Mailing Lists

An accurate list of the residents of your community can be your most valuable asset for building business. Mailings about sales, special purchases, availability of scarce merchandise, new products, and so on, invariably produce an extra volume of business. With a little time and effort, such lists can be compiled from voters' and taxpayers' lists, as well as city directories and reverse telephone books, which list subscribers by street and thereby permit you to select prospects in your own immediate neighborhood.

Display Items
in Related Groups

Often it is possible to gain additional sales by grouping items that supplement one another in doing certain jobs. For instance, a display of automobile polish should include chamois, car-washing brush-hose combination, and car-upholstery cleaner. A display of floor-waxing equipment can also contain heavy-duty detergent, the wax itself, plus pails, brushes, mops, and so on. A display of fence wire should also contain posts, a post-hole digger, and other items related to fence construction.

Important
Phone-Number
Cards

A Phoenix, Arizona, dealer distributes important-phone-number cards, which can be suspended conveniently from telephones and switchboards. Emergency numbers are printed, along with plenty of lines for the individual's use. At the bottom of the card is the dealer's address and phone number and a general description of the range of merchandise, e.g., Hardware, Appliances, Sporting Goods. This type of card is useful to the customer or prospect and serves as a constant reminder of where to purchase the merchandise carried by the dealer.

Cooperate with Shell Builders The building of home "shells" has become a big business in the past few years. A builder erects the basic structure of a house and sells it, leaving the finishing touches—accessories, wiring, appliances, paint, paper, and so on—for the owner to provide. A complete model home is usually finished attractively to serve as the builder's sales office. You can cooperate with a shell builder by supplying furniture, carpeting, appliances, or hardware for the model home, in return for which the builder agrees to display a sign advertising your store and its merchandise. The builder may help further by suggesting to buyers that your store is well stocked with the items necessary to finish their homes as attractively as the model house.

Tie-in with Noncompetitive Dealers A hardware dealer in Pittsburgh saves mailing costs by joining with a linoleum and asphalt-tile dealer as well as a lumber yard to produce direct-mail advertisements. Each dealer has a separate page to promote "specials," and the headline of the mailer is usually worded so as to promote all three dealers. A few sample headlines follow:

"Everything You Need to Build a New Recreation Room!"

"SAVE NOW on Hardware, Linoleum and Lumber!"

"Home Improvement Equipment that ave Dollar$!"

Free Piano Lessons A piano dealer advertises *Ten Piano Lessons Free* with the purchase of an instrument. The lessons are given to groups of six to eight customers at a time.

"One-Cent-Less" Sale A variety store runs an annual "One-Cent-Less" Sale, advertising in the local newspapers that two of each item listed can be purchased for "one-cent less" than the regular price of one.

Free Music-Appreciation Course Since many prospects feel that their lack of musical knowledge would make the purchase of quality stereo equipment an extravagance, one dealer advertises a *Free Music-Appreciation Course* which is given in the store one morning a week—and is embellished, of course, by the use of fine components.

Rent-A-Mink . . . Or any seemingly "unattainable" item that has occasional use. In this case a fur dealer advertises the possibility of renting a mink. Without listing either the rental price or describing the quality or style of the fur, the ad simply shows a cartoon illustration of a woman wearing a stole and looking proudly at herself in the mirror, while the written copy insists that *minks can be rented* for a much lower cost than one would think. The headline announces emphatically: "Everybody's Doing It!" *Which of your products can be rented effectively?*

CHAPTER THIRTY- TWO
ANALYZE YOUR STORE TRAFFIC

A SIMPLE CHECK-UP TO INCREASE EFFICIENCY . . . AND SALES

There's a goldmine of valuable information that can be derived from a study of your day-by-day traffic flow! With it, you can better arrange your hours, improve employee scheduling, and convert those "nonsales" into real sales. For example:

☐ Do you know what percentage of "walk-ins" who enter your store actually buy? And, if they don't buy—just why don't they?

☐ Do you know what hours of the day are "over-busy" ones, and what hours are "under-busy"?

☐ Do you know how to adjust your employee shifts to coordinate most efficiently with your specific traffic flow?

Exactly what can knowledge of your customer "flow" achieve for you? It may tell you that:

☐ You can perhaps open at a later hour than usual (due to sparse patronage during early hours).

☐ You should perhaps have a better stock-control system (to reduce non-sales due to frequent stock depletions).

☐   You should stagger your personnel hours—perhaps arranging for some to work only part-time—so that you have adequate help for "overload" periods, and minimum help during dull periods of the day.

☐   You should perhaps consider adding other items to your line—possibly related products that have proved to be "in demand."

☐   You should perhaps rearrange your own procedures (for example, the hours when you go to the bank or have lunch) so that they fit in more efficiently with your customer flow.

☐   You should perhaps remain open during evening hours (at least on certain days each week). This would be indicated if the bulk of your customer flow is in the late afternoon or just before closing. (Statistics obtained from varied businesses show that almost 50 percent of purchases are made after 4:30 p.m.) As families become more dependent on two incomes for survival, this trend will increase.

How can you "keep tabs" on your traffic flow for proper analysis?

We have provided a model for a simple chart that will enable you to get a clear picture of your store's traffic flow, analyze the situation, and do something about it. Proper analysis will help you determine what measures may convert nonsales into sales, and offer a guide to scheduling better personnel shifts and effective hours of operation.

Maintain this chart for a trial period of, say, sixty days. The chart records scientifically a typical day's activities at your place. It shows you: (a) traffic flow for each hour of the day; (b) dollar volume per hour; (c) number of people visiting your store; and (d) number of nonpurchasers.

We have prepared our sample chart to cover morning hours only. To obtain a clear, all-day picture, project the chart to show hours from opening time right through closing time. On various days, arrange to stay open an hour or two later than usual . . . just to get an indication of how many customers prefer these hours you'd normally miss out on!

TRAFFIC FLOW
AND SALES
ANALYSIS

Time	Dollar sales	Customers entering store	Customers making purchases	Strollers	Average sale (col. 2 ÷ by col. 4)	Nonsales (col. 5 × col. 6)
9-10 a.m.	$45.00	14	9	5	$ 5.00	$25.00
10-11 a.m.	35.00	7	5	2	7.00	14.00
11-noon	44.00	10	4	6	11.00	66.00
Noon-1 p.m.	30.00	4	4	0	7.50	.00
Morning summary	$154.00	35	22	13	$ 7.00	$91.00

SECTION THREE

NEW ADVERTISING CONCEPTS

CHAPTER THIRTY-THREE COMPOSING YOUR OWN EFFECTIVE ADS

Let's assume you're planning an advertisement for your business—one that you hope will achieve increased sales for your products or services. Initially, of course, you have a choice among media: Will it be newspaper or magazine? Radio or TV? Window and counter display, direct-mail, or neighborhod circulars?

"Hmmm . . . ," you say.

Quickly, before you get carried away with this heavy decision-making, let's make another assumption. For the purposes of this chapter, let's say you've decided on some form of printed material, and you're planning to design and write the copy yourself. (There are agencies that will gladly do this for you, but their rates may not be cost effective for a small business.)

GETTING IT ALL TOGETHER

From the moment you begin to grapple with the task you find yourself confronted with various problems, each a big one. What merchandise offer should you feature? What headline should you use? What sort of illustration should you select to dramatize your message? What layout will best capture the reader's attention?

One of two things can happen at this point:

(a) You decide the task is too tough for you and will take too much time from your regular work. In this event you'll probably set it aside for the "some other time" that rarely arrives.

(b) Undaunted, you press on with the project, even though you find that the ideas are slow in coming.

Now the fun begins. Somehow, no matter how you fight against it, irrelevant things keep popping into your head in place of the sought-after inspiration. Eventually, in desperation, you may seize upon some half-acceptable idea — one that proves to be inadequate for your needs. One businessperson expressed it this way:

"I know that constant advertising is vital to my business. Yet I do only a small part of my needed advertising because it takes me so long to think up acceptable advertising ideas. And even though I use an advertising agency, I prefer to generate initial ideas on my own."

And after a pause, we heard his wistful afterthought:

"If only there was some magical genie that could be summoned to give us the advertising ideas we need and when we need them!"

No such genie exists, of course. There is, however, an "assured" method for producing advertising ideas. By following a few simple procedures, you will find yourself able to generate an appropriate idea on almost any advertising project — and do it in a matter of minutes!

Our method organizes the mind, banishing unrelated thoughts and permitting concentration on the desired idea *only*. It requires adherence to the following steps:

1. **Know** specifically what *kind* of idea you seek.

2. **Organize** all available data relevant to the subject.

3. **Employ** "thought-nudgers" to arrive at the final idea.

To demonstrate: Let's say you're planning an advertisement for your local newspaper — one that will promote some feature of your products or services. You begin with Step 1 of the procedures given above.

KNOW WHAT KIND OF IDEA YOU SEEK

Do this: Jot down on a sheet of paper all the facts about your products or services that you consider good "sales points" — e.g., convenience, durability, appearance, operation, safety, delivery, taste, varied services, uses, and so on. Collect *all* the facts you can; examine your competitors' advertisements to make sure that no "mention-worthy" features have been omitted. (This will also ensure that you do not produce material that is similar to theirs in appearance.)

ORGANIZE YOUR MERCHANDISING FACTS

Go over all the sales points you have jotted down. Which of these do you consider MOST IMPORTANT? Is it *lower price* (e.g., a special sale of your products)? Is it *something else you can offer or do* that attracts attention and "scoops" your competitor?

Having selected your outstanding point, write it down. If, for example, you have selected *lower price* as your feature point, you'll jot down, "Show my prospects how they can get REAL SAVINGS by buying *my* products."

You have now boiled down your problem into a single sentence. You have one subject—and one subject only—to think about. Your mind is thus spared the waste-motion of irrelevant thought or of hop-skipping from subject to subject.

You are now ready for Step 3 (the most important step).

USE "THOUGHT-NUDGERS" TO ARRIVE AT THE FINAL IDEA

What are these "nudgers," anyway? A fair question. Briefly stated, they are any words and pictures that, when glanced at, serve to stoke your imagination into "quick flame" and to "pellet" your mind—in ping-pong-ball fashion—with a number of ideas pertaining to your advertising project.

The things that stir imagination differ among individuals; hence the nudgers you accumulate may be vastly different from mine, or from those collected by your best friend, Charlie. In time, as you practice using nudgers, you can gauge quickly which words and pictures are most effective for *you*.

Let's say, for example, that the first thing you "see" in your thought-nudger file is a picture of a magician. (Recall now that you are seeking some idea to dramatize the *lower price* feature of your products.)

You associate the two thoughts—*Magic . . . lower prices*. Suddenly you have a headline idea: "Like MAGIC—Prices Come Tumbling Down" (during this sale at your store). You'll include an illustration of a magician (top hat, cape, and all) waving his wand over a symbolic sketch of "tumbling" prices.

Perhaps you're featuring *a number* of items for this sale. To tie-in the other copy blocks with your headline, you'll insert smaller sketches of a magician's hat and wand, for example, before each offering.

Because the thought-nudger happened to be a magician shouldn't imply that you *must* embody a sketch of a magician in your ad. The thought of magic may give you secondary ideas for slanting your copy—you may prefer a magic carpet or even our elusive genie.

155

Not only secondary but also tertiary (third-order) ideas may suggest themselves from your nudger. Looking for words similar to *magic,* you think of *fabulous.* How can you symbolize the word *fabulous?* Into your mind pops Paul Bunyan—the *fabulous* mythical woodsman who did such supernatural things and told such tall tales! Presto! You have a novel idea for a *Paul Bunyan* sale of your merchandise. Now your headline may read: "Prices so fabulously LOW as to defy the imagination of PAUL BUNYAN!" You'll include a sketch of a huge Paul Bunyan (wood-axe in hand). Your copy will be in "exaggerated" style, reminiscent of the mighty woodsman himself.

This may lead to correlated ideas: miniature Paul Bunyan axes given free to those patronizing your sale, or premium-booklets containing various Paul Bunyan stories "tied-in" with merchandising facts about your products. Perhaps you could offer prizes to those writing "tallest tales," *a la* Paul Bunyan, about the benefits of your merchandise or services; the winner could be proclaimed the *Paul Bunyan* of your city.

All this . . . from glancing at one nudger of a magician!

Looking further into your nudger file, say you see a picture of machinery gears. An idea! Your headline reads: "GEARED to Give You LOWEST Prices." Your stylistic illustration centers on two intermeshed gears. In one gear you symbolize your business (picture of your store, factory, trademark, or some representative product). In the other, you insert a sketch representing *savings* (money bags, shattered prices, or stacked coins).

Some "Thought-Nudgers" to Practice With

To give you a head start, we're providing a beginner's list of nudgers and a brief discussion of ideas that may be developed from them. We're listing the primary ideas only; like the magician nudger, however, each one is capable of generating secondary and tertiary ideas that may suit your advertising project perfectly. Loads of other ideas will suggest themselves as you thumb through your own nudger file.

Chain links *Suggested headline:* "This Sale . . . LINKS You to Best Buys!"
Suggested illustration: Two chain links—picture of your establishment in one link and symbolic sketch of customer or of *savings* in the other link.

Doorway *Suggested headline:* "OPENS THE DOOR to Unequaled Bargains!"
Suggested illustration: Picture of your products or customers streaming through the open door of your store.

Ten-pins

Suggested headline: "This Sale . . . Scores a STRIKE on Lower Prices!"
Suggested illustration: Show ten-pins being bowled over by ball.

Tape measure

Suggested headline: "Prices TAILORED to Your Purse . . . Products TAILORED to Your Every Need!"
Suggested illustration: A tailor's tape measure shown rambling through your headline.

Magnet

Suggested headline: "A Sale . . . that Will ATTRACT Bargain-Seekers by the Thousands."
Suggested illustration: Picture of huge magnet (extending from your establishment) "attracting" large crowd of customers (swarming toward the entrance).

School chalkboard

Suggested headline: "ABC's of Good Value — Stock up on ALL Your Needs During this Great Sale!"
Suggested illustration: Hand with ruler pointing at large chalkboard on which headline is printed by hand.

Nutshell

Suggested headline: "In a NUTSHELL — the Greatest Buy Ever Offered!"
Suggested illustration: Picture of a big nutshell containing some sketch that symbolizes savings.

Invitation card

Suggested headline: "You're INVITED . . . to Accept $50!" In smaller print you'll explain this is what they'll realize in savings by purchasing your products.
Suggested illustration: Typical invitation card bearing script lettering pertinent to invitations.

Stocking

Suggested headline: "This is the Time for STOCKING UP — at Big Savings!"
Suggested illustration: Picture of transparent stocking filled with sale merchandise.

Horn of Plenty (cornucopia)

Suggested headline: "PLENTY of Bargains to Blow our HORN about!"
Suggested illustration: Picture of cornucopia crammed with sale merchandise items.

Bell *Suggested headline:* "Values that Really RING THE BELL!"
Suggested illustration: Picture of bell alongside headline. Perhaps each featured price shown on a smaller bell throughout ad.

Slide *Suggested headline:* "Prices Take a Downward SLIDE!"
Suggested illustration: Picture of children's playground slide with bunch of sale items sliding down.

Full House *Suggested headline:* "A FULL HOUSE of Bargains!"
Suggested illustration: Picture of a Full-House poker hand.

Axe *Suggested headline:* "Prices Fall Under the AXE!"
Suggested illustration: Picture of price tags being hit with axe.

Scissors *Suggested headline:* "We've CUT PRICES as Never Before!"
Suggested illustration: Pair of scissors cutting price tags.

Umbrella *Suggested headline:* "It's RAINING BARGAINS at Eugene's!"
Suggested illustration: Big umbrella with headline running across it.

Top *Suggested headline:* "These Values are the TOPS!"
Suggested illustration: Picture of big child's top alongside headline, with prices throughout ad shown on a top.

Parachute *Suggested headline:* "BIG DROP IN PRICES!"
Suggested illustration: Picture of bag of merchandise descending with a parachute.

Boxing gloves *Suggested headline:* "Look at These KNOCK-OUT VALUES!"
Suggested illustration: Fist with boxing glove hitting punching bag.

We could go on and on . . . but by now you have the idea! Unrelated as these nudgers may be to your business, see how quickly they supply you with dozens of specific ideas applicable to your advertising project. Merely select the one that best fits your needs.

Where do you get your own repertoire of nudgers? Almost everywhere! You'll find them through examining all types of advertising, through research concerning your business, and through constant observation of the world around you. Clip them out or jot them down whenever you see them. You'll soon have an adequate resource file, but don't allow yourself the luxury of ending your search for new ideas. The most effective advertising is current and topical. Each new trend or popular interest can provide nudgers to keep *your* ads one step ahead of your competition!

Here's why nudgers perform so unfailingly: They provide a "beachhead" for your thoughts, giving you a mental foothold from which you may proceed. They surround you with a multitude of ever-handy, stimulating *experiences* which are all-important for creative thought.

If you stop to think about it, most of your best inspirations in life have come to you through *experiences*—talking to a friend, seeing a movie, traveling, reading, feeling some deep emotion, and so on. Your imagination was aroused, your brain put to work.

In our busy day-to-day activities we lack the opportunity to accumulate all the experiences we need. Certainly we can't blithely leave our place of business to absorb new experiences whenever we want an idea. Herein lies the effectiveness of a nudger file—giving you a quantity of experiences in vest-pocket form, available at your beckoning, at the exact moment you need them!

CHAPTER THIRTY-FOUR PROMOTING YOUR BUSINESS THROUGHOUT YOUR COMMUNITY

Your Own Magazine

Issue a "magazet" (miniature magazine) to customers and prospects, containing chatty reading matter plus your advertising message. A Wisconsin firm issues a postcard-size magazine each week. An Ohio firm issues a 6×9-inch magazine—enclosing one with each monthly invoice. Such publications reap much reader interest and create goodwill.

Local Club Contacts

Publicize yourself through local clubs. A jeweler addressed service clubs on *the romance of jewelry*. One appliance firm arranged a homemakers' contest among women's clubs. A sporting-goods dealer addressed youth groups on the essentials of camping (and equipment needed). An insurance agent discussed educational insurance policies with members of a PTA.

Self-Written Press Releases

Are you really getting your share of free publicity in local newspapers and magazines? A Michigan undertaker publicized the fact that three generations of the same family were conducting business. An Indiana grocer merited a human-interest story because he knew all his customers by their first names. An upholstery firm, established 100 years, prepared an interesting write-up and pictures on its centennial celebration. What's "newsy" about your firm?

PROMOTING YOUR BUSINESS
THROUGHOUT YOUR COMMUNITY

Local Hobbies Within each community live many hobbyists. Why not sponsor a hobby exhibit, with the most interesting ones displayed in your window? It will attract the interest of passersby, invite local newspaper publicity, and generate goodwill.

Interior Display Signs Use interior display signs as an auxiliary sales force. A grocery firm installed a sign listing "Bargains of the Day," changing some featured items each day. An automotive supply store listed possible customer needs on a sign headed "Lest you forget. . . ." A furrier listed courtesy services available to customers. A bookshop listed its new books on one sign, current best-sellers on another. What type of sign will help *your* business?

Premium Booklets Can you issue a booklet that will be helpful to your customers? A jewelry firm issued one for their soon-to-be-married ring prospects: "16 Ways to Assure a Happy Honeymoon." A paper company conveniently provided "How to Select Paper to Fit your Specific Job." A duplicating machine company offered "124 Ways to Earn Money with your Duplicating Machine." A grocer supplied a booklet called "Food for Health." If the booklet is really instructive, it is long retained; hence it serves as a constant reminder of your firm's services.

Radio Programs Are your utilizing the promotional opportunities of radio? When a flu epidemic hit this community, *a druggist* volunteered time and expertise to a radio discussion on how to keep well. Following an increase of auto accidents in town, the owner of *an auto school* presented a program on safe driving. *A garage owner* discussed automobile safety measures. *A department store* representative, just before school opening, addressed parents about apparel and school equipment their children would need. If it's timely, this type of promotion can be unusually effective.

Local History We're all proud of our hometown; hence we are all interested in its historic lore. A Wisconsin real-estate firm used this appeal in its advertising: In each newspaper ad they pictured and described a local historical event, and subsequently issued a booklet on local history. Supplementing this, they offered awards to local school children who showed superior historical knowledge.

Telephone Contact A phone call is *personal* and serves as a good sales medium. One drygoods firm phones to tell customers of current bargains; a hardware firm phones past customers about new styles that might interest them.

Complete Package Plan Have you tried to tie-in related products and sell them as a complete package? An infants-wear shop sold a unit that included all needed items for the new-born. A hardware firm grouped and sold all products needed for kitchen painting.

Your Personnel as Salespeople

Don't overlook the salespower of your own personnel in store, office, or factory. Suggest ways in which they can promote your products among their friends and relatives. Sears-Roebuck Company, for example, has obtained some 75,000 extra customers through the efforts of its 14,000 personnel who were given "suggestion booklets" on outside selling.

Advisory Council

Why not a local "jury" to tell what's good about your products or services? A department store appointed a "youth council" to decide on college apparel needs. A flour manufacturer designated local "homemakers' councils" to judge the best ways to use its products. Another "jury" was set up by a distilling company to advise on liquor selection.

Get-Acquainted Day

Arrange a "get-acquainted" event for your firm. One department store ran a get-acquainted-with-our-buyers sale, picturing its departmental buyers in the ad. Another store conducted a get-acquainted-with-our-products sale—listing the many products it sold (some of which the public was unaware). Another firm ran a sale simply to "get acquainted with our low, low prices."

Institutional Displays

Arrange to install *educational* displays of your products or services in the local library, chamber of commerce, city hall, museum, and so on. A bank displayed odd coins. A beauty shop exhibited progress of hair styles and care methods in the past 100 years. A department store displayed changes in apparel styles. A sporting-goods firm exhibited "the largest fish" caught by local people.

Audio-visuals

A local jeweler offered slides on "adventures in gems" to be shown to clubs and schools. A bookshop showed slides on "books that will thrill you." A bank ran slides on "fascinations of thrift." How can *you* use them?

Cooperative Mailing

Merge your advertising with that of related, noncompetitive firms who seek to sell to similar prospects. A luggage shop shared promotional advertising with a travel bureau (since both sold to travel-minded people). A photographer (specializing in baby photos) teamed up with an infants-wear shop, and a jewelry firm with a bridal salon. You halve your expenses and reach a concentrated prospect group.

Charity Events

Act for the public good and the public good acts for you. Stores sponsoring charity events—United Fund, Cancer Crusade, March of Dimes, and so on—

find that they are performing a worthwhile public service and concomitantly gleaning invaluable goodwill. One department store allotted 25 percent of the proceeds of its sale to the community fund.

Sponsor Athletic Teams Why not sponsor one of the amateur athletic teams in your town—basketball, softball, football? Supply them with sweaters bearing your firm name. You'll be helping to promote local sports in addition to achieving effective self-advertising.

Enclosure with Invoice Each invoice can do a "selling job" if it's accompanied by sales literature—news of new products or a special sale.

Remembering Birthdays Nothing is more "personal" than one's birthday and nothing is appreciated more than another's remembrance of it.

Oddity Ads The unusual always attracts interest. A grocer regularly displayed "grocery oddities" in the store's window. A baker inserted oddities about local history and people in newspaper advertisements. A restaurant ran oddity ads about its customers and services, also installing an "oddity exhibit" in its window. What odd things about *your* business can be featured?

Awards for "Community Firsts" A leather-goods firm gives gifts to those who place "first" in things—first in athletics, first in scholarship, first in citizenship. This attracts much publicity and creates goodwill for the firm in its performance of a community service.

News Events What's "newsy" in your town? A Michigan merchant held a "Welcome to Our Visitors" sale during a local Elks' convention. A New York firm featured its line of water-saving products and devices at the time of a local water shortage. A Chicago firm conducted a Circus sale when the circus was in town.

Earnings Funds Clubs, churches, and charities are usually interested in earning funds for their various activities. Offer them a discount on your products or services that reverts to their club's earning fund. You will thus have recruited a large group of effective salespeople for your firm, besides aiding local charity.

Local Events How can you "link" your promotion to local celebrations? An Iowa merchant tied-in with the local Harvest Festival by featuring "bumper-crop values." On the occasion of Cheese Day a Wisconsin firm ran a "Food for Thought" advertisement (containing sales facts about the firm). An Ohio firm ran a "Congratu-lations" advertisement (giving discounts) to tie-in with the opening of a big local bridge.

Gifts to Local Graduates The high-school graduate is a valuable potential customer. One jewelry firm sends each graduate a certificate redeemable for $5.00 (on purchase of $25 or more). A bank sends a $5.00 bill to be used for starting a bank account. How can *you* attract this patronage?

Theatre Promotion What movies are now playing in your town? One retailer piggy-backed on the extensive local publicity achieved by the movie *Star Wars,* by offering *"out of this world values"* in conjunction with the movie and distributing *Star-Wars* souvenirs to customers. Another enterprising retailer took advantage of the *Superman* movie by offering "super values" plus a free autographed illustra-tion of Superman to customers.

Auction Sales There's challenge and interest in auction sales. An Indiana firm conducted daily auctions on the radio—highest bid received within five minutes obtained auctioned item. An Illinois merchant each week conducted a "mystery" package auction, merchandise contents undisclosed. Does this give *you* an idea?

Wish List We all have unfulfilled wishes. A New York department store did something about it. With each $5.00 (or more) purchase, a patron was entitled to submit his or her "wish"; each month the most interesting list was fulfilled. One cus-tomer "wished" to see her sister in Yugoslavia (from whom she had been separated for 15 years). An expense-paid trip was provided for her Yugoslav-ian sister to visit this country. A six-year-old girl "wished" that Santa Claus would remember her address, since he had neglected to visit her home last Christmas. A full-fledged Santa, loaded with gifts, appeared at her house as a wish fulfillment. A couple wished for a second honeymoon that they missed out on. They were given an expense-free trip to the Bahamas. In each case the collateral publicity value greatly exceeded the costs involved.

Budget Aids A department store gives away booklets containing budget guidelines. These tend to associate the firm with economical buying and also keep the firm's name in the customer's mind. A young-people's apparel shop distributes coin-banks to its customers; when filled, the banks are opened by the firm and applied to purchases.

Sponsor "Thrift Day"
Such sponsorship associates your name with low prices and wise buying habits. Conduct talks in local schools and clubs. Give awards for those demonstrating the practice of thrift. Advertise well.

Gadgets
Use of gadgets in your direct mail helps increase its salespower. Consider a miniature paste-on phone to emphasize your phone number; a paste-on feather to imply that the customer will be "tickled" at your values; a paste-on plastic turtle to tie-in with the heading "Don't be a slowpoke" (in availing yourself of these bargains). There are lots of ideas here.

Mathematical Tricks
From childhood we've been fascinated by tricks and stunts. An Oklahoma department store featured a mathematical trick in each of its ads. The copy above the ad would read "This is a trick" . . . and the copy above the merchandising message reads: "But this is *no* trick . . . You get best values here."

Post-Office Cancellation Marks
A Massachusetts jeweler linked his advertising with novel postmarks. One ad, for example, would show the postmark, *Bee, Arkansas* and read: "You'll *buzz* with excitement at these values." A *Clover, Virginia,* postmark was tied-in with the copy, "You'll be in *clover* when you get these bargains." Other postmarks included: *Little, Kentucky,* and *Rich, Mississippi.* You can get these postmarks by packaging your mail in bulk and addressing it to the selected post office, requesting them to cancel the stamps and forward to your addressees from their location.

"Thank You" for First Orders
A gesture of appreciation for an initial order can go a long way toward making a new customer a permanent customer. It can be a personally written letter, a friendly form letter, or even a postcard.

Foreign Mail
Mail from a foreign country! Most people are thrilled at getting such letters. A Washington firm capitalizes on this enthusiasm and dramatizes its imported products by having its letters sent from England bearing English postmark and stamp. Do you sell imported products? Consider this.

Rewards for Recommendations
The most effective and most extensive sales force a firm can have is the general public. Utilizing this idea, a large moving and storage firm has enlisted thousands of people as its sales force by distributing several million matchbooks offering (on inside cover) a series of monetary rewards *for recommending customers to them.* A coupon facilitates writing in.

166

"Smell" Ads
You have seen plenty of ads, but have you ever *smelled* one? A mint-julep firm "atomized" its advertisement so that the reader actually whiffed the tangy aroma of mint. Two senses are thus evoked—sight and smell.

Contests
Contests always attract interest, and there's a type of competition for *every* occasion. A New Jersey office-machine firm offered awards to those guessing the correct number of parts contained in each of its adding machines. A grocer offered prizes to observant window-shoppers who detected a misprinted label on a product carton. What kind of contest fits in with your operation?

Awards
Certificates printed on a sheet of paper cost very little. Yet, given by you to your customers or sales personnel, they assume important meaning. You'll find that people compete eagerly to win them. One Wisconsin firm awarded beautifully engraved certificates to the salesperson getting the largest monthly order. A credit jewelry firm awarded certificates inscribed with customers' names as "preferred charge-account customers" of the firm.

Safe Opening
A St. Paul jeweler crammed the safe with $1500 worth of merchandise and gave clues to the combination over the radio, inviting listeners to come in and "tinker" with the safe—offering its contents to the one who opened it. Many came to "tinker," many remained to buy.

Package Sales
Book-of-the-Month Club introduced a novel merchandising idea in supplying books to subscribers each month on an annual basis. A candy firm picked up the theme and promoted "candy of the month." A razor-blade firm promoted "razor blades each month" service (sending a monthly supply of razor blades). A beauty salon promoted "coiffure insurance"—for $15 a month ($40 a season) the customer gets any number of desired sets and combings.

Dates
A California grocery store announced its opening this way: Two luscious dates were packed in cellophane and distributed to local people. A card stapled to the package stated: "*You have a date* to attend the opening of our store . . ."

"Leave-Behind"
What should a salesperson "leave behind" for the prospect if the prospect is not in? A business card doesn't really tell the story. However, a novel combined calling-card/advertisement developed by a publishing company solved this problem. A 6×9-inch card contains a picture of the salesperson plus an advertising message. In the center is a sketch of a memo pad on which the salesperson jots down any personal message.

Customer
Entertainment

A Chicago clothing firm conducts regular afternoon musicales—playing symphonic recordings and serving tea and cookies. A Wisconsin carpet firm conducts lectures on "Know Your Rugs." Many prospective customers are attracted to these no-obligation events, hoping to learn something. A good number of them make their purchases from this dealer, who tries to sell each customer the rug specifically suited to his or her needs.

CHAPTER THIRTY-FIVE
AN ADVERTISING CHECKLIST

To determine how you should apportion your advertising dollar, you must have an awareness of the type of advertising that would be appropriate and the expense involved in its production.

The Approach   This checklist is intended as an aid in selecting and planning your advertising media. To obtain maximum benefits from the list—and the subsequent advertising—we suggest following five basic steps:

1. Decide *what* you want to advertise.

2. Decide *where* you want to advertise.

3. Establish an advertising budget (*see* Chapter 36). Get media rates from Standard Rate and Data (national media directory) or by contacting media directly.

4. Compose attention-getting ad copy (*see* Chapter 33). List all the consumer benefits you have to offer.

5. Keep careful tabs on which media bring best results per dollar expenditure. Augment this advertising and reduce it in less profitable areas.

The Media
- ☐ Newspapers
- ☐ Periodicals
- ☐ Radio or TV
- ☐ Business, trade, or organization journals
- ☐ Religious bulletins, papers, or journals
- ☐ School newspapers, yearbooks, journals, or programs
- ☐ Bus or subway cards
- ☐ Window posters
- ☐ Window displays
- ☐ Counter cards
- ☐ Store signs
- ☐ "Giveaway" novelties
- ☐ Booklets or brochures—in-store distribution
- ☐ Direct mail
- ☐ Cartons and labels used as advertising
- ☐ Catalogs
- ☐ Package inserts, when used as advertising
- ☐ Reprints of ads—used in-store, in windows, or for distribution
- ☐ All printed material used for advertising purposes

CHAPTER THIRTY-SIX

PLANNING YOUR ADVERTISING BUDGET

How much money should small businesses allot to their advertising each year?

Advertising is often approached haphazardly, and either too much or too little money is spent. With this lack of proper planning, your advertising program soon becomes desultory and you fail to receive maximum value from your advertising dollar. With a little foresight you can ensure that your advertising investment is proportionately right for your business and is wisely spent.

Below are listed eight ways to organize an advertising budget for a small business. Select the one that fits *your* needs.

1. **Percentage of sales:** A retailer decides to spend five percent of one year's net sales volume on the following year's advertising. If the previous year's volume is $100,000, the current year's advertising budget is automatically $5000.

2. **Unit of sales:** Your budget is based on the number of *units of a product or products* sold in the past year and the number expected to be sold in the coming year. For example, a vacuum-cleaner store may decide to spend $1.50 per cleaner for advertising. It hopes to sell 5000 cleaners during the current year, so its advertising budget is $7500.

3. **Objective or task:** In this method a retailer establishes the sales objective for the coming year and then computes the advertising cost to reach that objective. If the cost is too great, the retailer cuts down the objective.

4. **"Buying" prospect inquiries:** This method is popular with mail-order houses. The advertising is planned to *pay its way* as it goes along. The house may find that obtaining an order by mail costs $2. If they aim at 2000 sales during the coming year, the budget is automatically $4000.

5. **Following competitors:** A retailer finds that a competitor is spending twice as much on advertising and doing twice the business . . . so advertising is doubled to "keep pace."

6. **Arbitrary:** A retailer fixes an amount to be spent for advertising which seems reasonable in view of experience, profits, and hunches as to the coming year's business. Then the advertising program is carefully designed to fall within the budget.

7. **Goodwill advertising:** This is your "insurance" for retaining the business you now have. Every business insures its assets against fire; it's equally important to protect against deterioration of goodwill, and this is done through advertising. The cost of goodwill advertising usually is about 30 percent as much as hard-sell advertising. Therefore you purchase this type of "insurance" at relatively low rates.

8. **Combination:** Almost all of the above plans can be combined or varied to meet individual needs. The one absolute rule is this: *To be effective, your advertising must be planned carefully and budgeted wisely.* A haphazard approach will not work.

The Advertising "Leads" Evaluation Form that follows will help you to target prospect lead source, quality, and response activity. Thus the advertiser can evaluate what prospect leads have emanated from where, at what cost, and how effectively those leads were handled. Thus you can achieve maximum value from your per-dollar advertising expenditure.

As we previously stated, in prospecting for customers strive to be "systematic." Keep accurate files of responses, and reply methodically and quickly. The quality of your "reply fulfillment" influences the extent of customer-patronage continuity that is achievable.

ADVERTISING
"LEADS"
EVALUATION
FORM

Box no. _____

Date of ad _____

Publication _____

Ref. no. prefix _____

Size _____

Per-line rate $ _____

Total cost $ _____

No. of inquiries _____

Cost per inquiry $ _____

No. of prospects sold _____

Cost per prospect sold $ _____

Date Recd.	Ref. No.	Last Name	First Name	City	State	Contact Date	Sold Date
1							
2							
3							
4							
5							
6							
7							
8							
9							
10							
11							
12							

CHAPTER THIRTY-SEVEN YOUR BUSINESS CAN PROFIT THROUGH DIRECT-MAIL ADVERTISING

Direct-mail, properly planned and prepared, can help build your business. You get the undivided attention of the prospect and the required space to tell your story in its appropriate sequence.

The item that you mail can be one of several things—a letter, a brochure, a sample, a catalog, a postcard. Anything that is sent through the mail directly to your prospects with the objective of selling them something is in fact *direct-mail*.

WHO CAN BENEFIT FROM DIRECT-MAIL ADVERTISING?

Whether its basis is sales or service, every small business can benefit from the use of direct-mail. It's a business "must," especially in view of the keen competition afforded by ever-expanding chain stores and suburban shopping centers.

☐ **An electrician** obtained a steady flow of job leads by sending out a letter offering free lighting consultation.

☐ **A plumber** sent a "giant" postcard (6×9 inches) headlining this offer: "Complete plumbing insurance for the year—all the repairs you'll need for a fixed annual price." This mailing was directed toward building owners, naturally.

175

☐ **A paint dealer** sent a mailing on letterheads cut out from wallpaper swatches, thus each letter sent out symbolized and publicized the products.

☐ **A grocer** regularly mailed out a brochure listing his current specials.

☐ **A radio-TV service** enclosed an advertising leaflet in the envelope containing monthly invoices.

☐ **A beautician** sent out a monthly newsletter containing beauty hints to the women in her neighborhood.

These are but a few examples. There are many ideas that *you* can use to promote your business by the direct-mail method.

CHAPTER THIRTY-EIGHT

MAKING YOUR DIRECT MAIL MORE EFFECTIVE

Before you take a direct-mail package to the post office, examine it carefully and ask yourself some questions about:

Its value . . .
- ☐ Is your proposition a good one?
- ☐ Is the offer attractive?

Its appearance . . .
- ☐ Does the outer envelope have *appeal for the prospect* you are trying to reach?
- ☐ Does the outer envelope *create a good image* for your product and your company?
- ☐ Will your outer envelope motivate the recipient to look inside?
- ☐ Does the copy inside command *immediate* attention?
- ☐ Does the art treatment suitably and adequately reinforce the copy?
- ☐ Is your mailing typographically attractive and readable?

Its message . . .
- ☐ Is the copy clear and understandable?
- ☐ Does it have personalized appeal?

- ☐ Does it excite and invite continued reading?
- ☐ Does it properly dramatize what you are trying to sell?
- ☐ Is the tone conversational, rather than formally persuasive?
- ☐ Is the copy believable?
- ☐ Does it attract quick interest?
- ☐ Does it use every possible sales argument?
- ☐ Does it convince the prospect of the benefits?
- ☐ Is every detail made to appear as an advantage?
- ☐ Does it convey any air of "disinterest" on your part?
- ☐ Does it use the power of understatement?

Its appeal . . .
- ☐ Insofar as is relevant, will it appeal to the prospect's innermost desires?
- ☐ Does it make proper and subtle use of flattery?
- ☐ Does it convince the prospect as to value?
- ☐ Does it guarantee the prospect satisfaction?
- ☐ Does it give emphasis to salient points through repetition?
- ☐ Does it carry conviction and authority?
- ☐ Does it provide a logical reason for prompt response?
- ☐ Is it simple and convenient to order?

HOW MUCH SHOULD YOU SPEND ON DIRECT-MAIL?

In accordance with the type and size of the business and your average annual sales, the percentage of investment recommended for direct-mail varies. A general rule is to base your appropriation on a percentage of your past or anticipated sales for a one-year period.

A well-planned direct-mail campaign can result in accumlated goodwill and profits greatly in excess of your expenditure.

The following are national averages pertinent to various businesses. These figures show advertising expenditures for various types of retailers in percentages of the previous year's gross sales. These figures can guide you in setting up your own budget.

Appliances	2.5%	Gifts and novelties	1.2%
Automobiles	.7%	Grocery	.4%
Bakeries	.5%	Hardware	1.7%
Barber and beauty	2.2%	Jewelry	3.3%
Bars and taverns	.7%	Liquor	.3%
Building materials	.8%	Men's wear	1.9%
Cameras	1.9%	Millinery	1.0%
Candy	.4%	Nurseries	2.5%
Delicatessen	.6%	Paint and wallpaper	1.7%
Drugs	2.0%	Restaurants	.5%
Dry cleaners	2.5%	Service stations	.8%
Farm equipment	.7%	Sporting goods	2.3%
Floor coverings	1.8%	Toys	2.4%
Florists	1.8%	Variety	.5%
Furniture	3.5%	Women's apparel	1.7%

GETTING YOUR DOLLAR'S WORTH

Economically, it pays to promote several products or services in each mailing because of the fixed major costs—list procurement, postage, addressing, and stamping. Certain items or services may pay the costs of the mailing, while the others obtain a "free ride." This reduces the per-unit cost of your direct-mail advertising.

The use of color will enhance your mailing piece and can increase its selling power by 50 percent or more.

To what extent are pictures and descriptions needed? This can be answered best by asking another question: Is the merchandise *new* or *known?* Familiar merchandise can be sold with a minimum of pictures or descriptions, but new and unfamiliar merchandise will require illustration and detailed description for a strong "sell" at the time of its introduction.

Obtaining Mailing Lists

Good mailing lists are often free, or nominal in cost. Some sources are:

☐ Local voting lists (names and addresses by neighborhood).

□ Your *Yellow Pages* (names and addresses by business classifications).

□ Taxpayers' list (giving names according to property ownership).

□ Birth records.

□ Professional directories.

□ Lists of new residents can be obtained from telephone company and from local moving firms and real-estate agencies.

About
Test Mailings

If time allows, a test mailing is often helpful in determining the level of prospect reaction. The number of returns from a test mailing can be projected to indicate expected returns from a total mailing. To be tested effectively, a mailing piece need not require a mail response. Quite often, a mailer will produce increased store traffic, desirable because it brings the consumer into contact not only with the attracting product or service but also with your entire range of merchandise or service. If you are testing your direct-mail response, merely keep records of store traffic and sales for a period of time before the mailing, and compare them with similar statistics after the mailing has reached your prospects.

A Few Useful
Direct-Mail Tips

Best days Tuesday and Wednesday are the best days for your mail to *reach* your prospects.

Best months October, January, February, September, March, April, November, December, May, June, August, July—in that order, your mailings will elicit the most to the least response.

Pointers Seven out of ten men open their own mail. Average list depreciation is 17 percent a year. Change color of ink, paper, letterhead, and envelope often.

Follow-ups Best response usually received after the second or third follow-up. Cost of mailings should usually average about $5 per thousand mailed.

CHAPTER THIRTY-NINE
OBTAINING PUBLICITY
A GOLDMINE OF FREE ADVERTISING IS YOURS FOR THE DIGGING

YOUR BUSINESS "IMAGE"

No matter what type of business you run, it's vitally important that you develop a unique "personality image" that distinguishes you as an individual and your establishment as an extension of yourself. It is equally important that this image be given maximum exposre to prospects throughout your trading area.

Just starting your operation? Then it's wise to build your image right from the outset. Long-established? Let's hope you've already created a strong image within your community. If not, there's no time like the present to begin!

How, you may ask, does one go about doing this? How does one "create" an image? Just how can it be projected to the public?

There are two channels through which you can establish a solid business image. One is your program of paid advertising. The other is *publicity!*

Advertising can do only part of the job. From the standpoint of economy, the advertising budget of the typical small business must be limited to a figure approximating two percent of gross. But more important, advertising is frankly commercial, and the public recognizes this fact. Anyone who wishes to invest the capital can *buy* space or time—or mail letters—proclaiming their virtue. Publicity, however, is impartial. Without standing to gain anything, someone is taking the time (or space) to talk about your business.

PUTTING PUBLICITY TO WORK FOR YOU

Publicity is the catalyst that gives teeth to your advertising, that strengthens and documents the reliability of your claims and helps cement a favorable image that causes the prospective customer to prefer your store or service to that of your competitor.

Thousands of lines of FREE publicity (in many publications that reach your prospective customers) are available. You must, however, take steps to *ask for it!*

By publications, we mean: your local newspapers . . . shopping guides . . . radio and TV stations . . . trade magazines . . . company house organs . . . amusement guides . . . general interest periodicals . . . special-interest newspapers and magazines.

Now, chances are that you are already saying to yourself, "How does all this help me? Publicity means writing. I'm not a writer, nor can I afford to hire a publicity writer . . . so how can I get these FREE 'write-ups' in publications?" The answer is, you don't need any writing ability. The fact is that most newspapers and other publications are looking for newsworthy items, just as much as you are looking for publicity. The test is this: What is there about you, your organization, your type of business, or your personnel, that can be considered *newsworthy?*

Although your inclination might be to say "Nothing," the truth is that if you think for a little while, you will most likely find that there are dozens of possible news items—and maybe even several full-length feature articles—that could be written about you and your organization. Let's analyze a few write-up possibilities right here and now.

Your Business Itself

What are the human-interest aspects of your business? What special human-interest angle led to your own venture into business? What are some of the human-interest aspects of your customers, as a group and individually? Ask yourself these questions and see if you don't come up with some mighty interesting answers In the meantime, let us cite a few of the ideas that got a particular *Dunkin' Donuts* establishment into print quite a number of times. Among them were (a) the number of doughnuts consumed each month in the store; (b) the "romance" of doughnuts . . . how the doughnut was born . . . the background of the "hole in the doughnut" . . . the changing pattern of doughnut consumption (how it once was popular only among children and now is a favorite adult food); (c) the proprietor . . . the unrelated field from which he came . . . why he finds the doughnut business fascinating—like meeting people under friendly, relaxed circumstances and finding that his establishment has become an important meeting place.

182

Your Community Participation
It will be to your great advantage to participate in community activities, to become a "joiner" of various community clubs, groups, and organizations, and to become a sponsor of various activities such as Little League baseball, Scouts, races, art shows, and so on. Having a hand in such events lends itself to publicity.

Your Establishment
Unique displays, exciting counter arrangements, and unusual advertising can be incorporated into newsworthy write-ups.

Some examples are the automotive store or gas station that exhibits antique autos . . . the apparel shop that displays apparel of fifty years ago . . . the ice-cream store that features unusual local hobbies . . . or the handicrafts store that provides a gallery for its customers' completed projects.

Promotional Ideas
Events that you sponsor will attract community attention and make desirable human-interest write-ups: *Contests:* Doughnut-eating contest (prize to person eating most doughnuts in given time); contest for oldest customers, youngest customers. *Community-slanted events:* A furniture store tied-in with a "modernize City Hall" campaign by issuing a "Happy Dollar" for every ten-dollar purchase. Each "Happy Dollar" went to the modernization fund. An ice-cream store sponsors outings for handicapped children in the area, giving them a picnic once a year. A pharmacist attends the annual senior-citizens' Thanksgiving dinner and gives each senior a crisp five-dollar bill. *Prizes for merit:* Outstanding hobbyists . . . most promising students . . . most civic-minded person of the month . . . Boy Scout who performed best deed of the week.

Make a list of all promotional ideas you consider suitable for your particular business. Write up all the data in "rough" form and don't concern yourself with the fine points of prose. Your local newspaper is more interested in substance than in form. After all, they have their own writers who simply need to be fed ideas.

Timely Events
A prominent lawn-care firm tied-in with a community beautification program, providing material for a feature on the importance of beautiful lawns. A pharmacy publicized the store and performed a public service by supplying factual information for a write-up on 14 positive ways to avoid the flu during a local outbreak. An automotive-parts dealer helped his business and the general public when he spotlighted Fourth-of-July accident predictions with a publicity story on automotive parts that could make the difference between life and death. A slenderizing salon tied-in with a national physical-fitness program by preparing an article outlining 25 steps to physical fitness.

PHOTOS
ADD LIFE! Whenever you suggest a news story to your local paper, it will be mutually beneficial to supply some suitable photos. Pictures are always welcome. They bring a story to life and ensure the attention of many additional readers. If your market consists of many children or elderly individuals, photos are especially important.

WRITING YOUR
OWN MATERIAL If you have some writing aptitude, there are distinct advantages to be gained from originating your own copy for publication. One is that a well-prepared news release or feature article is virtually guaranteed publication—usually at an early date. Another is that you can control the exact slant or image you most desire to project to the public.

Keep in mind a few basic points of good journalism, and you're on your way to fame:

☐ **Identify yourself** at the top of the first typed page; indicate your name and where you can be reached for "further information." Note whether this is a feature story or news release—and if it's the latter, specify the date when it should be published. Number each additional page at the top.

☐ **Supply a headline**—but don't be too disappointed if it's not used. Editorial positioning often requires fewer (or more) words than you provide. This can rarely be determined ahead of time.

☐ **A lively first paragraph** is vital! In a news story, remember the "5 W's" (Who-What-Where-When-Why) and the "H" (How), if it applies. In a feature story, a colorful teaser about what is to follow does the trick.

☐ **Avoid adjectives** altogether in a news story. This is "editorializing," and strictly out of place in straight news. In a feature story make your adjectives and adverbs *count*, and try to rely on lively active verbs.

☐ **Quoted material** adds a lot to the flavor of personalities in your story and makes it appear less commercial. Don't be afraid to quote *yourself* at any point—your readers will not know that you're the reporter, and it brightens up your copy and serves to place emphasis. (When quoting others, be *sure* to have their approval. If you can't identify them with complete accuracy, use a general complimentary designation such as "a successful local gardener" or "one busy local craftsman.")

☐ **Be brief,** at least inasmuch as your story commands space. Use the required number of words to convey your message effectively, but don't ramble. Naturally, a feature story about some ongoing activity will require more coverage than an announcement of an upcoming exhibit. Use judgment.

Try to achieve the widest possible circulation for your news stories. Send your completed stories or your story suggestions to as many newspapers as possible in your trading area. After they have been published, further enhance their value to you by having them enlarged, framed, and displayed on your premises.

These suggestions for gaining publicity should serve to ensure that you and your organization are soon well known throughout your trading area. In turn, this familiarity should bring increased business. Take advantage of every possibility for publicity. Get yourself read about, talked about, and visited. Become a unique and vital part of the community.

CHAPTER FORTY A SUGGESTION LIST FOR ADS AND PROMOTIONS

One of the questions asked most persistently by those who own small businesses is this: "What can *we* do right away to get increased business?"

Our best advice it *advertise* and *promote!* This of course leads to many other related questions, such as the following:

☐ What type of advertising should we do?

☐ How much should we spend?

☐ How can we be sure that we've "touched all bases" with our advertising and promotions?

☐ How does one go about "thinking up" an advertising program?

Small businesses cannot afford the luxury of long-range advertising programs, large budgets, lengthy waits, costly trial and error. In many situations results must be achieved practically *overnight* if a small business is to maintain its solvency.

With this in mind, we've prepared a quick-reference suggestion list to assist in planning your advertising and promotion campaigns. It should provide a valuable starting point for your thinking and lead the way to a flow of additional ideas that apply uniquely to your business and its locale.

A SUGGESTION LIST
FOR ADS AND PROMOTIONS

The normal small-business advertising budget is about five percent of its annual volume. If you do a business of $100,000 annually, for example, it would indicate an advertising budget of about $5,000. This percentage varies, of course, for different types of businesses and areas.

PROSPECTIVE CUSTOMERS

☐ Manufacturers   ☐ Wholesalers
☐ Retailers   ☐ Jobbers
☐ Consumers

If Consumer, Which?

☐ General   ☐ Women
☐ Children   ☐ Men
☐ Teenagers   ☐ Senior citizens

Income Group

☐ High   ☐ Low
☐ Middle

Special Groups

☐ Householders   ☐ Conservationists
☐ Parents   ☐ Brides
☐ Mothers-to-be   ☐ Teachers
☐ Working mothers   ☐ Professionals
☐ Students   ☐ Salespeople
☐ Executives   ☐ Civil-service employees
☐ Union laborers   ☐ Hobbyists
☐ Retired people   ☐ Sports enthusiasts

APPEALS TO BE USED

☐ Comfort   ☐ Prestige
☐ Beauty   ☐ Utility
☐ Economy   ☐ Health
☐ Smell   ☐ Sentiment
☐ Taste   ☐ Upward mobility
☐ Sound   ☐ Luxury
☐ Intelligence   ☐ Scarcity

□ Necessity   □ Gift giving

□ Endurance   □ Security

□ Patriotism   □ Good judgment

RECOMMENDED MEDIA

□ Newspapers   □ Magazines

□ Direct mail   □ Displays

□ Radio   □ Television

□ Movies   □ Transit advertising

□ Publicity   □ Contests

□ Stunts   □ Premiums

WHEN TO ADVERTISE

□ Monthly   □ Morning

□ Daily   □ Afternoon

□ Weekends   □ Evening

□ Weekly

OCCASION

□ Vacation   □ School opening

□ Christmas   □ Valentine's Day

□ Thanksgiving   □ Easter

□ Mother's Day   □ Father's Day

□ Decoration Day

DIRECT MAIL

□ Catalogs   □ Broadsides

□ Folders   □ Labels

□ Letters   □ House organs

□ Brochures   □ Calendars

□ Blotters   □ Postcards

□ Booklets

A SUGGESTION LIST
FOR ADS AND PROMOTIONS

DISPLAYS

- Signs
- Counter
- Banners
- Lithograph
- Truck posters
- State fairs
- Sales portfolios
- Live demonstrations

- Dioramas
- Electrical
- Mechanical
- Silk-screen
- Trade shows
- Exhibits
- Neon signs

PREMIUMS AND NOVELTIES

- Mirrors
- Emblems
- Caps
- Toys
- Balloons
- Diaries
- Road maps
- Ball-point pens
- Billfolds

- Pencils
- Buttons
- Badges
- Games
- Rulers
- Calendars
- Memo books
- Card cases
- Souvenirs

STUNT PROMOTIONS

- Mobile sign
- Sample giveaways
- Skywriting
- Contest

- Man on stilts
- Sound truck
- Streamer by plane

PUBLICITY

- Written releases for newspapers and magazines
- Photo releases for newspapers and magazines
- Name "plug" on radio or television

190

NEWSPAPERS

☐ Daily a.m.	☐ Daily p.m.
☐ Sunday	☐ Sunday magazine
☐ Neighborhood	☐ Foreign language

SECTIONS

☐ Run of paper	☐ Amusement
☐ Society	☐ Financial
☐ Comics	☐ Sports
☐ Travel	☐ Book
☐ Classified	☐ Real-estate
☐ Garden	☐ Photography
☐ Shoppers	☐ Home
☐ School	

PERIODICALS

☐ General	☐ Quality
☐ House organs	☐ Men's
☐ Children's	☐ Women's
☐ Digests	☐ Comic
☐ Movie	☐ Art
☐ Science	☐ Fashion
☐ Humor	☐ Poetry
☐ Travel	☐ Labor
☐ Industrial	☐ Literary
☐ Adventure	☐ Photography
☐ Trade	☐ Western
☐ Song lyric	☐ Detective
☐ Sports	☐ Racing
☐ Pets	

A SUGGESTION LIST
FOR ADS AND PROMOTIONS

OTHER PUBLICATIONS

- ☐ Telephone books
- ☐ School yearbooks
- ☐ Theatre programs

FILMS

- ☐ Audiovisuals for salespeople
- ☐ Slides
- ☐ Trailers for paid advertising in theatres
- ☐ Educational films

RADIO AND TELEVISION

- ☐ National network
- ☐ Local
- ☐ Single stations
- ☐ Cities
- ☐ Small towns
- ☐ News
- ☐ Late morning
- ☐ Late afternoon
- ☐ Late evening
- ☐ Full hour
- ☐ Half hour
- ☐ Quarter hour
- ☐ Five-minute spot
- ☐ One-minute spot
- ☐ Early morning
- ☐ Early afternoon
- ☐ Early evening

TRANSPORTA-TION AND OUTDOOR

Car Cards

- ☐ Bus
- ☐ Subway
- ☐ Trains
- ☐ Timetables
- ☐ Posters
- ☐ Ball parks
- ☐ Dioramas
- ☐ Trolley
- ☐ Taxis
- ☐ Elevated
- ☐ Billboards
- ☐ Electric signs
- ☐ Stadiums

Terminals

- ☐ Bus
- Air
- ☐ Railroad

SECTION FOUR

NEW IMAGE-BUILDING CONCEPTS

CHAPTER FORTY-ONE

CREATING A MAGNETIC IMAGE

36 WAYS TO MAKE PEOPLE DO BUSINESS WITH *YOU,* AND *YOU ONLY*

It happens in every community. You see two stores. They sell the same merchandise and charge the same prices. They are as identical as "two peas in a pod," to use the old cliché. But one store is empty of customers and the other is full—people are constantly bustling in and out, and business is prospering. How do we account for the difference?

We might find an analogy among individuals. They appear alike. Many seem to have the same degree of ability. Yet some people succeed in everything they do, and others never seem to taste success. Why? What is responsible for this personal disparity?

It's not really that much of a mystery. I attribute the difference between the "winners" and the "losers," in both businesses and people, to one factor— IMAGE! The word may sound simple, but its meaning is not. Image is intangible in some ways, but tangible in many others. It is essentially *the collective impression created in the mind of the viewer.* The successful enterprise has an *image* that appealed to customers and stimulated their patronage. The unsuccessful one has an aura of failure about it.

It is the same with people. Everybody likes the image a winner creates. They sense it and respond to it. On the other hand, the loser's image is quite the opposite and just as apparent. People *see* indecision, irresolution, and aimlessness, and tend to avoid the individual who emanates these auras.

Never forget that the kind of image you create influences your prospective customer's decision to buy from *you* or from *your competitor.* And this spells the difference between eager, constant repeat business and casual, occasional sales.

But how do you acquire your image? How does one create an aura of success? How does one build goodwill? Why do some businesses have it and not others? Why do some people have it, and not others? Goodwill results from a favorable image, an image that radiates warmth, enthusiasm, and success. It sets your enterprise apart from your competitors. It is a place where people want to trade—again and again.

Central to any favorable image is the determination to succeed. If you tell yourself you won't succeed, you never will. If you tell yourself you *will* succeed, it is almost a foregone conclusion that you will! It is as simple as that. Create in your own mind's eye the image that you wish to attain. Eventually that image will project itself to others as well. It isn't something you can build overnight. You have to work at it, but it is worth everything you put into it.

A significant aspect of your favorable image is the manner in which you conduct yourself with customers. In the give-and-take of daily life, you make judgments about your customers. Just as surely, they make judgments about you. The resulting impressions add up to become an *image.*

To assist you in building a favorable image, we offer 36 comprehensive suggestions. Study these ideas. Apply them. They will mean money in your pocket and orders on your books. They will make the difference between repeat business and one-time buying. They will make people want to deal with you and *you only.*

☐ **Remember names and places.** Ever meet a business acquaintance after a long separation? If he smiled, grabbed you by the hand, and greeted you by name, weren't you impressed? On the other hand, if he seemed to have forgotten your name, it was not very flattering; the odds would be in favor of a negative result. Remembering names is good for your image. Try to develop the habit—it will pay dividends!

☐ **Be a joiner.** Socializing, mixing, and mingling with people can be fun. It gets you out of yourself. It broadens you. More important, it is *good business* to join clubs and organizations. It not only allows you to help others and be a good citizen, but also introduces you to people who can help you and your business. The contacts you make can be useful at some future time.

196

☐ **Be a good listener.** We all have problems. We are partial towards those who are willing to listen to them. People enjoy hearing themselves talk, and they like others who let them "sound off." If you become a seasoned listener, you'll get to know people better and you'll discover more about them. It is your way of showing your interest in them beyond the scope of the immediate transaction. If you listen when they talk, they'll listen when you talk—about your merchandise.

☐ **Play up the "you" appeal.** If you want the customers' business, show them how your serve *their* needs. If you are selling cupcakes to supermarkets, make sure you tell them about the new packaging material that gives cupcakes longer shelf life. This way of selling has come to be known as the *marketing orientation*. Though well-known in the consumer field, it is not embraced by heavy industry. It demands that you really get to know your customer's business, and it gives you a great advantage.

☐ **Be helpful.** There's a great deal to be said for those who help us without grinding their own axe. There are hundreds of ways to demonstrate your interest in the welfare of your business contacts, aside from your desire to sell to them. For example, one sales representative made it a habit to clip news items of importance to clients and send them along in the mail. If you pick up cogent information in your travels, you can pass it along. You are doing something for them. They won't forget it and they will probably find themselves wanting to do something extra for you.

☐ **Demonstrate your integrity.** Let people know that you keep your word. Live up to the promises you make. Over the long run it is a policy that pays off. The public is not inclined to tolerate shoddy goods or broken promises from business; retailers want more than merchandise from their suppliers. Integrity is a vitally important quality. Your reputation for integrity will spread quickly through the trade by word of mouth and will pay off in business referrals.

☐ **Be consistent.** In the prices you quote and in the claims you make, don't tell one customer one thing and another customer something else. I know an appliance dealer who gave three customers three different prices for a stereo set in a one-week period. As fate would have it, these customers were members of the same club. They compared notes, and the unfortunate (and unwise) dealer lost all three sales. Such inconsistencies cause serious damage to your image.

☐ **Give service.** Special attention and personalized service is appreciated. This extra interest will pay off in additional business. Take the case of Frank Murphy, a vacuum-cleaner salesman I know. He turned a disaster into a triumph. One day, by accident, he called at a house where a customer had already purchased a vacuum cleaner from another salesman representing his company. He was shocked when his friendly approach was met with a storm of abuse. The machine had not been used because of a mechanical defect. Frank brought it back to his firm and had it repaired. The service he performed for this customer won a permanent friend for the company and brought him several new customers by referral.

☐ **Be creative.** Keep thinking up new benefits your customer can derive through your product or service. Think of your customer's special problems and how your product or service can help in relation to them. A manufacturer of pantyhose became a multi-million-dollar organization, the world leader in its field, through such creativity. Attractive multi-colored plastic ice-cream-cone containers were designed for pantyhose. These were displayed on convenient, eye-catching "trees" in thousands of stores throughout the country. Packaged in plasticized baseballs, pantyhose were promoted for distribution in ballparks as a Mother's-Day gift. The baseball containers were also placed in fish bowls to encourage impulse buying. Many other such innovations provided this company with literally thousands of new customers, eager to buy the products.

☐ **Be systematic.** Organization, planning, and developing a system can make things far easier for you. The old exhortation, "Plan your work, then work your plan," is true today than ever. If selling is involved, plot the coverage of your territory from day to day, and plan your contacts in order to cover the maximum number of prospects. A map is very helpful. To target the map, use colored pins—red for customers, black for prospects, and green for "suspects." Then estimate the amount of time needed to cover the entire territory, based on the number of calls you can make each day. Subdivide your territory into areas in such a way that you can make a maximum number of calls with a minimum of travel. Adopting such a system results in a productivity gain that is certain to benefit you.

☐ **Be self-motivating.** Business is a constant "school of hard knocks." So many things can go wrong. Don't let adversity wrestle you to the mat. Take a positive attitude toward it. Remember the sun shines most brilliantly after a heavy shower. I remember a hardware jobber who had secured the largest order of his career; it involved portable hand tools. Suddenly his supplier was hit by a strike and couldn't deliver. My friend was fit to be tied. He was very depressed, but then his natural bounce asserted itself. He went out and found another supplier. And to top it off, his new source sold him the product for *less* than the old one! View setbacks in their proper perspective and set your business course with conviction and determination.

☐ **Be affirmative — not negative.** Nobody likes a "knocker." There's no sound reason for it. Elaboration on the deficiencies of a rival product invites suspicion. Instead, elaborate on what *you* and *your product* can do. You'll be more believable. When you focus on berating a competitive product — even though your comments may be true — there's a tendency for the listener to attribute your remarks to "sour grapes," rather than give credence to them.

☐ **Be thoughtful and considerate.** A friendly relationship with your customers will take you a long way. The best way to create it is through a genuine interest in them. A follow-up thank you note, a birthday remembrance, an occasional friendly phone call — these can create goodwill. At little cost in money or time, it broadens the entire relationship. Thoughtfulness of this kind not only will bring dividends, but also will give you personal satisfaction.

☐ **Be alert.** Watch for new ideas and developments in your field. Read the major business publications and the trade press. Find out what your competitors are doing. Think about how to improve your products and services by incorporating new materials, a new way of doing things, a new process. Most of all, see how these ideas can be turned to the advantage of your customer.

☐ **Be neat.** A businessperson makes the best impression when dressed in a fairly conventional manner. Sporting expensive jewelry, racetrack-type neckwear, disco dresses, or loud sports shirts can turn customers off. Customers like to deal with people who take their business seriously. Also pay attention to the grooming details of your daily dress . . . the tie that is ever-so-lightly stained, the skirt that is losing its press. The same is true of the presentations you offer. Nothing can be more harmful or discouraging to sales than furled and soiled pages in your presentation material.

☐ **Be patient.** Remember that potential customers don't know your product or service as well as you do. What you consider elementary may appear complex to them. Develop your sales pitch in stages with numerous valid reasons *why* . . . to be absorbed and digested a little at a time. Be patient also with people who work for you. Often employees need a little careful cultivation to turn out well. Finally, be patient with yourself. Don't be your own severest critic. Give yourself the benefit of the doubt.

- [ ] **Be logical.** Appealing to your prospect's intelligence can often carry you far. It is a firm foundation on which to build. We all know salespeople who depend only on emotion to sell. And we all know that too many of their orders are canceled when the prospect has second thoughts. Make your approach believable and avoid evasive answers to your customers' questions.

- [ ] **Be specific.** Avoid generalities. Whenever and wherever possible give specific figures and supply documentation to prove your point. Most businesspeople, particularly the successful ones, are "hard-headed." They want (and respect) facts. You must be specific to do business with them.

- [ ] **Be authoritative.** You must be the expert, you must display the expertise needed to "carry the day." You must read all the instruction material; moreover, you must understand it, so you can explain it clearly to prospects. You must familiarize yourself thoroughly with your products. In this way you can speak with confidence, customers can depend on you, and you can gain their respect and loyalty.

- [ ] **Show humility.** Though you should always maintain your aura of authority, there will be times when you haven't the answer. When this happens, admit it frankly instead of trying to bluff your way through. In such cases, merely say, "I don't know, but we have highly paid experts in our company. I'll be glad to consult them for an answer." Honesty and humility are qualities to be respected in any business relationship.

- [ ] **Be generous.** It is too easy to find fault with other people. Most often these faults are the faults of our own personalities. Look for the good points, not the bad ones, and you'll find you get along better with people. Be generous, too, with small attentions that show genuine interest. Treating the prospect to lunch will be appreciated. It will help each of you to know the other better. It will take a business arrangement and move it onto a new plane of friendship.

- [ ] **Be punctual.** Keep appointments on time. Remember, "Time is money." Lack of punctuality may be regarded as an insult by your prospects and an indication that you consider your time worth more than theirs. It is also considered a sign that you do not take your business engagements seriously.

☐ **Display good manners.** This may seem elementary, yet it is of vital importance in building a good image. Little things like asking permission to smoke, being considerate of the prospect's time and future appointments, apologizing for outside interruptions, and closing doors softly all help establish you as a person with whom it is nice to do business.

☐ **Be original.** Don't allow yourself to become dull or monotonous with the same unchanged sales talk and approaches. Boredom sets in quickly, not only for your customer, but also for you. Customers wonder why they should see you, since they already know your mechanical pitch. You find yourself giving your tired old sales talk with all the vitality of a robot. Constantly analyze yourself. You must seek to dramatize and to give excitement to your endeavors.

☐ **Be cheerful.** Maintain a cheery demeanor. Make every effort to keep your personal troubles out of your business life. Dejection communicates itself and dampens both your sales efforts and your prospects' interest. A ready, sincere smile is another way to impress others with your desire to be friendly. Good cheer has a way of spreading itself to others. It is infectious and reciprocal and encourages people to want to be with you.

☐ **Be a graceful loser.** Even if you don't get the order, show the same amount of cordiality as you did at the outset of your sales effort. Displaying irritation will only make matters worse. It will ruin your future prospects. Maintaining your equilibrium and being a graceful loser will earn you a measure of respect and chances are that you will have better luck next time.

☐ **Be brief and time-saving.** As noted earlier, time is an important coin of the business realm. It should not be wasted. Keep your sales pitch and visits as brief as possible. Prospects will regard you highly for it. They will welcome you back readily because they know you are a time-saver, not a time-waster.

☐ **Don't be a lecturer.** A sales encounter shouldn't be a monologue. The most effective ones are two-sided discussions, not one-sided lectures. Make yours conversational and invite your prospects' participation. Develop pauses and questions throughout to stimulate their involvement. In this way, they "sell themselves" by means of their own comments and ideas. A good rule is to let them do more than 50 percent of the talking. Encourage them to ask questions and answer them patiently.

☐ **Be an anticipator.** Before you see your prospects, anticipate the personal factors, the problems, the questions that may arise. Try to see what you can find out about their nature. Is this one the friendly, informal type, who likes to discuss things with you? Is another the authoritative type, who expects deference and formality from you? Is today's prospect a businesslike person who wants to get to the point quickly? Is tomorrow's a temperamental "prima-donna," liable to fly off the handle at the least deviation from his or her viewpoint? This kind of forethought will permit you to handle yourself better with the different kinds of prospects you meet. By anticipating, you may also be able to bypass the negatives and concentrate on the positives.

☐ **Be a notetaker.** For those of us who haven't total recall, taking notes provides an invaluable record which can be referred to in the future. It should include all the key points of any meeting. You can see what worked or didn't work. You can set yourself for the prospect's attitudes. You needn't take notes during the meeting, but do so immediately thereafter. And be sure they don't get lost. Be referring to your notes you will be able to establish correct follow-through.

☐ **Be friendly, but not overfamiliar.** There is a fine line between friendship and overfamiliarity. You need to be able to sense when you are overstepping it. Often it will depend on the nature of the one you are doing business with. What will be acceptable to some individuals will not be to others. When in doubt, fall back to a less familiar position. Remember, a prospect may feel pressured by overfamiliarity. It can create resentment that will ruin a deal.

☐ **Derive fun from your work.** If your work is a boring and deadly dull grind to you, you'll certainly fail at it. Success is rarely achieved through doing something you dislike but feel you ought to do, something that you have to push yourself to do each day. If you want your prospects to enjoy doing business with you rather than with your competitor, you have to learn how to *enjoy* your work. And very often this is merely a question of attitude. Joe Marshall hated selling because he did it badly. Every time he approached a prospect, he anticipated defeat. After four months of this, the company teamed him with one of its better sales reps, Beth Holzman. To Holzman, selling was "fun." Marshall couldn't understand it. How could selling be *fun?* Holzman explained that they were meeting lots of nice people, going into interesting homes, starting on new "adventures" — and being *paid* for it, besides. But what "fun" was there about having the door slammed in your face, asked Marshall. His friend said that this meant she had one less person to sell to, and that made her day easier. Marshall got the point; his attitude changed and he found his work progressively easier. After a while it became "fun" for him, too.

☐ **Display self-respect.** Place yourself on an equal level with your customers. They buy your product or service because what you supply is useful and valuable, not for any other reason. If you wish them to respect you, you must respect yourself. You must be polite but not servile. In this day and age, servility is *not* considered a virtue.

☐ **Be forthright.** Answer all questions fully and fairly — right on the line. Don't give inadequate half-answers. When your prospects realize you are not trying to "duck" or evade issues, they will respect you; that respect will be communicated to your product or service.

☐ **Exercise polite persistence.** A "turn-down" is no reason to be deterred from trying again. After a reasonable waiting period, you are free to make a polite renewal of your sales effort. It won't offend the customer and may well bring about a sale. Once again, it becomes a matter of being able to distinguish when persistence becomes offensive because of ill-timed *in*sistence and when persistence is genuinely warranted.

☐ **Don't misuse the hard sell.** I'm not suggesting that high-pressure selling be entirely avoided. Pressure must always be maintained to the extent that prospects understand the product fully. Don't overwhelm the customer with exaggerations, extravagent claims, or price-cutting that cheapens your product. Stick to the facts and make sure they're well understood. If you do this for qualified prospects, you'll have done all you can to sell them and still maintain goodwill. You'll be welcomed back the next time, rather than avoided.

By now you are aware of what goes into creating an image. As you see, *you* are the artist who paints the self-portrait. The manner in which you conduct yourself, the impression you give, the integrity you display, the consistency, the sincerity, the planning, are the main brush strokes on your canvas. They provide the reason why people want to do business with *you* and *you only*. They are your image.

Don't for a minute believe that the world has become so mechanical, so computerized, and so impersonal that human beings don't matter in business.

**CREATING A
MAGNETIC IMAGE**

The more identical products become, the more important are those who sell them. Your objective, then, is to build an image which is so positively radiant that it sets you apart uniquely from your fellows.

Undoubtedly you have been doing some of these positive things right along. But it's just as likely that this chapter has helped you spot a few areas which can be improved. With a little concentration on these, you can polish your image to a dazzle and enjoy the rewards of increased business!

CHAPTER FORTY-TWO: USING COLOR TO YOUR ADVANTAGE

Any store can become a more viable marketplace through the effective use of color to enhance its sales potential. Keep this in mind: *color creates emotional response!* If you doubt the proven credibility of this statement, consider the case of an Illinois hospital. Their policy places depressed patients in red rooms to lift them from their despair. Excitable patients are assigned to soothing blue rooms.

Here's a basic table of colors and the responses they elicit:

- ☐ Red—*activity, warmth*

- ☐ Blue—*serenity, coolness*

- ☐ Purple—*richness, dignity*

- ☐ Green—*nature, harmony*

- ☐ Yellow—*sunshine, cheerfulness*

- ☐ Pink—*good health*

How do you make these responses work for you? Here are specific examples of how other small businesses have done it:

- ☐ **A restaurant** increased profits by painting walls a cheerful yellow and installing warm lighting. This combination is flattering to the complexion and creates a sense of coziness that makes patrons relax.

USING COLOR TO
YOUR ADVANTAGE

☐ **A butcher** with a shrewd sense of color decorated his shop in green to bring out the naturally appetizing look of his meats.

☐ **A gift shop,** in confiningly narrow quarters, decorated the long walls in a cool blue, the narrow end wall a warm brown. This made the shop seem much wider. Customers no longer get the feeling of claustrophobia.

☐ **An air-conditioning contractor's** place of business and vehicles featured tones of cool blue to help put customers in the right buying mood.

☐ **A gas station,** which had formerly been a neat but inconspicuous white, "jumped" sales when it switched to an eye-catching combination of brilliant blue and yellow.

☐ **A beauty parlor,** once a drab brown, boosted profits when it redecorated in clean-looking light pink.

☐ **A carpenter and cabinetmaker** got a steady flow of new orders after installing a window display showing brightly painted samples of work. A previous display of unpainted items had failed completely to catch the eyes of passersby.

For their potential use in small businesses, we divide colors into the *warms* and *cools.*

COOL colors are light blue and light green and mixtures of them, such as turquoise. Cool colors

  a) are soothing,

  b) are relaxing,

  c) lend an air of spaciousness,

  d) are unobtrusive and make good background colors for walls and displays.

WARM colors are the yellows and reds and their mixtures, such as orange and brown. Warm colors

  a) are eye-catching,

  b) have an "important" feeling,

  c) lend a feeling of warmth.

Use colors in combinations of warms and cools. A cool background color brings out the vividness of brightly packaged merchandise. If the product is not likely to catch the eye, a bright red border around the display, or arrow pointing to it, will help it gain attention.

Avoid both black and white. Neither attracts attention and black is depressing, while white is bleak and promotes glare.

CHAPTER FORTY-THREE SELLING TO DISSATISFIED CUSTOMERS

A SALES FORTUNE AWAITS THE COURAGEOUS SELLER

Do you steer clear of prospects because you know they once dealt with your firm but stopped doing so after becoming dissatisfied? If you do, you're overlooking a potential sales fortune.

To be sure, it takes imagination, persistence, and boldness to walk where most salespeople fear to tread—into the hostile lair of an irate individual who dislikes your firm and anyone connected with it. But if you exercise these qualities courageously (and most salespeople can find them abundantly within themselves), it's possible to turn your firm's dissatisfied customers into your most profitable market.

A PERSONAL STORY

I, too, used to avoid calling on any prospect whom I knew to be hostile due to previous dissatisfaction. And it was only *by accident* that I found out what a mistake I'd been making! Here's how it happened:

One evening at a social gathering, a group of us started to talk business. In answer to a question, I mentioned the name of the firm for which I was working at the time. And when I did so, one of the guests (whom I hadn't known previously) literally turned *red* with anger.

Apparently the mere mention of my firm's name was enough to arouse the deepest resentments of Mr. Smith (as I shall call him). Not only to my amazement, but also to that of the other guests, he arose abruptly. With the comment, "No self-respecting individual would work for such a firm," he stalked from the room, put on his hat and coat, and *left* the party!

Believe me, my amazement was exceeded only by my extreme embarrassment—for myself, for my firm, and especially for my host of the evening. But I was also curious as to what lay behind this discourteous outburst. Having determined Mr. Smith's place of business, I resolved to call on him the very next day.

As I entered Smith's office, I felt he was about to have another outburst. There seemed to be not an iota of remorse or regret for his actions of the previous evening. In fact, from the look on his face, I felt that the passing of time had intensified, rather than abated, his resentment.

"Yes?" said Mr. Smith, with a growl implying that the utterance of one more word would unleash a torrent of vituperation.

"Mr. Smith," I began, "you may recall that during our meeting last evening you expressed resentment against my company, in the presence of people with whom we do business. Inasmuch as I shall probably be asked to explain your action on my next calls to these customers, don't you feel it might be wise for you to tell me your side of the story? Evidently you have some reason for resenting my organization and all who are connected with it."

"You're d— — — right, I do," Smith growled. "They're a bunch of no-good cheats and liars. Anyone who does business with them deserves what he gets!"

"Look, Mr. Smith," I said. "I have been representing my organization for over a year, and everyone I've called on has had the highest praise for our products, our service, and our business methods. Believe me, if I felt my firm had any desire to cheat or lie to anyone, I *wouldn't* be working for them. Now . . . evidently somewhere along the line, some kind of misunderstanding took place between you and someone in our organization. I don't know who it was, or what it was about, or who was at fault. I *do* know, however, that it wasn't I, and that my only interest is to set the record straight. And I know also that if at any time we have failed you in some way, the heads of our organization want to know about it . . . and to make amends in any way possible."

My evident sincerity, my loyalty to my organization, and the reasonableness of my argument finally had its effect. Smith conceded that he had been most unfair to me, as an individual, in showing his resentment at the party and projecting his dislike of my firm onto one employee. He apologized and explained that he had been "sold a bill of goods" by a former representative in

the territory, and that somehow the order for an entire season's merchandise
had been so badly handled that Mr. Smith's organization had suffered considerable financial loss through not having the merchandise on hand when it was
needed.

"Well, Mr. Smith," I asked, "did you ever contact anyone else in our
organization, other than that territorial representative, to complain? I'm sure
that if you had discussed this matter with our sales manager — or our president,
for that matter — steps would have been taken to see that you got proper satisfaction."

"I tried," said Smith. "I called your president twice and left messages
asking her to call back. But she never did. The sales manager, I remember, was
ill and couldn't be reached. I finally got fed up with the whole thing and can-
celled the balance of my order. But they delivered it anyway. So I simply paid
for it, hoping to sell it later on as a markdown."

By this time, I realized that Mr. Smith did have a justifiable grievance,
although his manner of expressing it seemed to be extreme. And it was then
that I suddenly got the urge to press the advantage which arose from his apology, and try to bring him back into the fold as a customer.

"Mr. Smith," I said. "I can truly sympathize with your feelings toward us.
Frankly, I don't know how it happened that our president didn't return your
calls, unless she didn't get the messages. And this, of course, is a possibility. At
any rate, now that I've heard the reason for your dislike of our organization, I
intend to do something about it. Your grievance is certainly justified, and I'm
going to investigate and report back to you *exactly* what happened . . . and see
if we can't do something to make up for it. Meanwhile, however, it seems clear
that the basic fault lay with the sales representative who serviced your account.
And that individual is out of the picture. I am now handling your territory, and
you can be sure that *every* order you give *me* will have my personal attention.
You'll be kept informed *every* step of the way if there is ever any reason why
your orders cannot be fulfilled exactly as specified. Incidentally, Mr. Smith,
we've just added to our line several items that you ought to know about. Here
. . . take a look at this catalog."

Smith was caught . . . both because of his feelings of embarrassment at
his treatment of me and my firm the previous evening, and by the audacity of
my approach to a sale, directly after I had acknowledged that he had cause for
grievance. He had to look at the catalog, if only out of the fear that by not
doing so, I would interpret his refusal as an unfriendly act and a continuation
of his feud with my firm.

Once he had examined the catalog, it was easy to get him interested in
the advantages of our merchandise. I walked out of his office with an order for

over one-thousand dollars worth of our products.

Later, after an investigation, I was able to report to Mr. Smith that our company's president had not in fact received his messages . . . that the firm regretted whatever loss or inconvenience had been caused by the previously poor handling of his account. I further informed him that our firm would try to offset the previous loss, at least partially, through certain future advantage in terms of advertising cooperation and merchandising help. Throughout the balance of my service with this organization, Mr. Smith was a loyal and profitable customer.

IT'S EASIER THAN YOU THINK

The moral of this story is that *it can be done* . . . you can regain dissatisfied customers if you can make the fullest use of your imagination . . . if you've got persistence . . . and if you have confidence and courage. The fact is, it's probably easier to resell the previously dissatisfied customer than to open up a new account. And here is the reason why:

Previously dissatisfied customers are familiar with your firm; they know its products, service, and sales story. Hence you needn't waste time in "educating" them on these points, nor in answering a large number of real or fancied objections they might raise. The chances are that their dissatisfaction involved but one or two occurrences. If you can give them satisfaction or make amends for these happenings, you will be able to regain their goodwill. On the other hand, when you're trying to sell a *new* account, you must take the time to provide a complete "education" about your product, your service, and your firm's policies. Then you must "spar" with them in answering all the many objections that they may think up in a last stand of buying resistance.

Yes, it will pay you to try to regain the goodwill of your firm's dissatisfied customers. In my own case, I now revel in them. Ever since my experience with Mr. Smith, I've asked *every* firm for whom I have sold to supply a list of the dissatisfied customers in my territory. It becomes my first order of business.

This is how I look at it: The way to handle a dissatisfied customer is similar to the way you would handle any single objection to buying. You let the customers vent their objections and this gives you the best possible clue as to how they can be sold. The difference is that new prospects will often throw up a smoke screen of *many* objections in their effort to resist your sales talk. On the other hand, dissatisfied customers will come right out with their real objection, the source of their previous dissatisfaction. Answer this satisfactorily and you're on your way to a sale.

Common
Complaints and
Smooth Solutions

In the following pages, I have listed most of the ordinary sources of dissatisfaction that you, as a sales representative, are likely to run into during the course of your sales career. They are accompanied by answers that have helped me (and other experienced salespeople) overcome them. If you will study this list and make these answers a part of your own sales equipment, you too will find that your previously dissatisfied customers are likely to become your most profitable source of business.

**You overcharged me on
my last order.**

"If you mean that I made an error in billing you, I'm very sorry and I'll be glad to look up your invoice and make an adjustment. On the other hand, if you mean that my price is more than that of competitive products, you'll find, in the long run, that it is more economical for you. It's like buying an automobile, Mr. Customer. You can buy a Ford . . . or you can buy a Cadillac. My product happens to be the Cadillac of our field—and while it costs more, it lasts longer and its top performance means greater economy for you in the long run!"

**I'm unhappy about
your slow service.**

"Really? That certainly surprises me! Most of my customers comment on how pleased they are with our *promptness*. But I'm not asking you to take my word for our service without some kind of guarantee. I know what we'll do! Here's my personal check for $2.00, made out to you . . . except I haven't signed it. However, I'm going to personally attend to the shipping of your order. And if it doesn't arrive on the exact date you specify, I'll sign the check and you can cash it the very day you call to say your order hasn't been delivered on time."

Another approach I might take is this:

"I *know* you've had trouble with our deliveries, and my firm is very sorry you've been inconvenienced. It's for that very reason that I have been assigned to your account—I've proven to my employers, ever since I've been with them, that I know the importance of prompt delivery to my customers. I make *every* effort to ensure that deliveries are on schedule, and that customers are informed in the event of the slightest delay. You can be sure that whatever orders you place with *me* will have my personal attention to see that shipment is made on the proper schedule and packed so that your merchandise arrives in perfect condition."

**My last purchase
didn't fit.**

"Really? Then you certainly do have a reason to complain. But I'm a bit surprised that you didn't let us know about it before this. We'd have given you a new one, or certainly refunded your money if we couldn't supply a proper fit. Today, of course, a bad fit is an impossibility as far as a purchase from my firm is concerned. Each customer's needs are individually analyzed by expert fitters to the point that *everyone* knows in advance the *exact* requirements and the *exact* specifications needed to fulfill them. Incidentally, if you still have that old

213

one . . . the one that didn't fit . . . lying around, I think some kind of trade-in arrangement can make quite a difference in the cost of your new one that fits. May I take a look at the old one?"

Your competitor gives us a better deal. "Well, I don't know exactly what you mean by a 'better deal,' unless you're talking only about price. Frankly, our price *is* a little higher than our competitors'. However, customers who have dealt with our competitors tell us they are glad to pay the small premium that assures the kind of service and satisfaction we provide. For instance, down-time on your equipment can be very costly to you in terms of lost production. But our unique system of emergency maintenance depots, located close to each town in which you have a plant, guarantees that you'll have the ultimate service and minimum down-time on each piece of equipment you buy from us. Again, you know that when you're buying our equipment you're buying the highest in quality. Other firms may cut their prices, but they also cut corners on quality. And in the long run, your 'better deal,' as you call it, is more costly and less satisfying than your deal with us. It's true that our original cost is slightly higher, but the reduction in equipment up-keep—*and* your production headaches—will more than offset your 'savings' on the 'better deal' offered by our competitors."

Your firm overstocked me. "Do you mean that we shipped you more than you ordered? If so, I'm sure it was an error . . . one that seldom happens . . . and we would have been glad to have you return the merchandise—particularly since our line has been in such demand that we've been unable to fill a large number of post-season orders. On the other hand, if you mean that our line hasn't moved properly, perhaps you haven't been utilizing it to its fullest potential. Maybe you haven't had time to digest the diversity of uses of our products so that you could readily point them out to your customers. Perhaps you haven't displayed our items to their advantage . . . or called attention to them in your advertising. Here, for instance, is a piece of literature listing a large number of uses for our products. I'm sure your customers will be interested in learning about them in your sales presentation and in your advertising. If you have a few minutes, I can show you a number of other uses that I, myself, have developed through a process of trial and error. Once you and your customers realize the many, many ways in which my product can help solve problems, I'm sure you'll have no trouble in selling any quantity we are able to deliver to you."

Your competitor's product must be better than yours, judging by how much better known it is. "Well, fame isn't always a sign of virture. And the ability to 'toot ones' own horn' through costly advertising and promotion campaigns does *not* necessarily mean that one's product is better than—or even as good as—one that is not so widely advertised. I will grant that at the present time my competitor's product is better known than mine. But that is because a great deal more is

214

spent on its promotion and advertising than has been spent similarly on our product. The truth is that we have turned back every available cent into research and development in order to ensure that our product is the finest quality you can possibly buy. The results rapidly are becoming evident from the many unsolicited testimonial letters we have received. Here are copies of several of them, for your inspection. Judging from the orders we're now getting through word-of-mouth advertising, our fame will soon be at least as great as our competitor's, without the expense of a costly promotional program — which, incidentally, cannot help but be reflected in either higher price or lower product quality. Which product do *you* want? The one whose price has been inflated through high promotional costs? Or the one whose quality can be guaranteed through better research and development? I leave it to you to make the choice."

My last purchase from your firm did not wear well.
"I'm both surprised and very sorry to hear that. The wearing qualities of our product have always been one of our chief sources of pride. But before we go any further, I'd like to examine the conditions under which our product was used. Possibly it was subjected to unusual stresses and strains for which it was not designed. On the other hand, if there was an actual failure on the part of the product itself, I may be able to get you a credit or a refund. Of course, I can't tell you exactly why our product didn't wear until I see the conditions under which it was used. And if I find that the fault lay with conditions, I'll be able to point out the difficulty so that it can be avoided in the future. Then you will not have a cause for prejudice against the product."

I had trouble with the last salesman your company sent to see me.
"I'm sorry to hear that. Of course, we try to hire only the best possible representatives for our firm. We're fully aware that we're judged largely by the integrity of those individuals who represent us. On the other hand, I'm sure you understand how difficult it is today to find qualified personnel — sometimes a bad penny slips in among the good ones. Possibly that is why the salesman you object to is no longer with us. However, I'm sure that, in all fairness, you are *not* going to hold the performance of one unpleasant individual against either my firm . . . or against me. I am now the firm's representative in this territory, and I pledge myself to make every possible effort to give you the kind of service you have a right to expect from a firm such as mine. In fact, I'd like to give you a guarantee, right now, that you'll be most happy with our relationship. Here is my personal check, made out to you, for $2.00. Keep it in your cash box or some other handy place, and if you ever think I have given you cause for trouble, take it out and hand it to me . . . I'll sign it for you. That's a fair deal, don't you think?"

215

**You take too long to
deliver my orders.**

"I know that our deliveries take longer than those of many of our competitors. But that's because our product is designed and manufactured to your specific requirements. We do not manufacture to what you might call average specifications nor do we expect our product to do just an average job. We go into production only after we know exactly what your problem is and how our product can give you maximum satisfaction in its solution. Our product is custom-designed and custom-built to your *individual* needs . . . and this often takes a little longer. But I'm sure you agree that perfection is worth waiting a little longer for. The efficient production and greater savings which our product makes possible for you is surely worth the small additional time that we take to deliver, isn't it?"

**Your representatives
don't give us the
help that your
competitors do.**

"My firm realizes that. Without your mentioning it, they felt that the representative who formerly called on you was not doing an adequate job of helping to acquaint you with our products, their uses, or with our company policies. That's one of the reasons they assigned me to your account. My firm feels that I do give the maximum possible help to my accounts so that they can use our products and our services to their best advantage. Just as an example, I make it a practice to write all my customers once a week just to keep them informed of special values, news developments in the industry, and new product applications for items they've purchased from me. Then, of course, I'll give you my home telephone number. You may feel free to call me at any time, at any hour, if there arises a problem with which I can help you. Fair enough?"

These examples just about run the gamut of dissatisfaction that you, as a salesperson, will encounter among your customers. To be sure, each business and each product will have its own particular version of the dissatisfaction and its own manner of presenting it. Details will vary. But most dissatisfactions or objections will fall into one of the categories we've outlined. And all you have to do is determine which one . . . and how the answers we've given can be adapted to the specific case with which you are dealing.

The amazing thing about these situations and responses is their flexibility. The same basic types of situations will arise in the lives of house-to-house salespeople and industrial sales representatives, in the sale of a simple retail product—say a pair of shoes—or of something as complex as heavy industrial machinery. Whatever your product and wherever your territory, you'll find essentially the same reasons for customer dissatisfaction—and the same ways of handling them will apply. All you need is the ingenuity, enthusiasm, and courage to adapt these answers to the problem at hand.

I find that it's good to keep in mind three basic steps when I tackle the challenge of previously dissatisfied customers.

1. I try to isolate the dissatisfaction . . . to establish *exactly* why my customer has become dissatisfied with our product or our company.

2. I try to zero in on the *source* of the dissatisfaction . . . to determine precisely what or who has caused it.

3. Then I do all I can to find a solution that will satisfy my customer.

These steps have paid off so well for me that I could live comfortably each year on my earnings from formerly dissatisfied customers only. For me, at least, previously dissatisfied customers represent a rich sales potential and are actually my best source of business.

You too can find an almost competition-free market in your company's files of dissatisfied former customers. Try it! Look within those files of the dissatisfied and you'll see a hidden treasure waiting . . . just for you!

CHAPTER FORTY-FOUR: MODERNIZING FOR EXTRA BUSINESS AND PROFIT

In today's climate of stiff competition—exemplified by shopping centers, malls, and expanding chain stores—the small-business owner can't afford to stand still. To keep abreast, it is essential to maintain a modern appearance. This may include such installations as a new store front, storage facilities, lighting fixtures, mirrors, floor covering, shelves, furniture, and air-conditioning.

Before proceeding with modernization, a retailer must consider the advantages to be gained from it. Examine its overall cost and compute the increase in business that will be needed to offset this investment. If a refurbished store front seems called for, it is important to select carefully the style or type that best meets the needs of the business and the ability to pay.

SHOULD YOU MODERNIZE YOUR STORE FRONT?

Your store front is *extremely* important. It is the "gateway" to the merchandise you have to sell; as such, it must attract and impress the public. It must make potential customers *stop*—to look at the goods on display, to look into the store itself, and, finally, to *enter* through the door. An effectively designed store front can create prestige and draw business. It is an investment that should pay off. A few simple tests will help you decide what to do.

Across-the-Street Test

Walk across the street. Now ask yourself: "If I were a shopper, would that store create a favorable first impression on me? Would I be *attracted* to that store? Would I *want* to go in?"

Next, watch people passing your store: Are they attracted? Do they stop to look? Do many actually *enter*?

Cash-Register Test

Now check your sales records for the last several years. Have your sales increased with the times? If not, or if only slightly, it indicates that your store is not attracting its share of increased consumer income.

Comparative Test

Do your competitors have better-looking stores? Have they been taking any substantial number of your old customers away from *you?*

Time Test

How long has it been since your last face lift? It's important that any store be modernized at least once in every 10 years. Otherwise it's similar to running the same newspaper ad day after day, or retaining the same window display for months on end.

IF YOU DECIDE TO MODERNIZE . . .

If these tests and your subsequent analysis say it's time for a change, there are four good points to remember as you plot your course of action:

1. Plan the project well in advance.

2. Employ competent professional advice and assistance.

3. Check your plans against similar projects already in operation.

4. Avoid actual construction during *peak* selling periods. Your slack season is a good time to begin.

PUBLICIZE YOUR MODERNIZATION

Take advantage of your investment in modernizing by giving it as much publicity as you can. Keep these thoughts in mind when planning the campaign:

☐ Emphasize your *community pride* and confidence, *loyalty* of customers, and your determination to create a "better store for better service."

☐ Display a sketch of the completed project. Customers will take a personal interest in your progress.

☐ Publicize each step of the project, leading up to some real event at the time of its completion. "Open House" is a terrific idea for the retail store. Music, refreshments, souvenirs, and prizes make the opening a gala occasion. Widespread publicity can draw new customers from many miles away.

FINANCING   Secure bids from reliable contractors. When the investment has been estimated, you may finance it from accumulated capital or through a bank loan. Divide your improvements into so many "stages" (e.g., Stage 1, front; Stage 2, interior . . .). *Amortize* the costs of each stage before starting additional improvements. When arranging a loan, justify your program by these methods:

1. Provide a complete financial statement of your operation over the past few years.

2. Submit the reliable bids.

3. Draw plans for future operations, showing expected increased sales volume. (Most retailers achieve a 20- to 30-percent business increase through modernization.)

ARCHITECTURAL   When selecting your architect, seek the assistance of your national
ASSISTANCE   or state Trade Association, your Chamber of Commerce, or your local chapter of the American Architects' Institute.

Architects specialize, so select one experienced in small-business design. Your architect will analyze your own unique problems, advise you on costs, supply you with sketches of your proposed front, layout of aisle space, designs and arrangement of fixtures. These drawings should be so complete that contractors will be able to submit bids on all or part of the proposed construction. The architect should assist you in securing, reviewing, and determining bids, and also check to ensure that the contractor is conforming to plans and schedules.

A wealth of information is also available from the *manufacturers* of fixtures, construction materials, floor finishings, paint, and so on.

THE NEW FRONT   Most modern fronts employ plate glass from floor to ceiling. Some use shadow-box displays to feature merchandise, creating interesting effects that attract passing customers. *Off-center entrances* are popular, with exterior masonry of stone or textured materials to help direct the eye toward the interior. Customers are drawn into a shop when they can observe the activity within an attractive interior setting.

Avoid the conventional two windows, divided in the middle by an entrance. Make your business front *eye appealing,* bright, and magnetic.

INTERIOR DECORATION

Choose colors for variety, contrast, and—above all—*harmony* with your merchandise. Improper colors will *detract* from your merchandise.

Depending upon its merchandise, clientele, and sales approach, each business has its own particular set of problems. Obtain specialized help on paint colors and treatments from paint manufacturers. Include a sketch of your business interior, together with a description of the *type of merchandise* you deal in.

Old varnish or paint can be removed to give a bright and modern appearance to your counters and fixtures. Light *natural woods,* with a durable polyurethane finish, retain their fresh appearance longer and require little maintenance. They create an aura of warmth, and their neutral tones blend well with virtually any decor.

Depending on your type of business, you may be able to use decorative posters, pictures, murals, and such. They add a great deal to decoration. Your own ingenuity plus some professional guidance can combine to effect a dramatic interior.

Flooring

Floors that are subject to a great deal of wear can be beautifully covered in heavy-duty vinyl. Less-traveled floors can be thickly carpeted for a luxurious effect. Floor covering manufacturers will be happy to provide free advice and suggestions.

Layout

How are you *using* your floor space? Customers expect to find merchandise fully and freely displayed and easily accessible. Aisles must be wider and your merchandise should be arranged so that the customer may view and handle it without waiting for a salesperson.

The following suggestions have proven valuable in actual experience:

1. Design your aisles at a sufficient width to allow free-flowing traffic and prevent crowding.

2. Set your displays *low.* Don't cut off the customer's view.

3. Make new shelves *deep* for good storage and display.

222

4. Plan floor units for *maximum display* and ready accessibility.

5. Use colors that *blend* with the fixtures, the rest of the interior, and the merchandise.

Lighting

The *effective use of light* is a major factor in your planned layout. Follow these seven guidelines:

1. Install proper *quality* and *quantity* of light.

2. Estimate cost of installation plus monthly electricity charges.

3. Have fixtures designed and placed to facilitate bulb changing.

4. Choose easily cleaned fixtures.

5. Don't fall prey to fads or experimental systems. Choose fixtures of a design that is likely to remain in style and that blends in with the atmosphere, decor, and merchandise.

6. Be careful of light which might *distort color values.*

7. Do not use *excessive light* on fast-fading merchandise. Rotate merchandise and allow sufficient air space to prevent such loss.

PARKING FACILITIES

As a modern store, you should provide adequate and accessible parking facilities. This can be accomplished by:

1. Making arrangements with existing privately owned parking lots and garages.

2. Securing the cooperation of local authorities to arrange for additional off-street or side-street parking.

3. Using the area in the rear of your own building.

NOW—ENJOY YOUR NEW SURROUNDINGS!

Through following the format that we have presented, we think you'll find the process of modernization less troublesome than it appears at first glance. In addition to increased business, you'll enjoy the psychological advantages of renewed enthusiasm that a rejuvenated work environment will bring to you and your employees. And since good spirits are contagious, your customers will be happier, too!

SECTION FIVE

EFFECTIVE ADMINISTRATION OF YOUR BUSINESS

CHAPTER FORTY-FIVE A MILLION DOLLARS' WORTH OF BUSINESS DATA

IT CAN BE YOURS FREE . . . OR FOR MERE PENNIES

If they are to survive, small-business owners must keep abreast of current methods, developments, and laws that may affect them. Many sources of information are available at little or no cost to you. We recommend that you explore this goldmine of material that may save—or earn—countless precious dollars.

Federal and State Government

A number of government agencies publish pamphlets and booklets designed to aid small business. They cover areas ranging from store and interior displays, management problems, advertising and promotional ideas, to financial advice. In many instances, they issue data for *specific* businesses (probably including yours). Their average cost is 25¢, a splendid bargain for well-researched, valuable information. Write to *Bureau of Publications, Washington, D.C.,* for a general catalog . . . and to your own state capitol for materials published locally.

The Small-Business Administration

This helpful agency furnishes a list of management aids and checklists. In addition, their 55 regional offices throughout the country serve to assist small firms with individual problems. Write to *Small-Business Administration, Washington, D.C.*, or consult the Blue Pages of your telephone directory for regional offices near you.

City Governments Larger cities publish helpful materials, available free or at little cost to small businesses. Write to the *Chamber of Commerce* of your closest city for a list of booklets and other aids they may issue.

Universities The business schools of most colleges and universities publish booklets containing small-business "helps," which again are available free or at little cost. In addition, many graduate students prepare theses on business subjects. These works contain unusually thorough and reliable information, since each represents over a year's research devoted to its preparation. They are available for inspection. Write to your local universities for lists.

Trade Associations What trade associations do you belong to? Nearly every one—in every field—is prepared to provide stimulating business information based on experiences of other members. You'll obtain many valuable, usable facts, so do seek them out.

Public Libraries No longer a hushed and imposing retreat for scholarly research, today's public library is a cheerful, lively place—filled with a wealth of up-to-date information on any topic you may possibly think of. Most libraries have at least one employee whose specialty is answering all kinds of questions, and they'll be delighted to answer yours, directing you to more free resources than you can imagine.

CHAPTER FORTY-SIX

MANUFACTURING IDEAS

Ideas! Ideas! Ideas! There is always a need for ideas—in every business—but especially in a small business that wants to grow and prosper. Original ideas are a virtual necessity. No matter what your operation, generating new ideas is an everyday part of its many facets. Consider these areas:

- ☐ Merchandising
- ☐ Purchasing
- ☐ Advertising
- ☐ Public relations
- ☐ Sales promotions
- ☐ Displays

Within each broad category a variety of approaches and special projects rely on a constant flow of ideas. Because of their intangible nature, it is a common belief that ideas are born of inspiration and are often stumbled upon more or less by luck or when least expected.

The truth of the matter is quite to the contrary! Most ideas are *created* as the result of studied and deliberate action. They *can* be produced or "manufactured" at will—actually made to order to fit a particular need or requirement. And like any other manufactured product, ideas are created by taking certain prescribed ingredients and following a carefully designed procedure.

The process or formula for manufacturing ideas involves various steps which, faithfully followed, result in precisely the idea you want and need. Let me outline those steps for you:

Step 1   In manufacturing a product, one obviously determines beforehand *exactly what is to be produced.* The building of a shoe, a table, and a tire are going to have different requirements. Similarly, in manufacturing an idea, you must know at the outset what kind of an idea you're seeking to create. So the first thing to do is write down—in one concise sentence—what it is that you want to think up an idea about. In other words, *what is your problem?* This may sound very elementary; yet you'll be surprised at how difficult it is to phrase your objective in a single sentence. Once you've done this, however, you'll also be gratified at how your thinking suddenly becomes clarified. Now, instead of your thought processes rambling and zig-zagging toward something nebulous, your thinking is directed toward a concrete and specific goal.

For example, if your aim is to create an idea for repeat business, your one-sentence summation might read, "What type of promotion would be most successful in getting old and current customers to make new purchases?" And now, having given succinct expression to your specific goal, you are ready to proceed to the next step.

Step 2   This is the *accumulation* phase in your idea manufacturing. It's the step in which you assemble all available facts and materials relating to the problem at hand. Arm yourself with as much information as possible from *every* source— whether your own line of business or that of others—as long as it has some relationship to the problem you are facing.

In the sample problem cited above, you would gather all promotional material (letters, brochures, stuffers, and advertising) put out by your competitors, as well as any likely looking material used by other businesses for the purpose of attracting repeat business. Now your objective is to boil it down into terse summary descriptions, so that you have all the information sifted down to essential outlines. You are thus equipped with the necessary *ingredients* for the manufacture of your idea.

Step 3   After you have carefully studied and reviewed the boiled-down versions of the miscellaneous promotional material, the recommended procedure is to *get away from it all!* In other words, after assimilating all the data into your subconscious mind, put the physical material away and try to dismiss it from your conscious thinking. You have now fed the necessary ingredients into your subconscious mind machine, and the thing to do is let the wheels and gears get into motion on their own.

After getting away from it all, *keep* away from it . . . *overnight!* This will set the stage for the final step in your idea-manufacturing process. This in-between phase might be called the "percolation" stage. Much like the perc-perc-perc of a coffee pot, the data you have absorbed now continues to bubble through your mind—even while you sleep—ultimately "brewing" into a distinct mental image.

Step 4 By morning you'll awaken with some clear-cut thoughts on which way to proceed toward completing your manufacturing process by producing the needed idea. Actually, this final step consists of two parts. The first is the elimination of everything unessential. By freeing yourself of extraneous thoughts, you permit ready access and a clear course to your goal. Thus the second part of the final step will be more or less automatic: Once your mind has eliminated the clutter of unessentials, the idea you have been seeking will suddenly stand forth in full view. The necessary idea has now been manufactured, and you are ready to shape it into practical, usable form!

After you have practiced this idea-manufacturing process a few times, you will find yourself automatically following the procedure. And soon you will fall into the natural habit of clipping and gathering all kinds of data and specimens for use in your future idea manufacturing. Your aptitude for spotting information will grow, and so will your collection of material for your idea factory. Your eye will automatically seek out and discover material pertinent to your particular problems, and your files will soon expand and bulge with a great and helpful variety of data. Magazine and newspaper articles . . . advertisements . . . notes about your competition and their procedures and promotions . . . your own notes and notations on conversations with others in your field, things you overhear or notice pertaining to your line of business . . . "flash" ideas that come to you from time to time . . . these are only some of the kinds of material that you may appraise as being of possible value in the future.

Frankly, this has been my own procedure in the creation of ideas over the years. It has helped me create and develop ideas ad infinitum, as (and whenever) desired, in almost nonstop succession. I started a long, long time ago and recall that after just six months I had accumulated notes, clippings, articles, ads, sales letters, and brochures numbering over one-thousand pieces and filling two giant-sized binders to their bursting point. Now, after years of following this practice, I have a *room* full of files carefully and minutely classified, set up in orderly fashion so that I can easily put my hands on whatever material or ingredients I need to feed into my idea-manufacturing machine. (Incidentally, my collection of material is still expanding.)

Before I started my file of idea material, I had to depend on the exchange of thoughts with stimulating friends and associates. Sometimes they would spark me to think up a suitable and workable idea for my purposes. More often, however, the spark was missing at the time I needed it most. By building your own resources you will be able to generate ideas independently and—more important—exactly when your need for them is most critical!

CHAPTER FORTY-SEVEN SELECTING A PROPER BUSINESS LOCATION

Let's start this chapter with a question:

How important is location?

The answer is an unqualified VERY! Few things have as much influence on your business as its location.

No matter how *excellent* the potential of your business may be, it can founder and fail if your location is ill-advised. And this applies equally to retail stores *and* service-oriented operations.

Naturally, there are many points you must consider. Here are a few basic ones:

1. **Is your business self-generating?** Is it a business that will *draw* people to its location so that it does not depend on location to attract customers? Some examples of self-generating businesses are drive-in theatres, discount outlets, supermarkets, beauty parlors, "big-name" stores (Sears, Roebuck, for instance), and franchised automotive suppliers. In most cases, these operations will *self-generate* their trade.

2. **Does your business depend on transient trade?** Some examples of this type of business are gas stations, drive-in restaurants, auto-repair shops, florists, and liquor stores.

3. **Does your business require trade compatibility?** In other words, should it be located among related businesses, where "togetherness" is a virtue and each shop helps draw trade for the other? For example, in New York City, one section of Grand Street is devoted almost exclusively to wedding-gown shops. Another street is devoted exclusively to furniture and home-furnishing stores. In Los Angeles there is a "Restaurant Row . . ."

In selecting your location, bear in mind that the more remote your location and the lower your rent, *the more you must spend in advertising* to draw customers to your place. Thus you may in effect pay the equivalent of a good-location rental without necessarily enjoying good-location benefits.

Also bear in mind that the expense of location should be measured in terms of a ratio of your rental fee to actual dollar sales, rather than in terms of monthly rental expenses alone. A low-rent location may prove very costly, if customers are scarce; a high-rent location may prove inexpensive indeed, if the flow of customers keeps your cash register constantly ringing.

Purchasing power of the area is, of course, another important consideration. The success of your business—and your anticipated sales volume—can be estimated with surprising accuracy by carefully assessing the economic status of the community. It is wise to be conservative in appraising the sales volume you believe an area will produce. The following factors should be carefully checked:

1. Volume of retail trade in the district

2. The number of telephone subscribers

3. Number, age, and make of cars owned

4. Number of bank depositors (and volume of deposits)

5. Census reports of rents

6. School and utility figures

7. Wealth produced in the area

In considering a location, be sure also to investigate *taxes and insurance rates.* Remember that local taxes add to your cost of doing business—as do certain licenses and fees imposed by communities. An otherwise attractive location might be inadvisable because of excessive taxes, fees, and insurance rates. *Transportation facilities,* too, are very important. The condition of railroads and highways can bear heavily on operating expenses.

Before deciding on your actual site, there are a few rather simple (generally reliable) ways of sizing up the location you are considering.

1. **Have a talk with the local mail carrier.** They are usually eager to supply sound information about conditions (pro and con) in the area they serve.

2. **Mail a questionnaire to a random selection of area residents.** Design your inquiry to yield candid answers concerning their desire and need for your product or service.

3. **Have a chat with your competitors** (either openly or incognito) to find out how they are doing.

4. **Interview noncompetitive local merchants.** Get their impressions of current business and general business conditions.

5. **Talk to the local banker and the local Chamber of Commerce.** Make any further observations that may be of specific value in your particular situation.

As you hone in on your actual location, be ever mindful of possible "dead spots." Traditionally, there are certain spots that shoppers just don't like to pass. These include lumber yards, coal companies, vacant lots, and, of course, strictly residential stretches where no businesses exist. Other spots that people generally avoid passing are those that are secluded, dark, closed, vacant or otherwise unattended, particularly during evening hours. These include parks, factories, public utilities, offices, churches, libraries. Such areas, usually dimly lit, tend to cause insecurity and to discourage traffic flow.

Once you have decided that all factors are favorable, it is wise to seek a long-term lease. A one- or two-year lease is a mistake if no provisions are made for renewal.

As a final guide in selecting a location refer to these booklets:

☐   Using Census Data to Select a Store Site (small marketers' aid No. 154)

☐   Using a Traffic Study to Select a Retail Site (small marketers' aid No. 152)

Copies are obtainable through the field offices and Washington headquarters of the Small Business Administration.

CHAPTER FORTY-EIGHT ENLIST YOUR SUPPLIERS' HELP IN PROMOTING SALES

DON'T MISS OUT ON THE VALUE OF FREE ASSISTANCE

Few small businesses are aware of the many "helps" most suppliers (wholesalers and manufacturers) can give them. Often you can obtain many thousands of dollars worth of ongoing free assistance merely for the asking.

Here's a checklist of some of the "helps" that may be obtainable from your suppliers:

☐ **Consumer services:** Your suppliers can furnish you with brochures and other literature about their products' features. You can pass these on to your prospects. Suppliers can provide helpful market-research data, as well.

☐ **Planning services:** Your suppliers can report business-sales outlook, by product, and advise you on competitors' progress and plans, helping you keep pace.

☐ **Financing services:** Your suppliers will advise you on management of money, and will suggest accounts receivable financing and investments. They can analyze your financial statements, advising you of weaknesses. Often they will help in financing new establishments.

☐ **Training services:** Suppliers frequently can suggest sources of new employees and will actually help train them.

☐ **Manager's services:** Suppliers will provide management booklets helpful to small businesses. They will advise on locations and give continuing management counsel. They will submit comparative wage scales.

☐ **Advisory services:** Most suppliers are glad to explain what it takes to start and succeed, giving you the benefits of their knowledge of your field.

☐ **Promotional:** Suppliers will advise on store management and such things as proper lighting. They frequently provide signs for street, window, and interior. Often they design window displays and dispatch specialists to install them. Most suppliers provide sales side and pass-out materials, and willingly share dealer's advertising costs when a sales campaign is being waged.

Other small businesses are taking full advantage of these free supplier services. Obtain *your* share!

SECTION SIX

KNOWING THE
ARITHMETIC
OF YOUR BUSINESS

CHAPTER FORTY-NINE CAREFUL RECORD-KEEPING BOOSTS PROFITS

. . . AND GUARDS AGAINST BUSINESS FAILURE

Most small businesses shun contact with the arithmetic of their operation—until circumstances *compel them.* And at this point it may be too late for remedial action. The fatal damage may already be done.

We remember when we conducted a Business Advisory Service for some 40,000 small businesses of all types. Typical of the inquiries we received was this one from an auto service station:

"All last year we worked an average of 12 hours a day, and because we were busy, we were *sure* that we were making money. Now my accountant has just given me the enclosed figures showing that we actually *lost* $850 during the last year. Where did we go wrong?"

Fundamentally, they went "wrong" because of poor record keeping. Among the things they lacked were:

☐ An awareness of the day-to-day progress of their business.

☐ An understanding of the "break-even point" of their business.

☐ An insight into comparative ratios of similar businesses to determine how they compared—for example, whether they were paying too much for such items as rent, advertising, and salaries.

☐   An awareness of how each *department* of their operation was doing, enabling them to pinpoint "loss" products or services that should be eliminated.

Temporarily, the arithmetic of one's business can be "shoved under a carpet out of sight." But at the stage when it does confront you, it may do so in an explosive manner. You may suddenly discover that:

☐   Where you thought you were operating at a profit—well-documented by long hours of drudgery—you are actually operating at a loss.

☐   You are not in proper control of what you are doing.

☐   You may be overpaying for certain things. In many instances these expenditures may be cut as much as one-half without impeding your business progress. Rent, advertising, and salaries are but three examples.

☐   You may be *under*paying for certain things that can help expedite business expansion.

☐   You may be overinventoried ... or *under*inventoried. (Both can prove damaging to your business.)

☐   You may be underpaying on taxes, subjecting yourself to severe penalties. On the other hand, you may be *over*paying these taxes, and throttling your business progress and earnings potential.

☐   You may have a series of wasteful "leakages" in your business—enough of them to "sink your ship" beyond the possibility of salvage.

In referring to the arithmetic aspect of your business, we mean your on-going process of *record keeping*—the way you maintain your books and day-by-day awareness of your business activities and status.

Proper record keeping is absolutely vital to the health of a small business. U.S. Department of Commerce statistics indicate that over 50 percent of small-business failures can be attributed to inadequate record-keeping systems.

Accurate figures are important for legal reasons, as well. Access to them is a *must* for:

☐   Your federal and state tax returns, including income tax and social security.

☐   Your applications for credit from suppliers and manufacturers of equipment, or for a bank loan.

☐   Your financial (profit and loss) statements about your business, if you should *ever* seek to sell it.

242

But for the sake of your business survival you must have the figures to tell you which way your operation is going and help you achieve increased profits. With an adequate record-keeping system—and it can be a simple one—you always can answer such questions as these:

1. How much business am I doing?

2. What are my expenses? Are any of them running too high?

3. What is my percentage of gross profit? Net profit?

4. How much cash do I have in the till, and how much in the bank?

5. What are my collections on charge business?

6. What is the condition of my working capital?

7. How much do I owe to my suppliers?

8. What are the trends in my cash receipts, my expenses, my profits, and my net worth?

9. What is my actual net worth—in other words, what is the value of my ownership of the business?

10. What is the relationship of my assets to my debts? What percentage am I earning on my investment?

11. How many cents of net profit am I making on every dollar in sales?

12. Is my financial position growing better or worse?

The answers to the above questions are in effect *directional signals.* They tell small business owners where they are going and whether they should do something to change the direction and course of the business. Once they understand the conditions that exist, they can take the necessary action to improve their position.

Whatever system you decide upon should enable you to keep your eye not only on sales, expenses, and net profit, but also on the balance sheet that tells how much money you owe and discloses the net worth of your business.

Here is how net worth is computed. First you list what you *own,* then what you *owe.* The formula is as follows:

ASSETS (Cash on hand, cash on deposit with your bank, merchandise, equipment, business property, and accounts receivable. List everything your business owns.)

Minus LIABILITIES (Accounts payable, taxes, notes payable. List everything you owe for either merchandise, equipment, or services.)

Equals your NET WORTH.

To verify that figure, you can check by the following method:

NET WORTH AT THE START OF THE PERIOD

Plus ADDED CAPITAL (Additional cash put into the business, value of new equipment invested in during this period.)

Minus WITHDRAWALS (Either cash or personal salary.)

Equals NET WORTH AT THE END OF THE PERIOD.

If your records are being kept correctly, your net worth as determined by both methods should tally. For a typical balance sheet, let us look at the following example:

ASSETS	Cash on hand	$ 500.00	
	Cash on deposit	3,500.00	
	Merchandise inventory	12,500.00	
	Equipment	3,800.00	
	Accounts receivable	1,900.00	
			$22,200.00
LIABILITIES	Accounts payable	$ 3,700.00	
	Notes payable	2,200.00	
	Payroll taxes	225.00	
			6,125.00
NET WORTH			$16,075.00

Now, let us see how *Net Profit* would be computed.

Sales (or gross income)	$2,400.00
minus COST OF SALES (cost of merchandise sold)	850.00

equals GROSS PROFIT	$1,550.00
minus EXPENSES	680.00
equals NET PROFIT	$ 860.00

Cost of sales in any business where merchandise is handled is generally computed by adding together the opening inventory plus purchases for the period, and then subtracting the closing inventory (figured on the basis of wholesale price, market value, or cost to you, whichever is lowest).

Next, it is important that you have an understanding and awareness of the *operating ratios* pertaining to your particular line of business—the figures from your profit-and-loss statement translated into percentages. This gives you a quick, visual conception of "how you're doing." It also exposes areas where you are spending too much or too little. Most important, it gives you a solid basis for comparing the expenses and income of your business with the ratios of similar-type businesses. Thus you can establish whether you are doing very well, fairly well, or poorly, in relation to what you *should* do in your particular enterprise.

Comparative operating ratios (pertaining to most types of businesses) are available from Dun & Bradstreet or from the Small Business Administration, Washington, D.C. Specialized sources (pertaining to specific businesses) also supply them; these may be trade magazines and trade associations for your field.

In analyzing your own operating ratios, consider first the ratio of *fixed expenses* (those expenses that generally remain the same month after month and vary only slightly, if at all); second will be your *variable expenses* (those that fluctuate from month to month, depending on the amount of business you do). A typical operating ratio might contain these categories:

Variable Expenses	**Fixed Expenses**
Outside labor	Rent
Operating supplies	Utilities
Gross wages	Insurance
Repairs and maintenance	Taxes and licenses
Advertising	Interest
Car and delivery	Depreciation
Bad debts	TOTAL FIXED EXPENSES

Administrative and legal

Miscellaneous expense

TOTAL VARIABLE EXPENSES

Let's look at the typical operating ratio of an automotive store:

Automotive Store	Percentage
Sales	100.00
Cost of sales	71.01
Gross profit	28.99
Variable Expenses	
Outside labor	.47
Operating supplies	1.18
Gross wages	8.69
Repairs and maintenance	.53
Advertising	1.11
Car and delivery	.93
Bad debts	.10
Administrative and legal	.49
Miscellaneous expense	.94
Total Variable Expenses	14.44
Fixed Expense	
Rent	1.46
Utilities	1.29
Insurance	.86
Taxes and licenses	.61
Interest	.37
Depreciation	1.20
Total Fixed Expenses	5.79
Total Expenses	20.23
NET PROFIT	8.76

CHAPTER FIFTY

FINANCING YOUR BUSINESS

To a small business owner (or franchisee) financing is often of paramount importance. If you are planning to purchase a business you may need financial help (a) for your initial purchase; (b) for subsequent inventory purchase; or (c) for maintaining yourself (covering your personal and family expenses) during the preliminary phase of your operation—often six months or more—until your franchise becomes self-sustaining.

If you are an established business, you may also need financial help either now or later for (a) desired expansion of your business; (b) increased advertising and promotional activity; (c) acquiring additional fixtures to increase your income and profit potential, enabling continued expansion.

Now comes the big question: *How do you proceed to obtain such financial assistance?*

Your prime source—usually most accessible to you—is a local bank or savings and loan association. Being local, they are acquainted with you and your operation, are familiar with your character and integrity. The guide they use for granting a loan is symbolized by "3 C's" . . . Character, Capital, and Capacity to pay.

Under normal circumstances most banks will be receptive to your request for a reasonable loan. Bank loans are most advantageous because their interest rate is generally lowest.

You may obtain short-term bank loans (payable in about 90 days) and long-term bank loans (extending for as long as 10 years). The following types of bank loans are among the most popular:

☐   **Straight commerical loans:** Usually payable in 30 to 60 days, these loans are made on the basis of your present financial statement. They are generally used for seasonal financing requirements, such as expanding inventories during peak sales periods.

☐   **Installment loans:** These are usually long-term loans, repaid on a monthly basis. Payments can be tailored to your business needs, with larger installments falling due during peak months and smaller ones payable during off-season periods.

☐   **Term loans:** Such loans have maturities ranging from one to ten years and may be either secured or unsecured. Repayment is made on almost any mutually agreeable basis—monthly, quarterly, semiannually, annually. Early increments sometimes are relatively small, with a large final payment. Many term loans are secured by collateral, and the lender will ordinarily require that your ratio of current assets to current liabilities —your "current ratio"—be two-to-one or better.

☐   **Bills or notes receivable:** Promissory notes are often given for purchase of goods. These notes are called *bills receivable* or *notes receivable*. If the credit of the notes' makers is acceptable, these can usually be discounted—that is, purchased by a bank at a discount from their face value. Your account is credited with the amount of the note less the discount. The bank will collect from the note's maker when the note is due.

☐   **Warehouse-receipt loans:** Under this form of financing, goods are stored in warehouses and the warehouse receipt is given to the bank as security for a loan to pay off the supplier. As fast as the borrower is able to sell merchandise, portions of the inventory are bought back.

☐   **Equipment loans:** These loans are made to finance the purchase of machinery or equipment. The lender usually retains title until installment payments have been completed.

☐   **Collateral loans:** This type of borrowing can be secured by such collateral as personal property under chattel mortgages, real property under real-estate mortgages, life insurance (up to cash surrender value of the property), or stocks and bonds that have not been purchased "on margin." Bank loans that are made with respect to bills or notes receivable and warehouse receipts, as well as with respect to machinery or equipment to which the lender holds title until installment payments have been completed, are, by definition, collateral loans.

If your banker says "No" to your loan request, contact your local Small Business Administration office, either directly or through your banker. One of the reasons for its existence is to assist small businesses in obtaining justifiable loans; it administers programs that can provide direct loans, guaranteeing 90 percent of a private lender's loan to a small business. If you haven't already done so, SBA will usually ask that you initiate your loan application through your local bank. Under the proper circumstances, SBA will undertake to insure the bank against loss with respect to 90 percent of its loan to you. Thus most banks—including the one(s) that refused your initial request—will cooperate with you on the basis of SBA's participation.

Another prime source of loans is the Small Business Investment Company, or SBIC. SBICs were established in 1958. They use part private, part federal money to provide capital for small businesses—through loans, direct stock purchases, the purchase of debentures convertible into stock, or some combination of these techniques. Along with their more specialized cousins, MESBICs, they give you a loan-financing opportunity formerly available only to bigger companies. These SBICs and MESBICs are private companies, but are regulated and generally partially funded by the Small Business Administration. Over 300 SBICs and MESBICs are currently in operation. Financing costs are generally higher than banks, but are lower than usual outside sources.

To obtain the names and addresses of SBICs in your area, write to Finance and Investment Division, *Small Business Administration,* 1441 "L" Street N.W., Washington, D.C. 20416, or to *National Association of SBICs,* 618 Washington Building, Washington, D.C. 20005

Other financing avenues open to your business include the following:

1. **Private capital:** Insert an ad in your local newspaper under "Capital Wanted." Through this medium you may attract private investors who regularly consult this column for investment opportunities.

2. **Factors:** In most communities there are factoring firms that make loans to all types of businesses. Their standards are lower than those of banks; hence they will be more inclined to extend you your desired loan (even though you may have been turned down by banks or government sources). Factors are recommended only as a "last resort," however, since their interest rates are often excessive.

3. **Veterans Administration loans:** If you are a veteran of the armed forces of the United States, you may be eligible to apply for a loan through your local Veterans Administration Office. Write to them to

obtain their detailed pamphlet on types of loans available and conditions under which they may be granted.

4. **Insurance companies:** Many insurance companies maintain loan departments as an integral part of their business. Their interest rates, although generally higher than those of banks, are much lower than the rates of Factors.

5. **Commercial investment companies:** There are many investment companies, privately constituted, that make loans, too. You will find them listed in the Yellow Pages of your local telephone directory. Their rates are generally on a par with rates of Factoring organizations.

When should you seek a loan? *Do not* seek a loan if you do not need the money for specific business purposes; you will only pay the penalty of high interest rates without obtaining proportionate benefits. Your rule-of-thumb should be an unqualified "Yes" to this question: *Will this money that I am borrowing help me to earn more money—in considerable excess of interest rates incurred?*

Do borrow money if it helps you establish yourself in business, accelerates your progress, and expands your profits. Bear in mind that it's always good economics to pay out "2X" dollars if you are able to obtain "10X" dollars in return—and expedite your business success momentum.

CHAPTER FIFTY-ONE BUILDING AN INSURANCE PLAN

POINTS TO CONSIDER ABOUT INSURING YOURSELF AND YOUR BUSINESS

Adequate *insurance* is of utmost importance to any business. Most of us are familiar with "personal" insurance (health, life, and property) and the protection it affords us. Business insurance, however, is much more varied and complex.

These facts are axiomatic:

Improper or inadquate insurance can spell the ruination of a business operation. Any one of a dozen unanticipated mishaps can completely *wipe out* the investment of the business owner.

Proper and sufficient insurance can give overall protection that spells continued security for the business owner. It can "cushion" him or her against most mishaps—business or personal.

In arriving at a formula as to how much insurance you should take for your business, always ask yourself this question: "How much can I *afford to lose* if wiped out by any type of disaster beyond my control?" Use your answer to this simple query as a rule-of-thumb. For example: If the assessed value of your property is $50,000, can you afford to take only $30,000 in insurance—absorbing a loss of $20,000?

There is another basic thing to keep in mind. As a business owner, you can't afford to rely on a collection of *individual* insurance policies—each purchased without regard to the other—as part of a basic program. You need an *overall basic program.*

Nor can you afford to overinvest in insurance; this, too, can become a ruinous burden. Often (in interest of insurance economies) you avoid gambling on possibilities . . . and invest only in *probabilities.*

There is no set rule as to how much to spend for insurance. This varies with different enterprises, locations, types of stock, and many other factors. The general small-business average is one percent of gross income. Thus, if your anticipated gross for the year is $100,000, you normally would not exceed an expenditure of $1000 per year for your insurance coverage.

Your agent or broker is prepared to render valuable assistance through "insurance survey" or "risk analysis," either of which will produce the facts necessary for intelligent insurance decisions.

RECOMMENDED COVERAGE

The types of business coverages that can save you money are described below. Always keep in mind that *you* are the beneficiary of insurance. As the owner, any uninsured losses would come out of your pocket. Fire, windstorm, explosion, or death are all recognized losses, but hidden and more disastrous losses can occur from interrupted business, terminated leases, and destroyed leases. "Losses" mean potential *future* damage, as well as immediate damage.

1. Fire Insurance

Have your property properly appraised so that it is insured for its full insurable value. Be sure that you reexamine your fire insurance periodically to make sure it covers new, current value. Add to the coverage as needed. If you rent or lease your business premises, it is advisable to determine to what extent, if any, your landlord's insurance covers you; then obtain your added insurance in the amount you wish.

2. Inventory Insurance

It is advisable that your inventory insurance coverage be for an amount slightly higher than the value of your normal inventory. To protect your periodical inventory fluctuations, arrange to obtain periodical extended coverage from your insurance broker. Keep an accurate account of inventory so that exact replacement value is known at all times.

3. Theft Insurance

To give yourself maximum coverage, bear in mind that this type of insurance includes protection against loss resulting from *three* categories of claims:

(a) **Burglary,** which requires *forcible entry.* For example, your safe is broken open or a person breaks into your place of business after it is closed (carrying off merchandise or office equipment).

(b) **Robbery,** which is the taking of property by *violence or the threat of violence.* When a business is held up or otherwise intimidated into handing over cash or goods, it has been robbed.

(c) **Theft or larceny,** which is the stealing of property while it is *unprotected.* For example, a thief finds the door of your business establishment unlocked; he or she enters and steals your property.

If you rent a store, a Storekeepers Burglary and Robbery Policy may answer your need. If you operate an office, you may want an Office Burglary and Robbery Policy.

4. Workmen's Compensation

This type of insurance protects employees against loss resulting from job-connected accidents (also against certain types of occupational illness). Generally, an employer is compelled by state law to carry this insurance. Premium rates are influenced by the percentage of weekly pay allowed as a benefit. Amounts paid for medical treatment are an important element of cost. The only way to reduce this insurance expense is to reduce accidents.

5. Accident and Health Insurance

This type of insurance helps reimburse an employee for expenses resulting from an off-the-job injury or a major illness . . . also for loss of income if he or she is unable to work. A sound health insurance plan will (a) act as an inducement to prospective employees; (b) help reduce employee turnover; and (c) promote better morale and loyalty to the company, thus increasing productivity.

6. Use and Occupancy Insurance

Should your business be interrupted or suspended due to serious damage, Use and Occupancy (or Earnings) insurance will provide you with the same profits you'd expect if there was no interruption at all. For collection of benefits, a total stoppage of business is not necessary. You can file claims on partial shrinkage of profits resulting from designated damage.

Such shrinkage of sales might result from damage by fire, breakdown of machinery, vandalism by striking employees, explosions, broken water pipes, plus a variety of other misfortunes.

7. General Liability Insurance

This type of insurance usually comprises two parts, *bodily injury* (which covers claims for the accidental injury or death of persons other than employees) and *property damage* (which covers accidental damage to property that is not owned, used, or under the care of the insured.)

Within this scope of general liability insurance, the following are among the most important:

(a) **Basic coverage,** which insures liability for accidents occurring on the business premises or arising from the use of the premises for business purposes. Ordinarily this is obtainable through the Owners, Landlords, and Tenants Liability Policy. The premium cost normally is figured on the number of square feet in the area to be insured; in some cases there is an additional charge for frontage. High-rish enterprises and/or locations, of course, would indicate variations from the norm.

(b) **Product liability,** which insures against liability for damage arising from the use of products or services. Some examples are accidents from defective electrical apparatus, poisoning from food or from dyes in textiles, and many miscellaneous hazards.

(c) **Motor-vehicle insurance,** with which you are probably quite familiar. There are two principle categories of motor-vehicle policies, *liability* and *property damage.* Liability insurance protects the vehicle owner or operator against damage suits arising from motor-vehicle accidents. A property-damage policy reimburses the owner for loss of or damage within the category of property damage: fire, theft, and collision.

(d) **Contractual liability,** which covers liability for negligence. While you will obviously take every step to avoid lawsuits, it is possible that some day you might be the loser in such a case, and coverage against this eventuality is well worth the investment.

A Comprehensive General Liability Policy is the most popular choice of insurance to cover all these areas. Such a package provides automatic coverages for many unanticipated hazards that may develop after you have purchased your policy. Your insurance agent will outline the one that is best tailored to your individual needs.

8. Business Life Insurance

Necessary for a business or for the family of a business owner is protection against financial loss due to the death of someone closely associated with the business. Maintain business continuity and your *full value in business* for your family by investigating these types of coverage.

Key-employee protection reimburses for loss upon the death of a key employee. *Partnership insurance* retires a partner's interest at death. *Corporation insurance* retires a shareholder's interest at death. *Proprietorship insur-*

ance provides for maintenance of business upon the death of a sole proprietor. *Credit insurance* covers the owner or key personnel during the term of a loan or the duration of a mortgage.

Finally, but perhaps most important is this: When the estate of a business person consists almost entirely of his or her interest in that business, a life-insurance policy payable to the family should be of a sufficient amount to provide them with cash to aid in liquidation of the business interest. Consideration also should be given to the possibility that the family may wish to maintain ownership of the business, whether or not they can actually operate it.

9. Fidelity Insurance

Losses of property and money because of fraud or dishonesty by one or more employees can be prevented through this type of insurance protection. Your best coverage may be a "blanket bond," which covers losses resulting from the dishonest act of *any* employee, regardless of name or position.

YOUR INSURANCE CHECKLIST

Here is a checklist that should prove helpful as you prepare to review your insurance needs with your agent or broker. Every phase of protection may not be required in your business, but it is wise to become fully familiar with the entire range of coverage that is available to you as a business person.

Buildings

- ☐ Fire
- ☐ Improvements and betterments
- ☐ Extended coverage
- ☐ Vandalism and malicious mischief
- ☐ Earthquake and flood
- ☐ Sprinkler leakage and water damage
- ☐ Glass
- ☐ Business interruption (contingent B.I. agreed amount)
- ☐ Extra expense
- ☐ Rent and leasehold
- ☐ Replacement cost
- ☐ Debris removal
- ☐ Demolition

Liability for wrongful actions

- ☐ Owners, landlords, and tenants
- ☐ Manufacturers
- ☐ Contractual
- ☐ Contingent
- ☐ Elevator
- ☐ Comprehensive general

255

BUILDING AN
INSURANCE PLAN

Merchandise	☐	Inland marine
	☐	Transportation, parcel post
	☐	Sales samples
	☐	Exhibition floater
	☐	Robbery and safe burglary
	☐	Installment sales floater
	☐	Ocean marine cargo
	☐	Burglary, robbery, and theft
	☐	Open-stock burglary
	☐	Money and securities, 3-D broad form
Business	☐	Key person life
	☐	Business continuation
	☐	Life: proprietorship, partnership, closed corporation
Employees (protection of human life values)	☐	Group life
	☐	Salary savings
	☐	Pension plan, company O.A.S.I.
	☐	Group disability
	☐	Medical payment
	☐	Workmen's compensation
	☐	Nonoccupational disability
	☐	Unemployment compensation
Equipment	☐	Boiler and machinery
	☐	Motor-vehicle property damage
	☐	Aircraft damage
	☐	Marine hull
	☐	Motor-vehicle liability
	☐	Nonownership
	☐	Neon sign
	☐	Use and occupancy
Protection against human failure	☐	Honesty, ability, and financial strength
	☐	Supply bond
	☐	Contract bond
	☐	License and permit bond
	☐	Schedule position bond
	☐	Blanket position bond
	☐	Primary commercial blanket bond
	☐	Depositors forgery bond

CHAPTER FIFTY-TWO
SHOULD YOU ALLOW CREDIT?

Most small businesses must extend some credit if they are to realize their maximum sales potential. Properly controlled, credit can stimulate sales, encourage larger orders, and build goodwill. (A recent survey showed that over 75 percent of small businesses do extend credit.) Credit requests range from occasional "charges" to regular installment budget sales.

In setting up a credit program, it is vital that it be organized methodically and maintained carefully. A well-monitored program can hold credit losses down to the vicinity of one percent.

For maximum success, follow this five-step procedure:

First At the time an account is opened, clearly inform the customer about your collection policy. Specify exactly when payment is expected. Do not vary your requirements.

Second Send out statements promptly. Follow through with additional statements (accompanied by letters) if the account is not paid. If these follow-ups are not answered, a personal visit or telephone call is suggested.

Third Set a specific credit limit per customer. Do not exceed this limit at any time.

Fourth If you deal with people who are transient and unknown to you (especially where large amounts of credit are involved), have them fill out a credit application, listing their place of employment as well as personal and financial references and the name of their bank. Such forms are available at most stationery stores or from your own bank. Check the references carefully—*in advance!*

Fifth *Maintain proper credit records.* A simple yet effective system begins with a *sales slip* that itemizes the transaction and is signed by the customer, who receives a carbon copy. The original remains with you.

Next, allocate each credit customer *a separate folder* in your file cabinet. Keep sales slips inside this folder, and on the outside rule off five vertical columns with these headings: *Date, Order No., Charge, Credit, Balance.* By recording all action *as it takes place,* you have a running record of charges— and constant, effective control.

The most important thing is to be punctual in both your billing and follow-up. Allow no variations in policy. Inform your customer clearly, in advance, when payment is due. This will reduce your risk of loss resulting from the extension of credit privileges.

CHAPTER FIFTY-THREE STOCK-CONTROL IDEAS FOR SMALL STORES

The basic function of any small retailing business is buying and selling merchandise at a profit. All other activities are carried on in order to facilitate the efficient performance of this function. Simple yet adequate stock-control records are *an absolute necessity* if you are to maintain well-balanced inventories. Only in this way can you buy effectively, meet customer demand, earn a profit, and reduce your investment in merchandise through a rapid stock turnover.

UNDERSTANDING THE LANGUAGE

An understanding of retailing terms is essential to any discussion of stock-control. Here are some of the most common terms:

- [ ] **Gross margin** is the difference between the actual selling price and the cost of the merchandise. It is expressed as a percentage of net sales.

- [ ] **Stockturn** is the rate at which the average amount of stock on hand is sold. Stockturn shows the number of times during a period (usually a year) that the average inventory is sold. Stockturn may be determined by dividing the net sales for the period by the average inventory (at retail prices) for that period. *To illustrate:* If your net sales for the year totaled $160,000, and your average inventory at retail (beginning inventory on

January 1 plus 12 monthly ending inventories, divided by 13) equaled $40,000, your stockturn was *four times*. This means your average inventory was sold every three months (or ninety days). In terms of cost figures, the rate of stockturn can be determined by dividing the *total cost of goods sold* for the period by *average merchandise inventory at cost.*

☐ **Markup** is the amount that is added to the cost to obtain the selling price. Thus if an item costs you $2 and you sell it for $3, the *markup* is 33 1/3 percent (or $1).

☐ **Markdown** is the difference between the last retail price and the proposed lower or actual selling price. Markdowns are expressed as a percentage of net sales. For example, if you take $500 in markdowns during a month and have a volume of $10,000 during that month, your markdowns amount to five percent.

☐ **Basic ("never-out") items** are those essentials that *every* department of any retail business *must* have in stock at all times. These are the items for which there is a relatively constant demand; hence they appropriately are called the basic or "never-out" items.

WHAT STOCK CONTROL WILL DO FOR YOU

Adequate records help you to maintain the well-balanced stocks that will satisfy customer demand, bring you greater profits, make buying more effective, and decrease inventory investment by ensuring rapid stockturn.

Stock records can serve as a guide for forecasting sales. They provide information on such subjects as the quality, quantity, styles, and types of items sold in previous periods. This information is valuable in planning purchases for the current year. It will also tell you when to build up stocks and when to lower them. During periods of low customer demand, stock on hand can be held at a minimum. In this way you can realize savings in taxes, insurance costs, interest, and space occupied.

Slow-moving items can be eliminated with the help of adequate stock-control records. Your selling job will become easier as your understanding of the important relationship between stock control and profits is developed.

DETERMINING BASIC OR NEVER-OUT ITEMS

All retailers must ask themselves, "What do my customers want that I should *always* have in stock?"

This is important in *every* type of retail store. A men's clothing store, for example, must *always* have on hand a supply of white dress shirts in the most popular sizes. A store selling ladies' ready-to-wear should *always* be ready to supply nylon hosiery of several basic styles and shades in the principal size assortments. To a customer asking for certain standard hand tools, a hardware retailer should *never* have to say, "Sorry, we're out of stock." For any of these retailers, to be out of stock in such basic items is to run the risk not only of losing a single sale—but also of losing a permanent customer.

If, however, the men's clothing store does not have a silk top hat, or the ladies' ready-to-wear shop can not provide a pink nylon tulle evening gown, or the hardware store does not carry fancy door chimes of a special type, the situation is different. Each may, to be sure, lose an opportunity to make a sale, but there is little risk of earning a reputation for being perennially out of basic items. Although the actual percentage varies with the type of store, basic items may account for as much as 75 percent of the entire sales volume. These standard items are the ones customers feel they have a *right to expect* your store to have on hand at all times. Taken collectively, these items represent the backbone of your retail operation. Although you will certainly carry other merchandise, you should consider this other merchandise a source of supplementary sales. Your buying must be patterned so that you have a constant supply of your never-out items.

From a profit point of view, it is just as unwise for you to be overstocked in unwanted sizes and colors as it is to be understocked in items which are necessary for your type of business. These are the questions not only of *what* to order, but also of *when* and *how much* to order. *Such questions cannot be answered without adequate stock-control records.*

Supply Factors Affecting Basic Items

Once you have developed your list of basic items, you must take into consideration a number of external factors. These will influence your ability to ensure that you have on hand a constant supply of essential goods:

1. *Some never-out items are SEASONAL in nature;* that is, at one particular season a retailer cannot afford to be out of stock. During the fishing season, for example, a sporting-goods store cannot afford to be out of certain basic items of equipment. In off-season months customers are not unduly disturbed at finding a limited assortment of fishing supplies, but they'll accept no excuse for anything less than a full line during the actual fishing season. Such customer expectations are quite logical; this means that the retailer must anticipate approaching seasons and place orders for basic items far enough ahead to ensure an adequate supply of a full selection.

2. *Delivery time from supplier to retailer directly affects the minimum level to which stock can deplete before reordering is necessary.* Clearly, if

goods can be delivered dependably by parcel post in three days, the minimum stock level can be set lower than if some slower means of transportation is required.

3. *Sales promotion may considerably increase the demand for a basic item.* A promotion may be initiated by the retailer, or it may be sponsored nationwide by a manufacturer. In either event, the retailer must anticipate the increased demand that will result from a successful promotion.

CHAPTER FIFTY-FOUR KEEPING TABS ON DAILY PROFITS

A SIMPLE SYSTEM ENABLES RETAILERS TO MONITOR PROFITS AS EFFICIENTLY AS DO LARGE CORPORATIONS

Larger business establishments, manufacturers, wholesalers, and jobbers are in a position to know the exact profits that they realize on sales from day to day. Retailers, however—especially the moderate-sized and smaller stores—are often hampered by relying on the annual or semiannual inventory, which often discloses that the expected profits have somehow vanished into thin air.

Despite the lack of personnel, and circumventing the cost of an extensive inventory/price-control system which volume may not justify, the progressive retailer can successfully set up a system for maintaining an accurate record of cash received and cash disbursed AND of stock on the shelves. While in larger stores, employee errors are checked by an efficient inspection system that accounts for every piece of merchandise, smaller merchandisers must protect themselves against the employee who may sell seven yards of goods as five yards, or ring up fifty cents on a dollar sale. The system described here is adaptable to the smaller merchant's needs.

"No merchant can hope to realize more for his merchandise than he has marked it when it is placed in stock," says a retailer whose scientific accounting system was designed especially for merchandise accounts. "Of course, the reverse is to be expected," he adds, "for frequent price reductions are necessary in order to keep odds and ends cleaned up, and it is just as necessary to keep an accurate record of all selling-price changes."

THE SYSTEM IN PRACTICE

This retailer does not find it difficult to keep his stock record straight, as he uses a system that keeps close tab on all of his activities. He always places after each item on an invoice, after it is checked in, the selling price of that article. By extending these items his bookkeeper easily ascertains the exact amount of revenue receivable on each bill of goods. Then the gross profit and the rate percent are readily determined. (How this is done is shown on Form 1, further along in this chapter.)

Keep a Perpetual Record

One invoice alone is not enough to judge the percentage of gross profit, so this merchant has a plan that takes a perpetual record. Double columns are provided for each department and each invoice is entered at cost and at selling values, as shown on Form 2. In this way the merchant is able to determine at all times the average profits that are made by a department. If they are not up to standard, he knows he must take steps to correct the condition.

In practice it is found that two factors determine the gross profit that may be marked on an article: competition and expense. If competition is not too great, it may be expedient to gradually raise the selling price until the rate marked safely exceeds the percentage of selling expense. Where competition is keen, the safest remedy lies in an increased volume of business.

Track Your Markdowns

The next step is to keep a record of the amount of the selling price that is lost by markdowns. For this purpose you should maintain a form on which is recorded the quantity, description, selling price before reduction price, and the extended difference. By subtracting this difference from the original selling value, the net gain on the transaction and the percentage of profit may be determined. This record is turned in to the office each week.

The amount of these reductions is then added to the sales of the department for the corresponding period, and the result is the original selling value of the merchandise disposed of. If the selling price on merchandise in any department averages 33 1/3 percent more than the cost, then, of course, by deducting 33 1/3 percent from the original selling value, the cost value of the merchandise sold is obtained. If, in turn, this amount is deducted from the actual sales, the *exact* amount of gross profit is obtained.

Figure the Weekly Profit

This amount divided by the sales gives the percentage of gross profit for the week. The gain or loss is the margin by which this profit exceeds or falls short of the cost of doing business. Here is a specific example that shows the method by which the difference between cost value of the goods and the gross profit is determined:

Sales for the period	$ 1525
Reductions	224
Original selling value	1749
Less 33 1/3 percent	583
Cost value	$ 1166
Difference between cost value and actual sales or gross profit	359
Percentage of actual sales	23 1/3 percent

If, for example, it cost 24 percent to operate this department, the loss for the week would be one-half percent or $7.62. On the other hand, if no reductions had been made, the cost to operate would have been reduced to 29.9 percent, and the net profit then would have been $217. This example illustrates the need to record reductions carefully at all times.

Departmentalize Stock Records

A perpetual stock account is kept for each department. Each department is charged with its inventory at cost and at selling values. From the selling value of the inventory, added to the selling value of any purchase made after inventory, the price reduction and the sales for the same period are subtracted. Then the balance of merchandise on hand at selling value at the end of the period is obtained. This amount is converted into cost value by deducting the average percentage of profit marked. This is specifically illustrated in Form 3. This merchant frequently verifies his stock record by an inventory of the stock at selling price.

Utlilizing this plan enables the retailer to keep an accurate check on the profits of his business as well as a complete record of costs and inventory value of stocks.

FORM 1
THE INVOICE

Upon receipt of every invoice the buyer places opposite each item the price at which the goods sell at retail. By extending these items, the bookkeeper ascertains the exact amounts that should be realized on each bill of goods, which is indicated in *red* ink to prevent possible errors in making payments. In this way, the gross profit and the rate percent is obtained. By subtracting the cost of selling the goods, plus any reductions that may be made, from the original selling value, the net gain on the transaction and the percentage of profit may be accurately determined. These invoices, checked in the manner shown, eliminate much of the usual difficulty in keeping the stock record straight.

THE JONES COMPANY

Date _____ 19_____

Sold to _____

_____

Terms:

Selling prices are entered
by the buyer

NO. 19062

DATE

REC'D BY

QUANTITY O.K.

QUALITY O.K.

PRICES AND TERMS O.K.

CALCULATIONS O.K.

TOTAL SELLING

TOTAL COST

PROFIT

% OF PROFIT

ENTERED
LEDGER

ENTERED
DEPT. RECORD

APPROVED FOR PAYMENT

FORM 2
THE
DISTRIBUTION
OF AUDITED
INVOICES

On this form is kept an
accurate record of all invoices
from each department for each
month plus the cost and selling
price of each item. The totals
are written in red ink, together
with the percentage of gross
profits, in order that a check
may be kept on the work of
each department.

—————— DISTRIBUTION OF AUDITED INVOICES ——— 19———

Dept. 1			Dept. 2			Dept. 3		
Inv. No.	Cost	Selling	Inv. No.	Cost	Selling	Inv. No.	Cost	Selling

FORM 3
THE PERPETUAL
STOCK
ACCOUNT

On this perpetual stock account each department is charged with its inventory at cost and at selling values. By computing the difference between the stock inventories, plus that bought after inventory, and the stock disposed of during the same period, the value of the stock on hand is determined.

_____ DEPARTMENT_____19 and 19_____

	Purchases			Disposed Of			Stock Balances	
	Cost	Selling		Sales	Reduc-tions	Total	Selling	Cost
Inventory Feb								
Purchases Feb								
Total								
Purchases Mar								
Total								
Purchases Apr								
Total								
Purchases May								
Total								
Purchases Jun								
Total								
Purchases Jul								
Total								
Purchases Aug								
Total								
Purchases Sep								
Total								
Purchases Oct								
Total								
Purchases Nov								
Total								
Purchases Dec								
Total								
Inventory Reductions								
Turnover—Cost								
Gross Gain								
Turnover—Selling								
Reductions Not Reported								
Total Stock Balances								
Average Stock								
Stock Turned Times								

CHAPTER FIFTY-FIVE UNDERSTANDING YOUR OPERATING RATIOS

Today, even though the opportunity for making profits for your business has never been better, there is a great need for basic control of costs and finances in small businesses.

RATIO ANALYSIS

Ratio analysis is a proven way to help you judge the financial condition of your business and observe any financial changes it may undergo. In most cases you will be able to spot the onset of any small trouble and correct it before your business suffers genuine financial harm. The ratio method is actually a "comparison of fractions" that will show you the relationship between two given items—usually between a complete item and one or more parts of it, or between two parts of the same item.

When you apply the ratio to your balance sheet or your profit-and-loss statement, you can compare items that are part of the same statement or compare various items from different statements. You can use this method to compare your firm with the rest of the industry, as there are "standard" ratios for all types of businesses.

Many of these proven financial comparisons can be valuable to you, as a businessperson. On the following pages we will define them and show some examples of their use. In all examples, *use the largest number that will divide each number evenly.*

Current Ratio: *A comparison between* **current assets** *and* **current liabilities.**

Current *assets* are those which will flow into cash during a normal business cycle, usually one year. They include cash, notes and accounts receivable, inventory, and temporary short-term and marketable securities. Current *liabilities* would include bills due within a short period of time (usually one year), notes, accounts payable for merchandise, bank loans, and taxes.

If a grocer has current assets totaling $3600 and current liabilities totaling $3000, the ratio would be found as follows:

$$\frac{3600}{3000} \qquad \text{(each divided by 600) equals } 6/5 = 1.2 \text{ to } 1.$$

Therefore his ratio would be 6 to 5, meaning that for *every* $6 of assets, he has $5 of liabilities or $1.20 in current assets for each dollar of current liabilities. The difference between current assets and current liabilities equals the company's working capital, in this case $600.

Net-Profit Ratio: *Compares* **net profits** *to total* **net sales.**

A druggist has total net sales of $1800 and the net profit from these sales is $600; comparison may be made as follows:

$$\frac{1800}{600} \qquad \text{(each divided by 600) equals } 3/1.$$

In this example, the ratio would be 3 to 1, $3 of net sales for *every* $1 of net profit, or 33 cents per dollar of sales.

When a comparison of your ratio is made with other firms in the same business, ratio results from a few years back can be just as useful as very recent ratios. The most important thing is to get started with a comparison standard.

Operating Ratio: *Comparison of* **total net sales** *to* **gross earnings.**

In the last example, we assumed that the druggist's total net sales are $1800. If gross earnings are $1200, this ratio would be

$$\frac{1800}{1200} \qquad \text{(each divided by 600) equals } 3/2.$$

This ratio shows that for *every* $3 of net sales, there are $2 of gross earnings, a 3 to 2 ratio or 66 cents of gross earnings for *every* dollar of net sales. Cost of goods may seem high simply because of a low selling price. For example, if sales are $10,000 and cost of goods is $8000, then gross profit on sales is 20 percent and the cost of goods sold is 80 percent. Now if net sales were increased by 25 percent and the cost of goods remained at $8000, sales would be $12,500, and the $8000 figure would represent *64* percent of sales.

Unit-Cost Ratio: *Comparison of the* **costs of production** *and the* **physical volume** *produced.*

If a manufacturer finds that actual production costs come to $300 for every 1500 cases of merchandise sold, the example can be compared as:

$$\frac{1500}{300} \quad \text{(each figure divided by 300) equals 5/1.}$$

Therefore, for *every* five cases of merchandise, the manufacturer has production costs of $1. This ratio is 5 to 1, for a production cost of 20 cents per case.

Capital-Employed Ratio: *Comparison showing how much* **capital** *was* **invested** *to product* **net profits.**

In our second example, the druggist's net profits were $600. If this individual invested $500 to obtain these profits, the ratio can be figured as follows:

$$\frac{600}{500} \quad \text{(each figure divided by 100) equals 6/5.}$$

On the ratio basis, we find that $6 of profits are received from *every* $5 of invested capital, showing an 83-percent capital investment for each dollar of profit.

If you compare your ratio to that of another business in the same line, and you find that the gross profit should be 25 percent, that does not mean you must average 25-percent gross for every single item you sell. Your competition may force you to lower your profit margin on some items.

However, there may be excellent business reasons for your company to be higher or lower than your competitor on certain items or ratios. The main consideration must be that you have a sound and well-balanced pricing policy.

Fixed-Property Ratio: *Comparison of* **fixed assets** *(fixtures, furniture, property) to* **total net sales.**

A plumber has fixed assets totaling $3600. Total net sales are $12,000. To find how much was invested to produce each dollar of net sales, the ratio would be

$$\frac{12,000}{3,600} \quad \text{(each figure divided by 1200) equals 10/3.}$$

The plumber finds that $10 of sales were produced for each $3 invested in fixed assets, or 30 cents in fixed assets for each dollar of sales.

The application of these ratios can be most helpful in comparing various items connected with the operation of your business. Through comparison, you will be able to identify weak points in your business and stop "overspending" on a particular item if you find that sales are not justifying your expense to produce them. You will be able to readjust items as they become costly in the operation of your business.

AREAS TO WATCH

In studying your operating costs, remember that certain areas deserve special scrutiny. These expenses are not as fixed in their determination as, for example, cost of goods. Let's take a look at some of them.

- [ ] **Management wages** or owner's compensation are items worthy of analysis. In a proprietorship or partnership, for instance, it is often the practice to compute profits *before* allowing any compensation to the owner or owners. After all other deductions, whatever earnings are left usually represent their compensation. This practice distorts the true accounting of the business: Unless assigned wages are deducted regularly, the owners are in effect making an involuntary contribution to the firm's capital. Results would not represent a true picture of profit or loss.

- [ ] **Employee wages and salaries** will naturally be a major item among the operating expenses on your profit-and-loss account. You will gain much when you know how others in your line are managing these expenses.

- [ ] **Occupancy costs** are important in all businessses but especially so to retailers. Every dollar paid in rent should bring a proportionate return in income. If your location costs are high in relation to your sales, they should be offset by correspondingly higher prices. Many "exclusive" shops with "elegant" locations take this principle for granted.

- [ ] **Advertising** is a powerful factor in attracting customers. Nearly every small business will find it profitable to allocate part of its expense budget for advertising. Many manufacturers also find that the money they spend for advertising attracts people to their names, products, and styles. If you discover that your former advertising budget was too low, an increase may increase your profits.

☐   **Credit sales** bear particularly close monitoring; you must watch constantly for bad debts. Credit is becoming the rule rather than the exception in all business today. Certainly it will boost sales, and—properly handled—there is money in it. Firms selling high-priced items find that, through credit, they are able to maintain high profit margins. In other firms, where markup cannot be increased, a larger volume of business offsets the credit risk. *Don't become careless,* however, in granting credit. Require credit applications and, as a rule, keep an account's credit within certain predetermined limits. The business that grants credit carelessly is asking for financial trouble!

TIME WELL SPENT

The time you take to determine the operating ratios of your business will be a wise investment, for it will provide an ongoing accurate picture of your financial status.

At all times you will have the information that enables you to operate your business with optimum financial efficiency. With this data constantly at your fingertips, you will have a definite advantage over your competitors, because you'll be maintaining the financial condition of your business on a *current* basis.

CHAPTER FIFTY-SIX
DETERMINING THE BREAK-EVEN POINT OF YOUR BUSINESS

One of the most vital factors in the continued health of your business is your constant knowledge of its *break-even point.* As the term implies, your break-even point is that particular spot in your business operation where you neither lose nor make money, but have just covered your expenses.

To make that still clearer, *it is the particular point where your gross profits exactly equal the total of your fixed plus your controllable expenses.*

Let us assume, for example, that you have a shop with a potential for doing a maximum business of $5200 a month, and you wanted to determine your break-even point. This, of course, is merely a hypothetical figure that enables us to convey an understandable "for instance."

Here is what you would do:

First   Ask yourself, what are your *fixed expenses?* They will include rent, utilities, insurance, depreciation, various taxes you must pay—all the items that remain constant regardless of your business volume. Let us jot down your total fixed expenses, let us say, at being $800 a month.

Second   Jot down your maximum sales potential per month. As previously stated, that is $5200.

Third   Figure out your *variable expenses*—the expenses that usually increase as your sales volume increases. These will include gross wages, outside labor, operating supplies, advertising, bad debts, repairs and maintenance, car and delivery, administrative, legal, and miscellaneous expenses.

Now let us assume your records indicate that your average sales for the month should amount to 80 percent of your maximum potential—in other words, about $4200. Further determine your variable expenses at, let us say, 67 percent of $4200—or about $2800.

Fourth   Add together your fixed expenses ($800) plus your variable expenses ($2800) and you arrive at a total expense of $3600.

Knowing these figures, you are now ready to make up your Break-even Chart. This should show you the point at which your business will break even —neither making nor losing money—under a given set of conditions.

INSTRUCTIONS FOR PREPARING YOUR BREAK-EVEN CHART

1. **Draw a blank chart** like that shown on p. 277, with equal horizontal divisions numbered 0, 10, 20, 30, 40, and so on, up to 100—these figures represent 0 to 100 percent.

2. **Mark your vertical divisions.** In this case they run from 0 to $5200, so let's make the vertical divisions represent sales in hundreds of dollars, with the bottom line representing $0, the next line $400, the next line $800, then $1200, $1600, and so on.

3. **Rule a diagonal line** running from $0 in the lower lefthand corner, to $5200 in the upper righthand corner, the line we show as A-B. Label this line SALES.

4. **Now rule a horizontal line** across the $800 mark. This indicates your fixed expenses, which remain approximately the same every month, no matter what your sales. This line is shown as line C-D and is labeled FIXED EXPENSES.

5. **Establish total expenses.** We stated above that the average expected sales would be 80 percent of maximum potential and that total expenses would amount to $3600. So run one finger up the vertical line at 80 percent, and another across the horizontal line at $3600. Place a dot at the point where the two lines meet. This we show as point E on our chart.

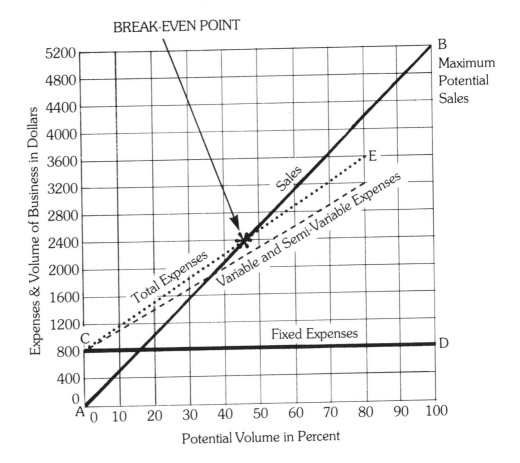

6. **Now draw a line** from $800 at 0 percent diagonally up to point E. This is indicated as line C-E, and we label it TOTAL EXPENSES.

7. **Where lines A-B and C-E intersect,** you find your break-even point. This we show as X.

    Point X in our example falls at $2400—or slightly over 45 percent of maximum sales potential. This signifies that you must do $2400 worth of business in order to break even. At this point you are neither making nor losing money, but just about covering your expenses.

HOW YOUR BREAK-EVEN CHART CAN HELP YOU

You can see from this particular chart that for any month you must achieve a sales volume of more than $2400 in order to make a profit. The chart can help you control your budget by indicating changes that may be necessary in order to bring expenses into line with income.

When your sales aren't all they should be, the chart will indicate this, too
—telling you that you should consider some changes in your methods, your
merchandise, or your staff.

Here are some other things the Break-even Chart can show you:

☐   How much business you can afford to lose before you run the risk
     of disappearing profits.

☐   What would take place if you increase or reduce prices.

☐   Whether you can afford to incur added expenses for making
     improvements.

☐   Which lines and items you should push and which you might be
     wise to drop.

Before the start of each month, determine through a break-even chart
how much business you must do that month. This will help you plan your way
to bigger, more consistent profits, and will tell you which way you are heading
at all times.

CHAPTER FIFTY-SEVEN
INVOICE CONTROL FOR THE RETAIL STORE

Incoming merchandise is invariably accompanied by an invoice form. Proper handling of these important sheets will facilitate tighter stock control. This can be accomplished by establishing a system that requires no additional personnel expense, merely a few efficient forms and a faithful routine for maintaining them.

Whenever merchandise is received, a clerk should fill out the receiving slip (Form 1) in triplicate, stamping both the invoice and the driver's receipt with the serial number that appears on the receiving slip. The receiving slip and the invoice are then dispatched to the order-checking department.

The duplicate receiving slip is forwarded to the invoice-control section in the controller's office, where it is listed on a card (Form 3) showing the receiving slip number, the department number, the money value of the goods, and the vendor's name. A new set of these cards is made out daily, so the card indicates the day on which the invoice came into the store.

The triplicate copy remains in the machine on which the receiving slip was written. At the close of the day, these triplicates are removed and taken to the controller's office for filing.

In the order-checking department—located in the office of the receiving and marking room—the invoice is checked against the original order for quantities and prices. It is then placed on the file for the buyer of the department to

"IMMEDIATE"
This slip is to be pasted on the invoice at once.

FORM 1
RECEIVING SLIPS

G17652

| Date | 19 | Our Order No. | Rec'g No. |

Received from

| Their truck | Our truck driver | Rec'd in Controller's Office |

Messenger

Quantity and description

| Invoice not rec'd with mdse. | For department | Amount of invoice | Dollars | Cents |

| Condition of shipment | | Receiving dept. | Receiving clerk |

| Rec'g point | Sent to Floor | Buyer |

No.

| Cost | Selling | | | $ |

| Checked with order | Quantity checked | Examined and approved by | Terms | Price and quality correct | Rec'g sheet checked |

| Rec'g dept. | Rec'g dept. | Rec'g dept. | Buyer | Buyer | Rec'g dept. |

| Extension audit | Re-checked audit | Voucher audit | Journalized audit | Ledger audit | Approved for payment | Special firm |

280

which the goods are going, and remains on this file until checked by the buyer. The buyer indicates approval by entering the retail price per article against each item. The entering of the retail price also indicates that the buyer has inspected the merchandise and pronounced it satisfactory.

As soon as the shipment has been approved by the buyer, the invoice is sent to one of the chief markers, who assigns it to one or more markers. They, in turn, verify the invoice by checking it with the merchandise for kind and quantity, and mark the merchandise in accordance with the prices indicated by the buyer.

When they finish their task, the invoice is ready for payment and is returned to the payment clerk in the office of the receiving and marking room.

The payment clerk lists the invoices on Form 2, which has space for 50 invoices. This form is made out in duplicate and both copies of the form, accompanied by the 50 invoices, are sent to the treasurer's office for counter signature. The counter signature is required at this stage merely so that the treasurer's office may be advised of how quickly invoices are coming up for payment, and thus be prepared to make the necessary financial provision. From the treasurer's office, the two copies of Form 2 (with the 50 invoices attached) are sent to the invoice-control section in the controller's office.

Here the invoices are checked against Form 2 to make certain all have been received from the treasurer, and then the original of Form 2 is retained in the invoice-control section; the duplicate is sent to the auditing section for audit.

You will recall that the duplicates of the receiving slip went directly from the receiving platform to the invoice-control section, where they were entered on cards numbered for each day. Only the first four columns of the card (Form 3) are filled out from the duplicate receiving slip. These entries are made on the day the invoice and the merchandise arrive at the store.

In the fifth column, *Date closed,* is entered the date on which the invoice is passed for payment; this date is determined in the treasurer's office, as we have noted.

After the extensions and totals on the invoice have been audited by the audit division, and after any deductions have been made, the auditing division fills out Form 4 and forwards it to the cashier. This form is an order to the cashier to make payment. The duplicate of the order is filed with the invoices listed on the order.

Each day a clerk in the invoice-control section goes over the cards and draws up a list of all invoices that have not been closed out within the allowable discount time from the date they were entered.

The *back list,* showing the receiving slip number, the department for

FORM 2

INVOICES READY FOR PAYMENT

No. 4900

Date _____

TO THE CONTROLLER

Attached please find _____ invoices as listed below.
The goods have been received and delivered to their respective
departments. The invoices have been examined, approved, and are
being delivered to the Executive Office

Signed _____ Department _____ Time _____

Dept. No.	Receiving No.	Amount of Invoice	Dept. No.	Receiving No.	Amount of Invoice	Dept. No.

I have received the above _____ invoices.

Signed _____ Dept. _____ Time _____

FORM 3

From						

To _____   Date _____

Receiving Number	Dept.	Amount	Name	Date Closed	Back List

which the goods were intended, the amount of the invoice, and the vendor's name, is sent to the receiving and marking room daily. The receiving department investigates these invoices and reports to the controller's office, then takes necessary steps to ensure that the bill is passed for payment in time to take the discount.

Charts are maintained in the office of the invoice-control section, showing by weeks the number of invoices received into the store, the number closed for payment, and the percentage of invoices on the back list.

This percentage is computed by dividing the number of invoices on the back list by the number of invoices received into the store each day, and then averaging the six daily percentages.

Three reasons why invoices may properly get on the back list are designated:

1. The shipment may be missing some merchandise, and payment held up pending investigation.

2. There may be some question about the merchandise, and the invoice is being held in the receiving room.

3. The delay may be due to negligence in the receiving department. As a rule, no goods are marked until the invoice has arrived.

FORM 4 We enclose our check in FULL PAYMENT of the invoices noted below. If discounts or other deductions are in error, check should be accepted by payee, and remittance notice returned direct to the Adjustment Division of our Controller's Office, stating the nature of the error. Errors will be corrected promptly through later checks. We endeavor to pay all bills promptly. If you have any charge against us of an older date than the invoices hereafter noted, please send duplicate invoices IMMEDIATELY noting our order number thereon. KINDLY NOTE INSTRUCTIONS ON OUR ORDERS. No goods are received by us except in accordance therewith. Unless countersigned by an officer of the Corporation, no order is valid for more than thirty days from date of issue.

Old Bal.	Date	Dating	Amt.	Invoice	Terms	Remarks	Deduc-tions	Balance Due
						Our check herewith		

Ent'd by   Figured by   Checked by

Goods purchased for special sale, however, may be marked and entered on a "hold-for-bill" sheet, which will be checked against the invoice when it arrives. The invoice does not leave the receiving and marking room until the goods have been marked at retail prices.

284

SECTION SEVEN

SALES AND COLLECTION LETTERS

CHAPTER FIFTY-EIGHT SIX SALES-LETTER RULES FOR SMALL BUSINESS

The balance of this book contains a variety of sample business letters. Among them you are certain to find several that fit your needs or suggest a suitable approach to some situation you face. When you select a letter for use, or when you originate a letter to one of your customers, remember the six rules outlined below. They are essentially the same rules followed by giant corporations and have helped many a small business to project an *excellent* written image.

1. **Remember what your product or service means to your customer**—not to you. The customers are the ones who will *buy* what you are selling and they will buy it for themselves.

2. **Write clearly.** This means that you must know your customers and write in such a way that they will understand you.

3. **Keep it short.** Your letter is competing with a thousand and one things for your customer's attention. Long letters usually are not read all the way through, if indeed they are begun at all.

4. **Know your product.** Thorough knowledge is essential if you are to write (and speak) convincingly enough to sell it.

5. **Know who your customers are.** It is possible to sell refrigerators to Eskimos—but not likely. So get the Eskimos off your mailing list and make sure that all your real prospects get on.

6. **Don't forget the commercial!** Always ask your customers to do *something* (look, listen, taste, touch, compare, consider, try). Otherwise, they might as well be reading a letter from Aunt Nellie.

1. What Your Product Means to Your Customer

Your customers' point of view about your product or service is quite different from your own—even though the customers themselves may be unaware of this fact.

Ask yourself *why* and *how* people benefit from using your product or service. Then, in your letter, tell them about those specific benefits.

A good way to get ideas, after you have searched your own brain for customer benefits, is through discussion with someone who is not closely connected with you (a person in another business, perhaps, or a distant relative). Ask why *they* would buy products like those you sell or why they patronize a store similar to your own. If you offer a service, listen to their reasons for subscribing to a similar service and consider these as appropriate benefits of yours, as well.

2. Write Clearly

Individuals often speak different languages, even if they live in the same town or next door to one another. Business executives and homemakers usually speak separate languages; young people and old people rely on totally differrent terminologies, as do lawyers and carpenters, mechanics and artists, engineers and musicians. So speak your customer's language—it is the only way to sell them.

Avoid complicated phrases—you are trying to prove that someone needs to *buy* something, not that you are well-educated. Use the language that you use *every* day.

Write well-organized letters and try them out on one or two friends before you mail them—objective comments will be valuable.

One of the most "result-getting" methods of capturing the attention of lost or strayed accounts is to tell them that you've missed them . . . and are eager for them to return to the fold. A note expressing concern of this kind flatters the customer *and* gives you a chance to list some current offerings. It also might evoke a response explaining the customer's reason for straying. Usually you can rectify the problem, thus saving a customer for your firm.

3. Keep it Short

Your customers are busy people. Jobs, families, health and financial concerns, education, community responsibilities, social commitments, hobbies, and pursuit of leisure activities—all these and hundreds of other attractions are constantly tugging at their attention. So—*do they have time to read a sales letter as long as an income tax form?*

NO, they do not! And there is no reason why you should discourage sales by making your sales appeal a long letter. Your proposition is simple: you want the person who reads your letter to buy something from you, for one or two good reasons. Tell them what those reasons are, and request them to buy. That is all there is to it. Don't think you are wasting paper and postage by being terse. The only time a sales letter is wasteful is when it fails to get its point across.

4. Know Your Product

You are asking your customers to respect your product enough to pay money for it; therefore you should respect it enough to be able to tell them about it.

Vague claims like "It's better" (better than *what?*), "It's different" (what's *that* got to do with the price of apples?), or even the time-tested "It's new," don't seem to be going down as well as they once did. In today's economy people value their money, so you must give them specific reasons why they should value your product.

Look at your product. Work it. Take it apart and put it back together again, if you have to. Then you will be able to make a "slam-bang" success out of selling it.

5. Know Who Your Customers Are

The best letter you ever wrote will sell nothing if it is delivered finally to some-one who once lived in your area but moved to Nome, Alaska, two years ago. You must keep your mailing lists up-to-date and accurate.

Maintain your mailing lists on cards, the ordinary filing kind, one card to a person. Get names and addresses from your own lists of charge accounts, dormant accounts, and from city directories and telephone books. City lists of school-age children are an excellent source for names and addresses of families who are experiencing their most active buying years. If people change their addresses, note it on their cards as soon as they tell you, or when the postman returns the letters you have sent to them.

Include on your cards such information as ages, number of children, occupations, birthdays, anniversaries, and other information that becomes available.

6. Don't Forget the Commercial

Except in cases where your promotion is for goodwill purposes only, always ask your prospects to take some action—and make it easy for them to do so.

Include checklists, stamped envelopes, postcards, premiums, and other attention-getters, and be sure your telephone number appears in your letters. These things prompt action and make it convenient.

Remember—if your customers are not asked to buy, they won't. Ask them to buy, to visit the store, to call you—ask them anything, but get them moving toward your product in some way.

CHAPTER FIFTY-NINE

LETTERS THAT SELL

LETTERS THAT ATTRACT NEW CUSTOMERS

People are always flattered when told their credit standing is recognized. The reaction is bound to be good when they find you are extending the courtesy of this privilege without their asking for it. There is a good chance that they'll stop in to pick up their card.

Dear _____:

Your credit is good at (firm name). Won't you drop in and pick up the credit card we've reserved in your name?

People like to do business with us. We think you'll agree that we make buying easier and more pleasant than ever.

If you would like us to forward your credit card by mail, or if you're interested in making a purchase now, just call us. Our phone number is _____.

Very truly yours,

An invitation to a party is always appreciated—and conveys a desirable feeling of friendliness.

```
Dear Friend:

      You are cordially invited to attend a TEA PARTY and
      FASHION SHOW on (day, date, and time).  We have
      reserved a gift for you as an additional incentive
      for being our guest.

      And ... we would like you to bring a friend along
      to enjoy the festivities and receive a delightful
      gift, too.  No--the gifts will not be alike!

      The occasion?  It is just our way of saying hello
      to an old friend, thanking you for introducing us
      to a new one ... and, at the same time, giving you
      both a chance to enjoy an exciting

           SNEAK PREVIEW of our LOVELY NEW FASHIONS!

      We have assembled, for the coming season, just
      about the most thrilling array of modes we have
      ever had the good fortune to purchase ... really
      glamorous styles of the kind seen at Paris and New
      York fashion openings ... and featured in fashion
      forecasts of leading national magazines.

      Do come and see these lovely fashions.  You will be
      as excited as we are.  You'll be even more excited
      over the low price tags on these wonderful crea-
      tions!  You will be under no obligation to buy
      anything ... because we won't even be taking orders
      that afternoon.

      So come ... have tea with us.  We'll be looking for
      you.

                                        Cordially yours,

      P.S.  Two invitations are enclosed.  The pink one
            is for you.  The green one is for your
            friend.  Just fill them in and present them
            at the door.
```

Simulated theatre tickets are attention-getters. People attach "value" to tickets . . . and the tickets that would go with this letter have definite value, since they are exchangeable for gifts. A good way to announce a special sale or event.

Dear Friend:

    These two tickets are sent to you with our compliments.

    They will admit you and a friend to our big MIRACLE SALE, which starts (day and date).

    You will find Miracle Values that will amaze you ... fill you with wonder ... and best of all ...

                  SAVE YOU MONEY!

    Don't forget the tickets ... because you can trade them for delightful SURPRISE GIFTS ... FREE!

    You don't even have to make a purchase! But we are sure you won't be able to resist the values.

    So, be our guest ... get yourself an eyeful of Miracle Values in our special MIRACLE SALE ... and enjoy receiving your gift!

                          Sincerely,

    The unmistakable bank-stock appearance of a check showing through a window envelope, with the recipient's name showing on it, will get 100-percent attention immediately! The recipient will also make every effort to "cash" it, if your proposition is legitimate and believable.

Enclose a real check, made out to name of prospect . . . fill in any
amount you wish. But leave the check unsigned! Have face amount of check
and name show through window envelope.

```
Dear Friend:

        Enclosed please find our check for (amount).

        It is a real check, all right ... and made out to
        YOU!  The only catch is ... the check is unsigned!

        Let us make an estimate on your (repair, altera-
        tion, air conditioning, roofing, landscaping, re-
        modeling, etc.) within the next fifteen days and
        show you how economically and effectively we can do
        the job!

        Then, if you decide to let us do the job for you,
        we will sign the check immediately ... and accept
        it as down payment for the job!

        That should make us both happy.  So phone us today
        --we will be delighted to give you that estimate.
        Of course, there is no obligation whatsoever on
        your part.

                                             Sincerely,
```

The use of a simulated check very effectively dramatizes the value of
special offers, sale savings, or special discounts such as this:

```
Dear Friend:

        THE ENCLOSED $2 CHECK IS FOR YOU ...

        That is the credit we will allow you, as a reward
```

for visiting our store, conveniently located at

_____.

This is a special GET-ACQUAINTED OFFER ... for new customers only. It is good for ten days after you receive this letter.

Come in, browse around the store to your heart's content! Look over our extensive selection of (description of your merchandise) ... all of outstanding quality, budget-priced.

Buy any items you like for a total of $3.50 or more ... and $2 will be deducted from your purchase when you show the enclosed check.

We know you will be thrilled at our large selection ... and we will be looking forward to meeting you!

Do come in during the next few days ...

Cordially,

STORE NAME

Pay to the order of bearer **2 DOLLARS**

NON-NEGOTIABLE   _Signature_

LETTERS THAT REVIVE INACTIVE ACCOUNTS

Dear Customer:

The other day, while browsing through my books, I noticed to my dismay that your business with us has fallen off considerably.

Naturally, this would disturb anybody who values old customers and is proud of a reputation for giving the finest service at the most reasonable prices. It certainly bothered me--enough so that I'm sending you this note.

Have we failed you in any way? Has something gone wrong that I know nothing about? I certainly would like to know the reason why your business with us has dwindled so. What can we do to regain your patronage and friendship?

Few things are more disappointing than the loss of a friend. So if anything is wrong ... if there is anything I can do to rectify any misunderstanding that may have cropped up ... please do not hesitate to tell me about it.

Right now, we have the finest collection of _____ (proceed to list a special line, a new service, or new list of items to capture the customer's attention).

I am looking forward to hearing from you very soon, so that we can resume our old friendly relationship.

Sincerely yours,

P.S. As a "reward" for your visit to our store within the next ten days, we have an attractive gift for you.

Dear Customer:

It's been much too long since we did business together. Because we miss you and value your patronage, I am going to make every effort to bring you back into the fold.

Looking over your account, I believe I can see the transaction that displeased you. There is really no reason why this matter should not have been amicably straightened out long ago.

As an effort towards "patching up" our past relationship, I have a special offer (or a special plan) that may interest you. We know that we have pleased you in the past and are confident we can do even better in the future.

So please telephone, or write to me, or better yet come in to see us today or tomorrow.

Sincerely yours,

Dear Customer:

Nobody wants to lose an old friend. I like to regard all our accounts as friends ... and treat them
as such. So, when I realized that it has been
quite a long time since you've done business with
us, I felt disturbed--and sad, too.

How can we get back on our old friendly terms?
What can we do to regain your valued patronage?

Right now we are featuring a special offer (list
here some special buy, service, discount plan, or
some unusual offer that will encourage your lost
account to make an inquiry or ask to see you).

We are very proud of this special offer, and if it
brings you back into the fold, we will be even
prouder. So phone or come in to see me. I am
looking forward to greeting you personally.

Sincerely yours,

Dear _____:

We'd grown accustomed to your face, your coming out
and coming in ... and we liked the idea of seeing
you frequently.

What happened?

Please let us know if anything about our products
or our service has disappointed you. We'll rectify
it immediately, because we would like to see you
back among our customers again.

Very truly yours,

Dear _____:

Old shoes are the most comfortable shoes, and
stores you have shopped in for years somehow fit
your needs most comfortably, too.

An old customer is more than a face in the crowd to
us. We know what you like, and we know we like
you. But lately you haven't given us a chance to
serve you.

```
Why not drop in soon and see what we have to offer?
It's the same familiar store, with the same
friendly people, but our merchandise is always
fresh, new, and exciting.  Come on in!

                                    Yours truly,
```

The magic of a 10-percent discount is hard to resist. "Courtesy cards," coupons, and certificates having monetary value have proven themselves over and over as business stimulators. If this card actually succeeds in getting an old customer back, the $1 cost is a bargain indeed.

COURTESY CARD

The bearer of this card is entitled to redeem it for a $3.00 discount on purchases of $10.00 or more.

Valid until December 5, 1982.

STERN BROTHERS
Highlands, Illinois

```
Dear Friend:

    The enclosed Courtesy Card is worth $1.00 in cash
    to you.

    If this be called "bribery" ... make the most of
    it.

    Yes, we want you back as a customer, and we are do-
    ing our best to influence you to rejoin our loyal
    following of happy, satisfied friends.

    Right now, you will find some of the most wonderful
    values you have ever seen.  In addition to the
    already-cut prices, we will allow you an extra
    $1.00 if you present the Courtesy Card with any
    purchase of $10.00 or more.
```

Did anyone ever accuse you of throwing money away?
Well, that's just what you will be doing, if you
don't cash in this Courtesy Card.

We'll be looking for you.

                                    Sincerely,

"Money in the mail" always draws immediate attention. This could be
the most profitable "penny" you have ever spent. It will, in most cases, get
results.

Dear Friend:

"A PENNY FOR YOUR THOUGHTS ..."

Actually, what we are trying to say is this: "Where
have you been lately?" We haven't had the pleasure
of doing business with you in a very long time ...
and we are really concerned about it.

A business is built on the satisfaction of its
customers. We have been trying to ensure this
satisfaction in every way, but obviously something
has happened to keep you away for so long. So we
are offering a pretty penny to find out why.

Enclosed is a Courtesy Card that entitles you to a
handsome gift. You don't have to buy anything ...
just bring it in and tell us "everything is okay,"
or let us know of any dissatisfaction that has kept
you away.

Please do come in for your gift ... we will be
delighted to see you again.

                                    Sincerely yours,

LETTERS THAT BUILD GOODWILL A *hand-written* personal note can go a long way towards cementing the new friendship between a store and a customer. It makes the customer feel important, and hurries him or her back at the first opportunity.

Dear Friend,

*Just a quick note to thank you
for your visit to our shop the other
day.*

*I hope you were pleased with
our service—and that you will come
back to see us very soon. It will
always be a pleasure to serve you and
your friends. Please ask for me, and
I'll give you my personal attention.*

Sincerely,

Customers like to feel that they belong to a privileged group that gets
advance notices and reminders offering them "first choice." This group is
usually very loyal to the store, and will take action if your notices arrive on a
regular basis.

```
Dear _____:
    It's spring (summer, fall, winter) again and
    (company name) is ready to help you solve some of
    the seasonal problems that roll around as surely
    as the hands on a clock.

    Here's a checklist of some of the housewares
    (drugs, services, car or lawn purchases, etc.) that
    people need now but often forget to buy.  Make sure
    that you are well-supplied.
```

300

Buy what you need ... but better buy before the
seasonal supplies run low. Give us a call right
away ... we'll deliver your purchase before the
day ends and you won't be billed 'til next month.

Yours truly,

The period that elapses between the letting of a contract and the actual
finished job is often long. In the case of a customer who is trying you for the
first time, and has contracted to lay out a considerable amount of money, this
period can be one of doubt and apprehension. Here is a letter that will help
bridge this period, inspire confidence, and set the customer's mind at ease.

Dear Customer:

It was a pleasure to obtain your "go-ahead" on
repair work. We appreciate it greatly and assure
you that the job will receive the attention and
concern that has built our fine reputation.

You will be pleased to know that our organization
is based on

HONESTY ... RELIABILITY ... PERFORMANCE.

HONESTY: Means that we give an honest, realistic
estimate on every job. We figure on the very
finest quality materials and employ only top experienced craftspeople. We do not quote one thing
and give you another.

RELIABILITY: Means that we do what we say we will
do and that if a job is not 100% perfect, or if any
mistake occurs due to any inadvertent carelessness
of our people, we will make good every time ...
without question.

PERFORMANCE: Means that we keep our promises ...
that we finish a job when we promise to finish it
... that carrying out our promises is our sacred
duty.

Our responsibility to you does not end when the job
is completed ... it just begins. Feel free to
phone or visit us at any time. We will be glad to
answer any questions or extend any further service.
There's no cost or obligation.

Sincerely,

Needless to say, the most direct way of getting to a parent's heart is through his or her children. When you take the trouble to show your interest and sympathy in the illness of a child, you have made a "hit."

Dear _____:

When I was a child, I hated being sick, mainly because I got so bored just lying in bed. Well, I have decided to do something about it.

Give me a call (after you have called the doctor) when there is sickness at home. I'll send over a kit I have made up to make illness more bearable for children and easier on the people who have to take care of them.

In the kit are balloons, bed games, comic books, and a couple of surprises for the unfortunate girl or boy who has been incapacitated. As a special treat, I will have a package of ice cream personally delivered to the child.

There is no charge for this. I am not in the business, but I do remember what it was like to be confined to bed when I was young.

Chalk it up to liking children.

Very truly yours,

Sending a friendly note in recognition and appreciation of a new account is a personal gesture that flatters your new customer and establishes confidence.

Dear Customer:

Thank you for your order and WELCOME to our long list of distinguished customers.

We assure you that your business is very much appreciated and that we want to do everything possible to sustain your continued patronage.

It is one thing to find new customers, but quite another to KEEP customers happy. And that is where our greatest efforts lie ... in keeping our customers satisfied and retaining their loyalty. It is our pleasure to "pamper" them with so much service that they wouldn't think of going elsewhere.

So, thanks again for your patronage and the
pleasant opportunity of serving you.

                            Cordially yours,

Dear Customer:

Right now, we feel like the guy who has been told
that he has just become the father of a new baby
... happy and excited and ready to pass out the
cigars.

Why do we feel that way? Well, we have just had a
new addition to our happy family ... YOU have
joined us as one of our privileged Charge Accounts
and we are delighted to welcome you and your
family into the hearts of our family.

As a member of our "good-credit" group, you are
entitled to all the courtesies and privileges we
extend to such customers and we hope you take full
advantage of our services and friendly cooperation.

Again, thanks for joining us. We hope to make you
happy with our service and quality merchandise for
many years to come.

                            Cordially yours,

Anniversaries are usually observed by family and friends. So when a firm
takes the trouble and interest to observe a business anniversary, it makes customers sit up and take notice. You'll lend a refreshing "human" touch to the
usually impersonal world of business.

Dear Customer:

The other day, for no particular reason, I was
looking through our customer list, and noticed that
you (your firm) have been doing business with us
for over five years.

The purpose of this note is to say "thank you." As
you know, we have always taken special pains to
give you the finest service possible, and you, in
turn, have rewarded us with more than a fair share
of your business.

That, of course, makes it mutually advantageous.
It is nice to have loyal customers, and I wanted
you to know how pleased we are with your longstanding account.

Sincerely yours,

Dear _____:

The day you opened your account with us (exactly
two years ago) was a big moment in the history of
this business.

Just for fun, we have reserved a free anniversary
present for you to show our appreciation for your
years of patronage.

Come in soon to pick up your present.

Yours truly,

What a surprise a note of *this* kind can be to a customer! With nothing
to promote or sell in your letter, its net effect can only be one of pure goodwill.
This is the kind of letter that "cements" long-lasting friendships between stores
and customers.

Dear Customer:

The mail you receive from us is usually related to
sales, discounts, special announcements, or even
bills. This is a different type of letter.

We feel that we have a lot to be thankful for this
year. One of those things, surely, is the fun we
get out of this business and the pleasure of dealing with nice people like you.

So this letter is to thank you for the business you
have given us this last year and to tell you that
we do appreciate the patience you showed when
things did not proceed with the perfection you
have learned to expect from us.

Sincerely,

Several times we've mentioned the personal touch that can be extended
to your customers through the observance of their birthdays. If you're unable

to obtain this information through the normal course of business, try a letter such as the following:

```
Dear Friend:

     We want to express our appreciation of your loyal
     patronage and remind you that whatever success we
     have attained is due entirely to customers like
     you.

     Because keeping in touch is important to us, we'd
     like to put your name on our Birthday List.  Then,
     when your special day comes around, we can send you
     a little personal remembrance.

     Please take a minute to fill in the enclosed card
     and mail it back to us.  Notice that we are not
     asking you how old you are ... merely the date of
     your birthday.

                                             Cordially,
```

```
+-------------------------------------------------------+
| MY BIRTHDAY IS:                                       |
|                                                       |
| Month: _____   Day: _____         |
|                                                       |
| Last name: _____  First name: _____       |
|                                                       |
| Street: _____  City: _____  State: _____    |
|                                                       |
|                        Signed _____        |
+-------------------------------------------------------+
```

LETTERS THAT GET REFERRALS

Human nature being what it is, people love to be in a position to do favors for their friends . . . to recommend them for something. It inflates their ego and gives them the feeling that they are "on the inside" and letting the friends in on a "good thing." Here are some letters that put this trait to use, and will reward you doubly: You will get the desired referrals . . . *and they will probably be good ones.* Your customers will be mighty careful to avoid recommending friends of doubtful credit reputation. Thus your new customers will come to you "prescreened."

Dear _____:

       Our best customers--and you are one of them--are
people who have come to appreciate the products we
sell and the manner in which we sell them.

       Because friends tend to share similar tastes and
needs, we feel that you may know many people who
would enjoy doing business with us.

       Therefore we are willing to waive our ordinary
credit-checking procedures on new customers whom
you refer to us. For instant charge accounts,
simply have them present one of the enclosed cards
indicating your friendship, and we will begin to
serve them immediately.

                                  Yours truly,

INTRODUCING . . .

John Jones,

who is personally known to us and is recommended as
deserving of full credit courtesies, usual discounts, and
other company perquisites extended to your preferred
customers. Your cooperation is appreciated.

Signed _____

Money never fails to "talk." We know that one of the best sources of
new customers is *old* customers. A suitable reward for their efforts will bring
truly amazing results. The reward can be either money or merchandise, and
the following three letters show how this might be done:

Dear _____:

       The magic word is MONEY!

       We cannot afford to advertise on big television
programs ... but we can reward you handsomely if
you help us get our name around to the right
people.

Here is how to play the money game:

Tell five people whohaven't yet opened an account
with us about our store. Then fill in their names
on the enclosed card, drop it in the mailbox, and
wait....

If any of the five people whom you have contacted
opens a charge account with us during the next
thirty days, we will pay you $____ for each of
them. (By the way, you are not limited to five
people ... the proposition goes for as many of
your friends as possible.)

Why not start telephoning now?

Yours truly,

Dear _____:

Here is a business proposition designed to put
extra cash in your pocket.

As always, we are looking for new customers. In
the past, we have found that our old customers ...
people like you ... are our best source for
attracting new ones.

If you send us the names of five people whom _you_
think might be interested in doing business with
us, and if only one of those five actually opens a
charge account with us, you will receive an attractive, useful "thank-you" gift.

You like our service--you must know other people
who would, too. You'll benefit us ... them ...
yourself!

Yours truly,

Dear Friend:

No advertising is as effective as the recommendation of a satisfied customer.

We are grateful for your past patronage and hope
that we have made you happy with our service. But,
in addition to keeping you as a valued customer, we
would appreciate your help in recommending your
friends to us.

And--to show you how much we appreciate this aid, we would like to give you a valuable gift for every customer you send to us. The enclosed business cards are for the purpose of introduction.

Any customer who comes to our place carrying your name on the back of our business card will earn for you (or your organization) a gift of anything in our store up to 10% of the value of the purchase he or she makes.

We will automatically credit your account for the 10%. When you come in, you may choose your gift, or apply the amount as payment on your account.

Does that sound interesting to you?

Sincerely,

P.S. Please be assured that our offer is of a strictly confidential nature and will be kept that way.

LETTERS THAT ANSWER COMPLAINTS

A forthright admission of a mistake inspires confidence and acts to "close" the case. It might even benefit you further by attracting new customers. You can be sure that customers will tell friends that your firm is a pretty good place to do business, because you "settle complaints quickly and don't give an argument." The following three letters are examples of ways to approach the problem:

Dear _____ :

We know that you are angry, and the important thing, besides making sure that such an incident never recurs, is to make you happy with our service again.

We will call you to arrange satisfaction of your complaint as soon as possible.

Sadly for us, it is often easier for you to remember that one unpleasant experience than the thousands of happy experiences you have had with a company.

We hope that you will have thousands more pleasant experiences with us. One might be the new (name of product) that we have just received. I would like

to show it to you personally. Please ask for me
when you come in ... soon.

Yours truly,

(Fill in face, except
eyes, with red magic-
marker)

Dear _____:

Is our face red. After studying your complaint, we
can see that you have a great deal of justification.

Above everything else we value your patronage--and
will strive in any way to maintain it. Next time
you visit our store, we have a little gift reserved
for you ... as a further humble indication of our
good intentions.

We look forward to seeing you soon.

Yours sincerely,

Dear _____:

You are absolutely right!

You have my sincere apology, but I would rather do
more than apologize. Won't you please call me, so
that I can do everything in my power to satisfy
you?

Yours truly,

People like to feel sought after and important. They will bear goodwill
towards the firm that conveys this feeling . . . that makes them feel important
as both individuals and customers. Below is one type of letter that helps
achieve this effect:

(Obtain gold seals and some red gift-wrap ribbon at local stationer. Paste them on your letter.)

... That's why when weeks have passed and we don't see you around ... we miss you.

How much? Well, enough so that we are willing to give you an incentive just to see you again--a useful gift that we are holding at our store in your name.

Feel no obligation to buy. Just stop in and say "hello" and give us the pleasure of presenting your gift, which we hope you'll enjoy using.

We look forward to seeing you soon.

Sincerely,

LETTERS THAT ANNOUNCE SPECIAL EVENTS

Here's a novelty approach that has great attention-getting value. Enclose an actual paper bag (penny-candy size) in your sale announcement! The element of mystery as to "what's in the bag" is hard to resist. The actual paper bag enclosed with the letter could contain descriptions of typical items to be found in a special sale—or it might be used to introduce new items. It is inexpensive, too, since ordinary paper bags can be used.

Dear Friend:

It's in the bag!

Yes--if you will look inside the enclosed paper bag, you will find something of real interest to you.

If you like what you see inside, come quickly-- don't waste any time. There's lots more wonderful news inside our store ...

Sincerely,

Ordinary government cards will do. No printing is required. It can be produced at home or during slow periods of the business day.

Here's an attention-getting announcement that is extremely simple and inexpensive, ideal for a small shop with practically no advertising budget.

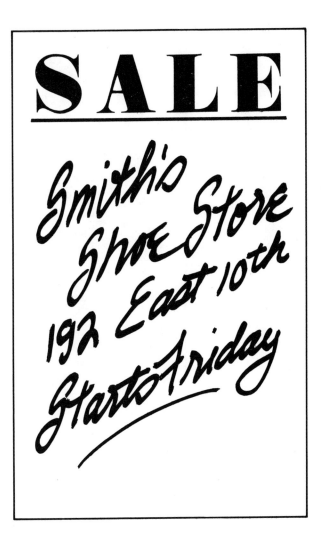

The "scorched letter" has novelty and dramatizes the event described. It is not likely to be thrown aside quickly—and probably will be shown to friends. It helps to turn an ordinary clearance-sale announcement into something quite exciting.

Dear Friend:

This is the HOTTEST NEWS IN TOWN!

In fact, it is so hot that it scorched
this letter ... as you can see.

Here's why! Starting this Saturday,
and continuing for only 5 days, we
are staging a ...

BLAZING INVENTORY SALE!

"Blazing" because every value is so
"hot" it will warm the heart of anybody
who appreciates a real bargain.

This inventory sale comes just once a
year. It is important to us, because
it clears the decks and makes room
for NEW MERCHANDISE. And it brings
many old and new customers into our
store.

EVERYTHING MUST GO!

So get on your fire wagon ... and come
help put out the big blaze.

Sincerely,

A telegram always gets attention, and simulated telegrams are nearly as good if they're printed on yellow paper and mailed in yellow envelopes. Imprint your enevelope with a catchy phrase to eliminate the possible "scare" that some people associate with a telegram.

MOST EXCITING SALES EVENT IN TOWN	**IMPORTANT AS A** **TELEGRAM**	BIG SAVINGS EXTRA SALESPEOPLE

JUST ARRIVED.   CARLOAD OF NEW MERCHANDISE
SPECIAL PURCHASE AT LOWER THAN MARKET VALUE.
WE ARE NOW PASSING ON THESE SAVINGS TO OUR
CUSTOMERS. SENSATIONAL LOW PRICES ON QUALITY
BRANDS.   COME EARLY FOR BETTER SELECTION.
SALE STARTS TODAY ... ENDS ON SATURDAY.

(Name of Store)

(address)

ONE HUNDRED YEARS AGO NEXT THURSDAY NOTHING
HAPPENED.   BUT (name of store) IS HAVING AN
ANNIVERSARY SALE ANYWAY AND A HUNDRED YEARS
FROM TODAY PEOPLE WILL STILL BE TALKING ABOUT
THE VALUES AT THIS SALES EXTRAVAGANZA.   GO TO
(name of store) NEXT THURSDAY FOR THE SALE OF
THE CENTURY.

CHAPTER SIXTY COLLECTION LETTERS

STANDARD APPEAL COLLECTION LETTERS

Admission of possible error:

Dear _____:

In view of your excellent credit rating, we were a bit surprised when your account became past due. Our billing is usually accurate, but every now and then a mistake will occur.

We have appreciated and enjoyed your business and look forward to many future associations with you, (customer's name). Will you please let us know if there has been any mistake in your invoice, so that we may correct it immediately. If there is no error, please send your check, or pay at our office, to bring the presently outstanding account up to date.

Sincerely,

Dear Customer:

According to our records, you owe us a little money. However, there is a chance that we may be guilty of a bookkeeping error and perhaps owe <u>you</u> an apology.

Since this balance is standing on our books, we know that you will be glad to cooperate in getting the account cleared up.

With this thought in mind, will you be kind enough to fill in the information below and return it to us in the postage-free envelope.

With thanks,

                                    Credit Manager

Balance Due $_____.

RE: Bill of $ _____.

____ I am enclosing check.

____ I will send check on _____ 19____

____ I do not owe this sum. Explain: _____

_____

        Name: _____

        City: _____

        State: _____ Zip _____

Dear Customer:

  <u>P</u>robably you have overlooked your account.
  <u>L</u>est it slip your mind again, won't you please
  <u>E</u>nclose your check or money order and mail it
  <u>A</u>t once? Your cooperation in this way will be
  <u>S</u>incerely appreciated, and it will maintain your
  <u>E</u>xcellent credit standing with us.

  Balance now due is shown on enclosed invoice card.
  Please return this card with your remittance.

                                    Thank you,

                                    Credit Manager

316

IMPORTANT:

Be sure to return the enclosed invoice card with your payment to ensure proper credit to your account.

For use on single-item direct-mail sale:

Dear Customer:

Thank you very much for your order for _____. We hope you are enjoying the use of it.

We were pleased to bill you for the $_____ cost as you requested and are looking forward to serving you in the future.

To make it easy to send in your payment, we have enclosed a postpaid reply envelope. So, why not take care of it right now--while you are thinking of it?

Sincerely yours,

Frank, firm, understanding approach, suggested for long-time customer who becomes delinquent:

Dear Customer:

Unfortunately, I find it impossible to visit personally with you for a friendly talk, so I ask you to accept this letter as the next best thing.

This is not a "pay-up-or-else" letter, nor is it an attempt to minimize the serious situation. You owe us $_____ which is long past due, but we feel that there must be some special reason for your delay in payment.

I believe we have had a long and friendly relationship, one that we wish to continue for years to come.

How can we help you over this rough spot? We want our money, of course, but perhaps we may be able to help you in some way. I suggest that you write me in full confidence. Between us, we probably can agree on some plan that will enable you to take care of this past-due account without undue strain.

We might even be able to provide you with some
immediately needed merchandise.

I have written this letter frankly and ask only
that you grant me equal frankness in your reply.

If you will use the enclosed, self-addressed
envelope, your reply will come to my desk unopened.

Sincerely,

FRIENDLY COLLECTION LETTERS

"Open-door" letter to customer in financial difficulty:

Dear Customer:

Has some unforeseen difficulty arisen since your
purchase from us? Why not call us or come in and
tell us about it?

Naturally you have an obligation to meet, but we
think you'll find us very reasonable. Your continued silence implies an unwillingness to cooperate,
which can only worry us and possibly hurt you.

Let us remain as friendly as we were when you
received this credit. For your own benefit, we
suggest that you act now. Please pay the balance
of $_____ or write us regarding it today.

Very truly yours,

Appeal for partial payment:

Dear Customer:

What is worth more than a pocket full of money?

<u>Good credit reputation!</u>

The person whose word is truly as good as his or
her bond has a most valuable asset indeed. Unfortunate circumstances may get such people down, but
they never stay down--there are always many "helping hands" within their reach.

We believed you would pay us in full for your
purchases when we extended you the privilege of a
charge account. We still believe this.

Even though you cannot pay your past due account in full, why not make a partial payment now, however small? You can make additional payments at stated intervals.

Come in and talk it over with us, or drop us a line. We would deem it a real pleasure to help out in any way we can, and you will find us not only friendly but mighty fair.

Sincerely yours,

Credit Manager

Balance $_____

Dear Customer:

Perhaps I should be saying "thank you," instead of "please." "Thank you for your check," that is, instead of "Please will you sent it today."

For it may be that your check has crossed this letter in the mail. If that is so, please consider this letter unwritten.

Otherwise, it will be a very real help to us, and will save you another intrusion of this sort, if you'll just forward your remittance for $_____.

Cordially,

Frank request for payment:

Dear Customer:

Are we being unreasonable in asking for payment on your past-due account? A payment request is not the most welcome letter in the world, but let's be fair. Our business rendered you a service and we have paid for the materials, supplies, and labor which made that service possible.

We have done our part; we have paid our bills. Please do your part by sending or bringing in your payment today so that we will be able to clear up this old account.

Sincerely,

Balance $_____.

Due from _____, 19___.

Appeal to fairness:

> Dear Customer:
>
> Balance only $_____.
>
> It is easy to carry one newspaper ... but have you ever tried carrying a big bundle of them?
>
> Similarly, you may feel your account is trivial and of little importance. But when a large number of the hundreds of accounts we carry feel the same way, it becomes a "big bundle" ... much too burdensome for us to carry.
>
> When this situation exists, you can readily see that it becomes difficult for us to maintain the high quality of our service and the low prices that benefit you.
>
> Undoubtedly you have overlooked our previous reminders about the past-due condition of your account. If there is any other reason, will you please write or phone us today about it?
>
> Your prompt payment TODAY will clear your account record with us. We suggest that you send your remitance attached to this letter--for prompt credit to your account.
>
> Yours sincerely,
>
> Store Manager

NOVELTY AND HUMOROUS COLLECTION LETTERS

Letters of this type will often succeed in bringing in money from neglected small-balance accounts and occasionally from the larger delinquent accounts. However, even the experts in collection correspondence do not agree on the wisdom of trying to be funny about the grim business of money. Some are deadset against humor. Others claim that humor does work.

Perhaps the best system is to try out a series of humorous letters on your poorest-paying accounts. If they work with these customers, then try such mailings on a wider scale.

Small balance:

Dear Customer:

Have you ever had a litter of kittens running
around your home? If you have, you know that even
though they are small, they certainly get in the
way.

One of the "kittens" in our office is your unpaid
account of $_____. It has been "getting in the
way" since the due date.

You can help us find it a nice home in our Paid
files by sending your check or money order by
return mail.

Thank you.

Cordially,

P.S. If this "kitten" is not yours, please let us
know on the back of this letter why you do
not owe this balance and mail it back in the
enclosed postpaid envelope.

Dear Customer:

Remember the story of the nine blind men? Each
touched a different part of the elephant, and each
had a different impression of how an elephant
looked.

Perhaps your impression about this indebtedness
differs from ours. Perhaps you have reasons for
this delay in payment. If so, we would like to
hear about them.

Our impression is that we have given you outstanding merchandise and service and fullest cooperation, and that we are entitled to prompt payment.

We will expect to hear from you within five days.

Very truly yours,

Novelty approach:

Dear Customer:

| This letter | in a new | called |
| is written | block form | SQUARE SPAN. |

COLLECTION LETTERS

Supposedly it is much easier and faster to read once you are used to it. In theory the eye and mind can grasp each block in one quick glance without the jerky left to right sweeps that conventional printing requires. Because we have not been receiving payments on your account, I thought perhaps my letters, saying this amount must be cleared up without further delay, must not be reaching you. So I chose this style of letter in the hope it would catch your eye and cause you to open your check book or come down to our store with the overdue balance of $_____. If it is more convenient to mail the payment, please use the enclosed postage-paid envelope, but please act today to settle this long overdue account.

Sincerely yours,

Dear Customer:

Abner, on his first trip to the big city, was bewildered at the sight of a store called "Eagle Hand Laundry."

"Imagine!" he exclaimed. "They even have places here where eagles can come down to wash their hands!"

```
We, too, are bewildered ... at the sight of your
unpaid debt.  It is difficult for us to understand
the reason for your delay.  Certainly we gave you
all possible cooperation--sending you the merchan-
dise you ordered at the time you wanted it.  There-
fore we deserve prompt payment in return.

It is still our feeling that this nonpayment is an
oversight on your part, and we will expect your
remittance within the next ten days.

                                  Very truly yours,
```

```
Dear Customer:

     How do you do?

     Some pay when due.

     Some pay when overdue.

     Some never do.

     How do YOU do?

     Balance $_____

                                  Very truly yours,
```

Many firms have used original "stunt" ideas in their collection letters.

☐ **Telegram:** A "pay-up" telegram sent to debtor, impressing him with the urgency for quick action.

☐ **Paper clip:** An ordinary paper clip is attached to a letter to "hold the money you are planning to remit."

☐ **Looped string:** Piece of cord is looped through corner of letter to remind customer to remind self to pay debt.

☐ **Letter upside-down:** The text of the letter is written upside-down to indicate how "upset" the firm is not to receive payment.

☐ **Straw:** Piece of straw is attached to letter. Shows "last straw" reached in firm's patience.

☐ **Postage stamp:** A 15¢ stamp is tipped onto the letter, to "nudge" debtor to reply.

☐ **Two sides:** There is a picture of an open book; one page, titled "Our Story," is where firm tells why it deserves prompt payment. The other page, labeled "Your Story," is for customer to explain when he or she is going to pay—or if not, why not.

☐ **Use of color:** A red notice is sent first, indicating that the firm will be in the "red" if payment doesn't come; a blue notice follows, showing how "blue" they are about not receiving payment.

Such stunt ideas should be used with discretion. They prove unusually effective with some people—attracting attention and jolting them into payment in a way the usual letter does not. With other customers, they may prove considerably less effective.

FRANK-APPROACH COLLECTION LETTERS

```
Dear Customer:

    There is something wrong and I cannot figure out
    what it is ...

    Our books show that you still owe us a balance of
    $_____.  We feel certain that this represents the
    correct balance due us.  Is there some reason for
    the delay which you have not brought to our atten-
    tion, or has this bill just been neglected?

    Each month we have to pay our own bills.  If we are
    to meet our obligations and continue in business,
    we must have a response from our customers to whom
    we have extended credit.  I have tried to give you
    equal consideration with every other account on our
    books ...

    Still--you owe us a balance that is now overdue.
    This is the third time we have written to you.  We
    want to be fair in our transactions and think we
    can expect the same treatment from you.

    If you do not owe this money, tell us and we will
    straighten things out.  If you do, please send us a
    check in today's mail or come in person and settle
    this account.

                                        Sincerely yours,

                                        Auditor
```

Implied threat of further action:

Dear Customer:

RE: Overdue amount of
$_____

Undoubtedly you will be surprised to learn that our records of your account show that payment is over ninety days past due. Time does pass rapidly and sometimes we lose track.

We have not received any reply to the several reminders and letters that we sent to you about your account, and we're at a complete loss to understand why they have been ignored.

We always dislike having to take further action on any account, but we feel that you have been accorded every opportunity and additional time in which to remit the balance shown.

Please send your check or pay in person within the next ten days; otherwise we shall be forced to act further.

Enclosed is a postage-free envelope which you can use for your prompt payment. Or, payment can be made at our store from _____ a.m. to _____ p.m.

Sincerely,

Manager of Accounts

(Copy in Pending Action File)

"Guard-your-credit" appeal:

Dear Customer:

Your Credit is your most valuable asset. Your most treasured plans for the future, ownership of a car, a new home, may all hinge on one thing--your Credit.

The entire business world puts its faith in your Credit Record and in your ability and willingness to pay according to agreed payment terms. Don't damage a good Credit Record by negligence, forget-fulness, or slow payment. Your Credit Rating is most important to you.

Send in that past-due payment today and resolve to be prompt with future installments. Protect your good Credit Record.

Very truly yours,

Credit Manager

P.S. Payment necessary to restore your
favorable Credit Rating: $_____

LAST-RESORT COLLECTION LETTERS

"Last-resort" letter signed by firm official:

Dear Customer:

The folder containing your account has been placed on my desk with the recommendation that I instruct our attorneys to proceed with the collection of $_____.

In your folder I see many requests for payment without any response from you, and therefore I really cannot blame the credit manager for making this referral. However, I honestly believe this account became delinquent through your oversight, and for that reason I'm taking the time to send you this letter. It is my sincere hope that you will liquidate this balance immediately.

I am placing your folder on my desk while awaiting your prompt reply and remittance. Please do not fail me, as I am making this an exception to our usual credit department rules.

Very truly yours,

Dear Customer:

Here is an ordinary rubber band--like any rubber band you have seen.

(Attach rubber band to letter here.)

Stretch it to here . . . . X and it will snap back.

But stretch it to here . . . . X and it may break!

Similarly, a credit arrangement such as the one you made when you purchased merchandise from us has "stretched" ... up to a point.

Seriously, your delay in paying on this account is beginning to stretch your credit dangerously close to the breaking point.

Won't you send in your payment today? And please try to make future payments when they become due.

Sincerely,

Balance $_____.

Setting deadline for a no-payment account:

Dear Customer:

On (date of original purchase), you contracted for an obligation of $_____ and as of today, no payment has been received. This is certainly long enough to wait ... don't you think so?

I approved your credit promptly and felt justified in doing so, but your lack of action has given me some cause for serious doubt.

I have been very lenient with you and have tried to give you a "square deal," but all of my letters have been ignored. What conclusion can I come to?

Unfortunately, your silence has taken matters out of my hands. Your account will be forwarded to our attorneys for collection unless we satisfactorily hear from you before (date).

I sincerely hope your immediate return reply will make this legal action unnecessary.

Yours very truly,

Credit Manager

cc: Legal Assignment File

"Final-notice" letter—send five days after previous letter:

Dear Customer:

Regretfully we find that you have not responded to

our last letter, which allowed you only five additional days in which to settle your account.

I use the word "regretfully," for no other word
seems appropriate in such a situation. Our
friendly relationship with our customers is our
most valued possession. We endeavor to be worthy
of that friendship and expect only the same in
return.

Possibly you have been ill or away from home and
have been unable to properly answer our previous
letters. With that in mind, we have telephoned our
attorneys to hold your file for an additional five-
day period before starting litigation that may
prove financially costly and will impair your local
credit.

If this five-day period expires, we must definitely
resort to correcting this situation according to
law. We shall feel justified in knowing that we
have done our best to settle this matter by more
friendly means.

Unfortunately you will not receive further notice
prior to being served with the appropriate legal
papers.

Please do no make it necessary for us to embarrass
you in this manner. Do send your check in full
payment at once.

                                  Yours very truly,

Introducing an outside agency:

Dear Customer:

We have a working agreement with the _____
Collection Service of _____, and under the
terms of this agreement we are obliged to notify
them of our delinquent accounts.

Your account shows a past-due balance of $_____.
We hope you will help us avoid the need of turning
your account over to them, but soon we will not
have any choice in this matter.

Please save yourself this embarrassment--and additional expense--by sending your check in the next

mail or by calling at our store within the next 48
hours.

                              Sincerely yours,

                         Manager of Accounts

Notice: Rubber-stamped reply envelope
             "Personal Attention: Manager of Accounts"